The Cult of True Victimhood

# The Cult of True Victimhood

*From the War on Welfare to the War on Terror*

Alyson M. Cole

Stanford University Press
Stanford, California 2007

Stanford University Press
Stanford, California

Printed in the United States of America on acid-free, archival-quality paper

Library of Congress Cataloging-in-Publication Data

Cole, Alyson M.
The cult of true victimhood: from the war on welfare to the war on terror / Alyson M. Cole.
   p.   cm.
Includes bibliographical references and index.
ISBN-13: 978-0-8047-5460-6 (cloth : alk. paper)
ISBN-13: 978-0-8047-5461-3 (pbk : alk. paper)
   1. Political culture—United States.   2. Discourse analysis—Political aspects—United States.   3. Victims—United States.   I. Title.
JK1726.C62 2006
306.20973—dc22

                                           2006004580

Typeset by G&S Typesetters in 10/14 Minion

*For Tammuz*
*(TMF)*

# Contents

Acknowledgments ix

1 Situating Anti-Victim Discourse 1

2 Shaming the Victim: The Anti-Victimist
Campaign 20

3 Victims on a Pedestal: Anti-"Victim Feminism"
and Women's Oppression 47

4 Blue Lester: Two Faces of Victimhood 79

5 Therapeutics of Blame: Blaming Victims and Victims
as Blamers 109

6 9-1-1: The Nation as Victim 144

Epilogue 169

Notes 181

Index 233

# Acknowledgments

WHILE WORKING ON THIS PROJECT I benefited from the support, advice, and critical commentary of numerous individuals. As a graduate student at the University of California at Berkeley, I was privileged to have Michael Rogin, Hanna Pitkin, and Mary Ryan as advisors. Many parts of my work bear the distinct imprint of this intellectual parentage. I remain indebted to Michael Rogin in countless ways, both academic and personal. His pioneering scholarship, sparkling wit, and boundless creativity were matched only by his generosity of mind, spirit, and time. Mike was an eminent teacher, a vigilant reader, a vigorous critic, and a devoted friend. I hope this book serves as a modest tribute to his memory. How might I explain what a great impact Hanna Pitkin had on my thinking about political questions? Often through seemingly simple queries (e.g., "Do you really want to use the word 'community'?") she challenged me to pause and rethink. While dissertating, I relied on her precision and rigor, as well as her wondrously literal sense of humor. Mary Ryan was an invaluable source of information and good judgment. I was fortunate to have a historian involved in my project, especially one who would use the pronoun "we" during our discussions about the modern women's movement.

Incisive criticism and thoughtful suggestions from Mary Hawkesworth and George Shulman improved this book immeasurably. I am incredibly grateful for their guidance. John Bowman carefully scrutinized several segments of the manuscript and offered valuable advice, for which I am very appreciative. I am also thankful for the wise counsel David Katzman, Lenny Markovitz, and Norman Yetman offered on Chapter 4. Phil Green has been a reliable interlocutor since I first began the study of political thought with him as an undergraduate at Smith College.

The Clyde Sanfred Johnson Memorial Fellowship and University of California Regents' Dissertation Fellowship supported my research in its earliest phases. Later grants from the PSC-CUNY afforded me a brief reprieve from some of my teaching responsibilities so that I could complete this project. An additional fellowship from the City University of New York's Office of Compliance and Diversity Programs served as my entrance to a spirited group—Karolyn Koh, Patricia Mathews, Valli Raja, Michelle Rief, and Ed Snajdr—who read drafts of two chapters and offered useful remarks. Stephen Steinberg orchestrated our meetings. Since indulging in sentimentalities will certainly embarrass Steve, suffice it to say that he has been a wonderful mentor—piercingly critical at times, but unwaveringly supportive, generous, and an all-around mensch.

No such restraint is possible, however, when it comes to Oz Frankel. Oz read countless drafts, debated nearly every nascent idea, and held my hand during all the rough moments. Although the term "partner" often seems an awkward designation for one's spouse, Oz really has been my partner—my dearest friend, my best companion, my most reliable confidant.

Writing is frequently a shared endeavor, even when only one name is credited as the author. Inspiration and support come in various forms, all of which are indispensable to the process of producing a book. In this vein, I would also like to acknowledge those who offered encouragement and camaraderie along the way—from teachers and colleagues: Tony Affigne, Jesse Berrett, Tom Burke, Alex Byrd, Stephen Cole, Jenny Felmley, Judy Gruber, Vicky Hattam, Jamie Martel, Nelson Polsby, Andrea Roberts, Don Scott, and Barbara Simerka—to the members of my department at Queens College: Ziva Flamhaft, Tito Gerassi, Andrew Hacker, Judith Kimerling, Michael Krasner, Peter Liberman, François Pierre-Louis, George Priestly, Pat Rachal, Alex Reichl, Joe Rollins, Yan Sun, and Burt Zwiebach—as well as my friends and family: Jeanette Byrd, Barbara Cole, Debra Cole, Jonathan Cole, Tsilly Dagan, Sara Frankel, Yair Frankel, Marc Foster, Tom Graham, Rafi Mann, Varda Mann, and Mimi Rosenberg.

I also want to express my appreciation to Stanford University Press and especially to Kate Wahl, who is everything authors hope for in an editor—dynamic, forthcoming, and exceptionally dedicated. Special gratitude is owed to Rebekah Sheldon for research assistance during the summer and fall of 2005; in particular for taking on the painstaking task of tracking down several inadequately cited sources. Azmina Jasani deserves mention as well for helping with an elaborate LexisNexis search during the summer of 2003.

Additional thanks to the discussants and co-panelists at the following conferences where I presented segments of this work in progress: "Re-Blaming the Victim: A Critical Examination," American Political Science Association Conference, 1996 (for Chapter 2); "On Female Suffering and Third Wave Feminism," Western Political Science Association Conference, 1997 (for Chapter 3); "Therapies of Blame: Victim Blaming and the Psychologization of American Politics," American Political Science Association Conference, 1997 (for Chapter 5); "Black Mask, Jewish Soul: Julius Lester's Conversion," American Political Science Association Conference, 2002; and "Triangulating the Black/White Divide," National Association of Ethnic Studies Conference, 2003 (for Chapter 4).

Earlier abbreviated versions of Chapter 3 appeared as "Victims No More (?)" in *Feminist Review* 64 (February 2000) and "'There Are No Victims in This Class': On Female Suffering and Anti-'Victim Feminism'" in *National Women's Studies Journal* 11 (Spring 1999). The material is reprinted in revised form with the permission of Indiana University Press. A modified version of Chapter 4 appeared as "Trading Places: From Black Power Activist to 'Anti-Negro Negro'" in *American Studies* 44 (Fall 2003) and is reprinted courtesy of the copyright holder.

The Cult of True Victimhood

# 1 Situating Anti-Victim Discourse

"VICTIM" HAS BECOME A KEYWORD in the American political lexicon and ubiquitous in the culture at large. Since the end of the 1980s, the victim idiom has been pivotal to fierce disputes over the welfare state, civil and criminal justice reform, as well as the so-called culture wars. Difficult questions concerning what harms and injuries merit recognition, what such recognition entails and, as importantly, the power and risks of fashioning political identities around suffering fuel these diverse controversies. I contend that the recasting of familiar conflicts in terms of victimization—by employing concepts such as "victim" and the recently devised "victimist" and "victimism"—is politically significant and requires thorough scrutiny. We cannot fully understand how the welfare state was dismantled, why the culture wars periodically erupt, or even what prompted George W. Bush's response to the events of September 11, 2001, without excavating the meanings victimhood and victimization have assumed in contemporary U.S. politics.

On the surface, American society appears ever more responsive to suffering. We have established a multitude of new agencies, crafted new laws, and allocated more public funding to ameliorate suffering of all kinds, from domestic violence and hate crimes to natural disasters and ethnic cleansings. Even the decorum governing how to talk to those who endured great harm about their injuries has been refined in recent decades. The prohibition against holding individuals—for instance, victims of crime—responsible for their plight now seems so thoroughly entrenched that we often forget that the expression "blaming the victim" was coined only thirty years ago. Popular culture and the media provide additional evidence of a vigorous public appetite for narratives of

1

harrowing experiences. Confessions about torment and devastation may be pro-spective routes to celebrity status. The commemoration and museumification of genocides, slavery, and other atrocities increasingly occupy the national pub-lic sphere. Have we become, as Charles Sykes cautions, a "nation of victims"?[1]

This book endeavors to dispel this misperception. Victim talk is indeed om-nipresent, but American political discourse is dominated not by claims of vic-timization as much as by claims against victims. Along with new institutional and cultural attentiveness to particular forms of harm, I argue, victimhood has been vilified. In an outpouring of books, articles, and political speeches, a com-mon warning rings: "victimism" infects every corner of our social body, endan-gering our national well-being. Thus, the columnist John Taylor asserts:

> It's a strange phenomenon, this growing compulsion of Americans of all creeds, colors, and incomes, of the young and the old, the infirm and the robust, the guilty as well as the innocent, to ascribe to themselves the status of victims, to try to find someone or something else to blame for whatever is wrong or incomplete or just plain unpleasant about their lives.[2]

In articulating their concern politicians, scholars, and journalists alike turn "victim" into a term of derision, an epithet. In contrast to most previous uses, they deploy "victim" to dismiss, ridicule, and condemn. Pundit Larry Elder's sneer is typical: "Get it? The joys of victimhood. . . . [V]icticrats feel a sense of moral superiority. . . . This creates a sense of power, of entitlement, of a club to be used against 'oppressors.' The comfort of underdog status."[3]

The best evidence of the success of the crusade to shame victims may be that now even those whose victim status would be readily acknowledged under the most stringent criteria perform linguistic gymnastics to disavow the desig-nation. Consider, for example, the case of Nicole Barrett. A deranged stranger smashed in her skull with a six-pound paving stone in the middle of the day in midtown Manhattan. Barrett's head presently bears four major scars, a crater-like dent, as well as two metal plates held in place by screws; and she suffers from severe short- and long-term memory loss, depression, and frequent "sensory jumbles." Nonetheless, she proudly tells the *New York Times* that she is "not a victim" because she "does not want to dwell on the past."[4]

While it is rare to find many self-designated victims these days, there are legions of "survivors." The brutalized Central Park jogger, Trisha Meili, waited fifteen years to come forth to narrate her tale of survivorship, which she de-scribes as a "story of hope and possibility."[5] Professional victim advocates encourage this trend of renouncing victimhood. A study published in the *National Law Journal* found that social workers recommend renaming victims' services—battered women's shelters, for instance—survivors' agencies. This new classification, proponents explain, is "less passive, negative, and disempowering."[6] That victims and their supporters purge the term from their vocabulary is more than a matter of arbitrary word choice.

This book explores the contours and content of the campaign against victims—its ideological underpinnings, its historical genealogies, the cultural sensibilities it promotes, and the political alliances and policies it sustains. Much has been written about "the victim problem" in American politics. In contrast, I make this literature itself into the subject of my investigation. As I argue, anti-victim discourse shapes victim talk by foregrounding and perpetuating particular and rather new understandings of victims, victimization, and victimhood. It is this campaign that associates victimization with weakness, passivity, dependency, and effeminacy. Conversely, it also depicts victims as manipulative, aggressive, and even criminal, at times, as actual or potential victimizers, a danger to themselves and society. The sheriff of Milwaukee County, Wisconsin, David Clarke, succinctly articulates this view: "They adopt victimhood as an identity and exaggerate it. They give failure, lack of effort, and even criminality a tacit stamp of approval. This is done not with a view towards forging solutions but to foster and nurture an unfocused brand of resentment and sense of alienation from the mainstream."[7]

"Victim" serves as such a sharp insult today because anti-victimists transformed discussions of social obligations, compensations, and remedial or restorative procedures into criticisms of the alleged propensity of self-anointed victims to engage in objectionable conduct. Though forged during debates over domestic policies, in the wake of 9/11 President Bush applied this conception of victimhood to characterize terrorism.

> Defeating the militant network is difficult, because it thrives, like a parasite, on the suffering and frustration of others. The radicals exploit local conflicts to build a culture of victimization, in which someone else is always to blame and violence is always the solution. They exploit resentful and disillusioned young men and women, recruiting them through radical mosques as the pawns of terror.[8]

The phenomenon that I term "anti-victimism" appears at first to be little more than a reaction to the perceived excess of victim claims, or perhaps yet another skirmish between the political Left and Right. Such a view is woefully facile. Whereas anti-victimists persistently target racial politics, feminism, and other forms of oppositional politics, the anti-victim sentiment is not unique to conservatives. Presumed victim-defenders betray a similar aversion to victimhood. The trend within many progressive movements has been to strip adherents of any latent attachments to suffering, to prevent them from being so "victim-oriented." The Democratic Leadership Council, for instance, devoted an entire issue of *The New Democrat* to the theme of "Getting Beyond Victimization." Contributor Errol Smith sums up the thrust of the essays addressing the pervasiveness of "victim mentality" among African Americans, Latinos, women, gays and lesbians, and even inner-city mayors: "If we do nothing else in the next decade except reject this victim identity . . . the nation will have taken a quantum leap forward. The more detached we are from 'victim' mentality, the more responsible for ourselves, the less likely we will become victims." [9]

It is one of the ironies of American politics today that as the Left desperately struggles to disengage from "victim politics," the Right jockeys to carve out a place within it. While conservative critics deem victimism to be a pervasive threat and call to restrain victims, they nevertheless become in effect practitioners of victim politics by devising and promoting new groups of victims. Perhaps the most striking example is the victims' rights movement. Paradoxically, many of the same individuals who bemoan the proliferation and empowerment of victims enthusiastically support this effort to substantially alter the criminal justice system by granting victims of crime robust new rights and corresponding roles in criminal proceedings. This movement recently succeeded in codifying fetuses' status as victims into law by amending legislation designed to reduce violence against women to include the Unborn Victims of Violence Act of 2004 (the so-called Laci and Connor Peterson amendment). Consequently, offenders can be charged with two crimes for injuring a pregnant woman. My argument, in brief, is that anti-victim discourse subsumes the ostensible opposition between victim-claimers and victim-blamers.

One way to reconcile these seemingly incongruous positions—how those who demonize victimhood come to engage in victim politics themselves— might be to follow Michael Rogin's theorization of political demonology. The current drive against victimism continues a long tradition of suppressing groups that challenge the status quo by casting them as a subversive threat to the stability of the nation. Rogin contends that the battle to repress subversives has often assumed the form of identification, desire, and impersonation.

Taken inside, the subversive would obliterate the American; driven outside, the subversive becomes an alien who serves as repository for the disowned, negative American self. The alien preserves American identity against fears of boundary collapse and thereby allows the countersubversive, now split from the subversive, to mirror his foe. Countersubversive politics . . . imitates the subversion it attacks.[10]

With one hand, anti-victimists strive to knock victims off their holy mantle. They forge victimhood (or victimism) as a subject position and then target it for ridicule. With the other hand, however, they place victims on an even higher pedestal by advancing what I call the Cult of True Victimhood (in tribute to the famous depiction of the nineteenth-century gender ideology, "the cult of true womanhood").[11] In this way, anti-victim discourse goes beyond the ambiguity of countersubversive splitting and mirroring, for its practitioners reify and exalt the very status they revile.

True Victimhood is defined in opposition to victimism: a victim is "true" because the victimist is evidently a bogus victim. However, contrasting victims and victimists has less to do with the veracity of petitions or the facts of injury than with the sufferer's personal qualities, which may be classified according to the following categories: propriety, responsibility, individuality, and innocence. *Propriety:* The True Victim is a noble victim. He endures his suffering with dignity, refraining from complaining or other public displays of weakness. *Responsibility:* The True Victim commands his fate; he does not exploit his injury to excuse his failures. He assumes victimhood reluctantly or, even better, rejects the status altogether. *Individuality:* Victimhood is an individual status even when a group is injured collectively. A True Victim is not a victim by affiliation or by engaging in "victim politics"; victimization must be immediate and concrete. *Innocence:* This is the most important virtue of True Victimhood. Anti-victimists apply the category of innocence in two distinct ways. First, with respect to his victimization, the victim's innocence must be complete and incontrovertible. True victims have not contributed to their injury in any way. Second, the victim is morally upright; he must be pure. This totalizing conception of innocence encompasses every facet of the True Victim's character.

The Cult of True Victimhood's construction of innocence serves to limit victim claims. Accordingly, philosopher James Bayley argues that the designation "victim" should be reserved for individuals who vigorously resisted their injury and were entirely powerless to prevent it. The possibility of having acted otherwise disqualifies sufferers from victim status: "Victims are helpless; if they are not helpless they are not victims. . . . It is false to the meaning of victimhood to take the entire array of ills visited upon African Americans by bigoted people [for instance] as victimization." Bayley further specifies that the term "victimization" accurately applies only to instances of suffering resulting from actions prohibited by law and brought about by an "identifiable cause." [12]

As in Bayley's formulation, anti-victimism superimposes a highly rigid juridical model of victimhood on all types of victimization. In doing so, it stifles the majority of victim claims, radically narrows the scope of those who might rightfully seek victim status, and confines redress to retributive actions by the state. When charges of social injustice are recast within notions of blamelessness and guilt that emanate from the courtroom, members of marginal groups must provide the equivalent of forensic evidence to demonstrate that they are in fact disadvantaged.

At times, True Victimhood invests suffering with an added, if not transcendent, meaning amounting to an anti-victimist martyrology. Foremost in the pantheon of true victims are those individuals who have been ostracized, censored, and punished in other ways by political correctness, affirmative action, hate speech codes, and similar manifestations of injurious victim politics. Their anguish is especially poignant because it exposes the sinister forces in American society that hide behind the liberal mask of tolerance, inclusion, and equality.

That anti-victimists cast victimism as a form of victimization exemplifies the demonological penchant for doubling and circularity. This book addresses the affinities between anti-victimism and demonology, including practitioners' deep-seated investments in the victim/anti-victim dynamic. My ultimate concern, however, is the political effect of anti-victimism. The Cult of True Victimhood serves to undermine collectivity and depoliticize challenges to injustice. For even as they prop ideal forms of true victimhood (and assume the mantle themselves) in the final analysis, anti-victimists aim to suppress, negate, and erase most victim claims. The truest of True Victims are victims who refuse to be victims.

## Identity and Politics

Anti-victimists conceive of almost any form of collectivism as inherently victimist, since it undermines individual autonomy by encouraging a profound dependency on the group or the state. Here anti-victimism couples a market-oriented view of individualism and another conception of individuality that opposes the conformity of mass society, or the stifling conventions of "group think." However, the "ism" in victimism is not a designation of ideology as much as of psychology, for anti-victimists construe victimhood as evidence of a personality type. Claims of victimization are scrutinized through a diagnostic lens as symptoms of an impaired character rather than as matters of verifiable facts. In this regard, it is telling that both Shelby Steele and Wendy Brown—two critics of contemporary identity politics who speak from opposing political perspectives—draw upon Nietzsche's concept of *ressentiment* (in Steele's case only implicitly) to explicate destructive investments in suffering.

Nietzsche warned against a psychological reliance on one's suffering, which he viewed as a will that wants to escape life itself. Civilization, he explained, deprived us of our natural instincts of terribleness, strength, and joy. Because all instincts that cannot be released turn inward, instead we created a "bad conscience" to war with and torture. The duality of "good and evil" expresses the rancor and *ressentiment* of the weak against the "will to power" of the strong. The revenge of the weak is precisely the bad conscience, whereby even the once strong and "primitive" must turn their wills against themselves to live in society. In contrast to those consumed by a backward-looking dependence on the past, Nietzsche challenges us to embrace *amor fati*, to "want nothing to be different, not forward, not backward, not in all eternity."[13]

Steele addresses the melancholic black man who cannot disengage from the past of slavery and discrimination to face the possibilities of the present.[14] Brown warns against what she calls "wounded attachments." She posits that weaker groups recruit the state to protect them from discrimination or to allocate benefits. Through the process of legislation, however, the state comes to define the form of these groups, the substance of their identity, and thus inscribes their public standing as victims. "Legal 'protection' for a certain injury-forming identity," she writes, "discursively entrenches the injury-identity connection it denounces. . . . [S]uch protection codify within the law the very powerlessness it aims to redress."[15] Intertwined with Brown's Foucauldian concern about the license permitted to the state in the inscription of identities is her presumption that all forms of enduring identification are suspect. True freedom entails liberation from the fixity of identity; individuals should engage in continuous and uninterrupted recomposition. Other anti-victimists, albeit in a far less sophisticated manner, likewise view victimhood as a form of identity and that identity as evidence of weakness, fatalism, a rejection of life's promise, and a surrender of individual will to others.

Anti-victimists do not simply probe the victim's mentality to uncover her real affliction; many also prescribe remedies to rehabilitate victimists. Anti-victimism thus becomes another venue through which therapy enters politics. First employed to evaluate individuals, therapeutic logic then colonizes public debates about matters of social policy. This radical inversion of the personal as political belittles political demands by casting them as matters of attitudes or feelings, or other individual inadequacies. In this way, anti-victimism operates as an individuating, atomizing discourse that hails, or as Louis Althusser might put it "interpellates," its subjects by calling into question their personal innocence, moral stature, and strength of character, while ignoring their common condition and history.[16] When the startled subject turns back and replies, "I am not a victim I am . . . (something else)," she too is ensnared by anti-victim discourse. Anti-victimists ignore that, as the political theorist Judith Shklar remarked, victimization "happens to us, it is not a quality." [17] The victim persona they demonize and dissect is largely their own creation.

Identity politics, so goes the argument, is conducive to the victimist personality for it builds on little else beyond a sense of injury, real or perceived, historical, present, or merely potential. The other facilitator of victim politics is the much-dreaded welfare state. This link between victimhood, on the one hand, and victim identity or mentality, on the other, should not be taken for granted. It requires decoupling. After all, acknowledging oneself or one's group as targets of victimization—and properly understanding the means that justify and naturalize such injustice—is arguably a necessary first step toward political action, not an indication of a paralyzing infatuation with misery or of endemic powerlessness. "Suffering and citizenship are not antithetical," Susan Bickford elucidates in her critique of identity politics' opponents, "they are only made so in a context in which others hear claims of oppression solely as assertions of powerlessness. A conception of citizenship adequate to the world in which we live must recognize both the infuriating reality of oppression, and the continual exercise of courage with which citizens meet that oppression." [18]

This conception of consciousness-raising has lain as the cornerstone of radical politics at least since Karl Marx. According to Marx, the proletariat's evolution from "a class in itself to a class for itself" was essential to doing away with class inequality. The Marxian emphasis on an unsentimental recognition of injustice and the precise mechanisms that perpetuate it was meant to facilitate the future revolution; it was not intended to make workers view themselves as eternally exploited. In Marx's vision, the inevitable ascendance of the proletariat would allow laborers the freedom of detaching themselves from the monochromaticism of factory employment and the possibility of experiencing myriad productive and self-productive opportunities. The end of workers' alienation—from their power to labor, the products of their labor, and their "species-being"—would permit a diversity of activities and correlating affiliations. In one of his few descriptions of life after capitalism Marx explains, "[I]t is possible for me to do one thing today and another tomorrow, to hunt in the morning, fish in the afternoon, rear cattle in the evening, criticize after dinner, just as I have a mind, without ever becoming a hunter, fisherman, shepherd or critic."[19]

Late-twentieth-century identity politics in the United States and postcolonialism elsewhere encapsulated a similar promise. Dismantling the forces that sustain hierarchies of gender, race, ethnicity, and sexuality would free individuals to explore and sustain new possibilities through new identifications. Consciousness-raising sessions among early modern feminists, for instance, were not conceived of as therapeutic venues for desperate and confused homemakers to complain and possibly adapt. On the contrary, such gatherings sought to catalyze transformative action. As Carol Hanisch famously asserted in her defense of personal politics: "Therapy assumes that someone is sick and that there is a cure, i.e., a personal solution. . . . Women are messed over, not messed up. We need to change the objective conditions, not adjust to them."[20]

At the same time, some forms of identity politics gave rise to an opposing approach, the transvaluation of old cultural forms or even stereotypes. In the African American declaration that "Black is beautiful," the feminist celebration of "maternal thinking," or assertions of "gay pride" we may find indications of apprehensions about the radicalism of the future or the desire to cohere around "positive" content rather than merely the anger awakened by injustice. As problematic as such gestures of reverse affirmation may be, they did not amount to an embrace of victim identity. Similarly, whereas anti-victimists charge that American scholars are obsessed with ferreting out real and imaginary past wrongs along lines of gender, sexuality, race, ethnicity, and class, in fact over the last three decades there has been a marked shift in academic work to stress agency over oppression.

Scholars researching the past have been looking for historical junctures where minorities or women played a major role in shaping their own destiny as well as that of others. The focus of much research on American slavery, for instance, shifted from emphasizing subjugation to highlighting how slaves resisted their oppression and created their own distinctive culture.[21] A congruent change may be observed in women's historiography, from documenting women's oppression to uncovering how women empowered themselves as individuals and as a class.[22] Some of these efforts to demonstrate the subversive agency of oppressed groups ascribe such immense powers to victims that the fact of victimization becomes overshadowed, if not lost entirely.[23]

The desire to locate agency in the experience of oppression may also inadvertently carry on the legacy of Marxian thought that rejected the philanthropic calculus of pain and compassion in favor of "scientific" analysis. The working class's claim on history derives not from its collective suffering, but from its production value. Recall that Marx's admiration for the proletariat was matched by his disdain for the lumpen-proletariat. The lumpen were unproductive and therefore devoid of historical significance.

## Historical Context

What circumstances contributed to the rise of anti-victimism and the Cult of True Victimhood? Clearly a cardinal factor was the ascendance of a new movement on the political Right that combined a fierce commitment to a market economy with social conservatism. Both positions targeted the liberal federal state, including the social services it provided, from welfare to education. Another branch of the federal government, the Supreme Court, also drew great attention. Decisions about racial justice, criminal procedure, privacy, and even reapportionment galvanized and united conservatives of all ranks. They viewed the Warren Court's decisions about the rights of the accused, for example—securing counsel for the indigent or establishing Miranda rights—as benefiting criminals, creating loopholes for defense lawyers to abuse, and increasing lenient sentencing.[24] To counter the rapid expansion of criminals' rights, President Ronald Reagan declared that the 1980s would be the "decade of the crime victim."

The victim of crime is one among three archetypes of suffering that the invigorated conservative movement promoted, the second being the proverbial casualty of reverse discrimination and other progressive policies, and the third, and most potent, the aborted fetus. In 1973, in *Roe v. Wade*, the Burger Court continued in the footsteps of its predecessor's efforts to expand civil liberties by uncovering in the penumbra of constitutionally enumerated rights a temporary window of privacy that might permit a woman, in consultation with her physician, to terminate her pregnancy. Some fifteen years later, Reagan rallied the troops in a "personhood proclamation" in which he pledged to fight the decision and, as a first step, decreed Sunday, January 17, 1988, National Sanc-tity of Human Life Day. In contrast to its role in *Roe*, in the 1978 *Regents of the University of California v. Bakke* decision the Court helped create a poster boy for the newly minted grievance of "reverse discrimination."[25] Charges that the state engages in massive discrimination in an effort to ameliorate minority fac-tions prefigured the anti-victimist complaint that victims and their defenders have become victimizers.

Concurrently, the welfare state (and the policy-driven social sciences that thrived in tandem) was attacked by both sides of the political spectrum for either "blaming the victim" or for facilitating what would later be termed "victim poli-tics." The authority of academic social experts declined as a consequence of this turn in public discourse. In their stead arose a cadre of advocates who abandon the posture of neutrality based on empirical research of old and uninhibitedly dispense moral guidance, for example, Dr. Laura instead of Dr. Spock, Mother Teresa instead of Daniel Patrick Moynihan. Faith in the power of science to address social crises began to falter. Neo-conservatives called for reintroducing morality to public policy. Historian Gertrude Himmelfarb, for instance, advo-cates reviving the Victorian sensibility that distinguished between the deserving and undeserving poor. She finds particular promise in Jeremy Bentham's no-tion of "less eligibility" that guided the notorious Victorian workhouse to prod the poor toward a life of productivity rather than continuing dependency.[26] Such unvarnished nostalgia for early Victorian moralism provides one of the most vivid manifestations of the postmodern engagement with the past. The "condition of postmodernity" that brought back modes of labor, public issues, and aesthetic forms considered artifacts of the past, such as sweatshops, TB epidemics, or even ornamental architecture, may also account for the revival of (anti-)victim talk.[27]

The crusade against the welfare state, identity politics, affirmative action, and "political correctness" has been in full force since at least the late 1970s. (Some date the emergence of contemporary conservatism to Barry Goldwa-ter's failed campaign of 1964.) However, only at the turn of the 1990s did many of these issues receive an added impetus and urgency in the form of anti-victimism. Only then were the anti-victimist terms and ideas that are famil-iar to us today coined and elaborated. Despite the demise of the Soviet Union, declarations about the cold war victory, and a jingoistic spectacle in the deserts of the Persian Gulf, America found itself a decade before the onset of a new millennium, once again, in the depths of malaise. Economic recession further contributed to fears of decay and loss of national stamina, especially when Europe (Germany in particular) and Japan were obviously prospering. Events such as the Los Angeles riots in the wake of the Rodney King beating in 1992 gave rise to concerns that the country was falling apart at the seams. In this context, the anti-victimist tirade emerged as another instance of the jeremiad tradition in American public culture, bemoaning the decline of the nation and calling for renewal by redeeming the past.[28] Then came Newt Gingrich's 1994 "revolution" and its evocation of angry white men, the spread of the "culture wars," and even more vitriolic condemnations of big government as the bogeyman of American society. This was the backdrop to the anti-victimist onslaught and to what I characterize in the next chapter as the drive to remasculinize America.

At the end of the decade, during the 2000 presidential campaign, George W. Bush peddled "compassionate conservativism" as a significant departure from the thornier aspects of the Contract with America and Gingrich's caustic personal style. Some complained that after winning office Bush abandoned his promise of compassionate policy making since his programs deviated little from the core principles of neo-liberalism. What such critics neglect, however, are the profound consistencies in the administration's approach. Compassionate conservatism was always a perpetuation of anti-victimism rather than a deviation. Bush pledged only to assist those who comply with the principles of True Victimhood, those who accept the fundamentals of our market-driven social system and make claims for help as individuals. By introducing compassion as the chief principle of policy, Bush actually offered "victim politics" as a substitute for the welfare state.

## Genealogies

True to the jeremiad form, anti-victimists present victimism as a dramatic break in American history, the triumph of liberal elites in their radical departure from traditional American values. However, the politics of suffering and its discontents are neither new to American public life nor exclusively, or even predominantly, the domain of the Left. One thread in the history of politicizing suffering leads back to philanthropy and social reform at the beginning of the nineteenth century. Public drives to combat pauperism, child labor, prostitution, and drunkenness often relied on post-Enlightenment humanitarian sentiments and also had deep roots in the evangelical tradition, for instance, by appropriating its conversion testimonials to narrate experiences of deprivation.[29] Exposing bodies in pain and dramatizing moral degradation were dominant themes in the effort to convince the public of the need to assist the most vulnerable.

Middle-class white men and women, "friends of" the oppressed, managed such philanthropic campaigns, which typically involved paternalistic efforts not just to help the downtrodden, but literally to speak for them in public forums. Antebellum reformers who represented slaves, asylum inmates, and "fallen women" often explicitly used the term "victim." Harriet Beecher Stowe's 1852 antislavery novel *Uncle Tom's Cabin*—the most popular novel of the century—drew connections between the saintly Uncle Tom and Jesus Christ, rendering Tom's death both inevitable and of great moral significance for, like the original victim, he died for the sins of society. The pro-life movement, whose proponents speak for those who cannot speak for themselves, may be the most striking contemporary rendition of this nineteenth century sensibility. Another historical link that affiliates nineteenth-century middle-class reform (even in its most radical permutations) with neo-conservative politics of today is the desire to instill the ethos of the marketplace among the less fortunate and to acculturate them in the ways of the bourgeoisie, by educating the illiterate, civilizing the Indian, reclaiming the criminal, or rescuing the poor.[30] Contemporary efforts to reform victims entail similar principles of individualism, self-sufficiency, and moral rectitude.

Historian Patricia Nelson Limerick makes the case that the West was built on the bedrock of victimhood. White women murdered by Indians, farmers ruined by nature, pioneers exploited by promoters and boomers, served as powerful scenes of violation fueling Westerners' sense of victimization, their view of themselves as simply innocent conquerors. Increasingly, another oppressor came into view, federal officials. The federal government retains the role of villain in the Western imagination today. In an ironic appropriation of the experience of Native Americans, even corporations portray themselves as martyred innocents. As one businessman declared: we are the "new Indians . . . [but we] will not be herded to the new reservations."[31]

Still, the largest segment of the nation that persistently viewed itself as victimized was arguably the post-Confederate South. From the 1860s and through the 1960s significant swaths of white society in the South condemned the Civil War and especially Reconstruction as the foundation of its subjugation. Even now these views have purchase in that region.[32] No wonder the Confederate flag continues to function in some parts of the country, including those far removed from the South, as a symbol of resistance, defiance, and antiestablishment. The North's most horrendous crime was not its victory in the struggle to preserve the Union, but the radical Republicans' design and sponsorship of the campaign to restructure traditional Southern society during Reconstruction in the late 1860s and early 1870s.[33] The cult of the "lost cause" did not seek specific remedies or reparations, but sustained a fatalistic culture of memory and stagnation—vividly depicted in William Faulkner's prose—that would (or should) be a feast for the modern anti-victimist. Rallying around the "lost cause" justified a wallowing in regional despondency to the point of paralysis and even decadence. It also legitimized the continuing discrimination of blacks throughout the period. (In this sense, "victims" certainly were victimizers.)

Indeed, the confluence of suffering and politics has been so central to American history that we can conceive of this past in terms of successive vocabularies of oppression. American culture provides iconic imagery and paradigms that assisted different groups by framing their contingent experience according to readily available templates of sacrifice, martyrdom, and injury. Suffering might thus be explained and invested with redemptive value. To give a famous example, the two hundred individuals who died at the Alamo in Mexico in 1836—a motley crew of adventurers, speculators, prospectors, and settlers—became in the country's collective consciousness Americans "who died for our freedom." Thus, a historical episode became an epic myth deployed ever since to justify, for instance, American involvement in the First World War, the cold war, and Vietnam.[34] More recently, and more implicitly, the idea of dying for freedom has been used to frame the meaning of the three thousand or so lives lost on 9/11, as we will see in Chapter 6.

Of course, no discussion of the role of suffering in American political culture can ignore the contribution of Christianity in this regard. Jesus' time on the cross has nourished rich iconography and conceptions of suffering repeatedly employed to grapple with personal and collective injury. In the political martyrdom of Abraham Lincoln and Martin Luther King Jr., for instance, we can detect traces of Christ's sacrifice.[35] (The phenomenal success of the *Passion of the Christ* (2004)—the ultimate victim film of our era—provides further confirmation of the reign of the Cult of True Victimhood in American culture.)

In the early republic, slavery provided the cardinal symbol of repression. It corresponded well with late-eighteenth-century (as well as the Jacksonian) fears about tyranny and with the underbelly of the republican sensibility, with its anxiety over the aggregation of power and the dangers posed to the commonwealth by menacing outsiders. The revolution of 1776 was forged in such an atmosphere; a context that latter-day commentators consider excessive and even inexplicably paranoid, especially since rich and powerful slave owners and other prominent colonists bemoaned new taxation as their ultimate enslavement.[36] The fervor of their grievances certainly seems incommensurate with the injustice they endured. Might it be that the "founding fathers" were the first practitioners of "victim politics" on American soil, the originators of "the culture of complaint"? By the nineteenth century, slavery inspired coinages such as "wage slavery" and "white slavery" to designate the abuse of (white) laborers, and, at the end of the century, the worldwide traffic in Caucasian prostitutes.[37] (We should also remember that pioneering nineteenth-century feminists often regarded women's plight as a form of enslavement.) Even causes that had little to do with slavery, such as temperance, deployed the vocabulary of human bondage.

By the middle of the twentieth century another manifestation of racism emerged as the most potent symbol of subjugation—Jim Crow's regime in the South, whose moral violations the civil rights movement publicized and attacked. Modern emancipatory movements that addressed the oppression of women, Native Americans, Chicanos and Latinos, lesbians and gays, among other Others, turned first to the African American experience in search of models of mobilization, strategies, and identification. Of course, the civil rights movement also provided inspiration for the tactics and self-conception of politics on the Right. The Life Center of New York, Inc., for instance, celebrated its twentieth anniversary with a keynote speech by Dr. Alveda King. In case the connection between the civil rights of African Americans and those of fetuses was not obvious to all, the press release for the event explains that their doctor King is the niece of Martin Luther Jr., and that she presumes her work on behalf of the pro-life cause continues his great legacy.[38]

By the 1970s, Auschwitz and Hiroshima supplemented (and, to an extent, supplanted) slavery and racial discrimination as icons. Most important was the Holocaust of the Jews in Europe. Several scholars have documented the pervasiveness of the Holocaust in American public life. Peter Novick, for example, assembles persuasive data showing how fully American society incorporated the Holocaust into its official history.[39] The plight of the European Jews during the Second World War reshaped views about suffering, trauma, testimony, and memory itself. Several survivors and commentators have pleaded against sentimentalizing their experiences and depicting death camp inmates as heroes by pointing to the "gray zones" of complicity and transgression that made surviving possible.[40] Nevertheless, the Holocaust survivor has become a model for grappling with adversity, especially in the recent preference for the designation "survivor" over "victim." The Americanization of the European Holocaust may also be at the roots of the late-twentieth-century "passion for the real," that thirst for rapturous, authentic experiences that, according to Slavoj Žižek, prepared Americans for the spectacle of September 11, 2001.[41] One way or another, the European Holocaust became a yardstick that, in its rarely matched extremes, dulls other forms of victimization and mutes—while also foregrounding—contemporary victim claims.

## Keyword

A Latin word, "victim" (*victima*) was first liberally employed in English by the Rhemish (exiled English Catholics) translators of the bible (1582). Beyond Scripture, the term has been in general use only since the end of the seventeenth century. In its earliest uses, "victim" denoted a living creature sacrificed to a deity. In this context, "victim" often appeared in reference to the scapegoat whose banishment cleanses society of its sins. It was later applied to Christ. Application of the term through the centuries has been reserved for instances of acute loss, either in body or property, such as a person cruelly put to death or subjected to torture. Beginning in the eighteenth century another sense of "victim" took hold to denote less severe types of suffering, injury, or merely hardship.

English scholar Maurice Brown suggests that these shifts in meaning, as well as the emergence of new forms of the word such as "victimize" and "victimization," signify a departure from the idea that the needs of the collective arbitrate morality and prescribe personal experiences. Society may no longer freely consign blame to particular individuals or animals.[42] While the original designation accentuated the act of sacrifice (and collective cleansing), now "victim" and "victimization" denote suffering that is presumed to be subjectively determined. The modification Brown observes toward more individualistic assessments of suffering should not be overstated, however, since even subjective experiences are understood through socially defined mediums.

"Victim's" affinity with "scapegoat" lingers in common use. Indeed, the two terms frequently serve as synonyms. As we will see, some critics allege that by abusing others as well as public resources, "victimists" render society a scapegoat for their personal inadequacies. Similarly, when sociologist William Ryan warned against "blaming the victim," he condemned victim blamers for turning the poor into scapegoats for the malfeasance of an entire socioeconomic system.[43] With some fundamental concepts, as Raymond Williams writes, "[e]arlier and later senses coexist, or become actual alternatives in which problems of contemporary belief and affiliation are contested."[44] According to Williams, the significance of what he calls "keywords" is rooted not in the clarity they bring to public discussions but just the opposite: their very susceptibility to diverse, indeed, opposing, interpretations and applications. The centrality of these terms and their opacity facilitates contestation and renders keywords pregnant with meaning. Controversies ignited by the use of keywords, and over their denotations, cannot be understood solely by analyzing the terms, but the specific words do matter.

> [M]ost of the social and intellectual issues including both gradual developments and the most explicit controversies and conflicts, persisted within and beyond the linguistic analysis. Yet many of these issues . . . could not really be thought through, and some of them . . . cannot even be focused unless we are conscious of the words as elements of the problems.[45]

In accordance with Williams's conception of keywords, this book explores the places "victim" occupies in American parlance today. I am attentive to the manner in which the word is deployed, when and by whom, as well as how it transforms the meanings of harm, injury, and responsibility. At the same time, my investigation extends beyond the concept to incorporate a cluster of closely associated terms, such as "blame," "innocence," and "agency," for "victim" is ultimately a sign for an entire discourse whose effects transcend the word itself and no longer depend on its presence.

This book aims to reveal a semantic terrain, to show how Americans currently use the language of victimhood, and how that language rests on a grammar that controls what can be said about personal and political experience. I will also show how these rules structure and create coherence among what appear to be conflicting positions or dichotomous ideas, for instance, the conceptual affinities between anti-victimists and those who warn against victim blaming.

Chapter 2 identifies and dissects anti-victimism in its most overt form in the burgeoning popular literature proclaiming that America has become a "nation of victims," dominated by a "victim culture," with its "victim morality" and "victim-speak." These writers warn that the proliferation of groups and individuals who allegedly use their self-proclaimed victim status to justify special privileges and to excuse everything from violent crimes to their own personal failings imperil the nation. Despite the authors' diverse subject matter, these texts share a strategy of argumentation as well as particular rhetorical devices. Their campaign against victims slides from blaming those who wrap themselves in the victim mantle to denying that these are victims at all.

Using the modern women's movement as a case study, the next chapter turns to the presumed victim-practitioners and examines contestations over victimhood as a group identity. As against those who condemn the supposedly recent ascendance of "victim feminism," I show that since its inception the modern movement has wrestled with how best to politicize women's oppression. Chapter 3 delineates the various forms victim controversies assumed within the movement, from conflicts over difference feminism to the effects competing victim claims have had on coalition building and group cohesion. The genealogy I construct traces the origin of victim debates among American feminists back as far as *The Feminine Mystique* (1963), for Betty Friedan also engages simultaneously in victim claiming and victim blaming.

Chapter 4 considers victimhood as a personal identity through careful scrutiny of the writings and autobiographies of Julius Lester, a former Black Power advocate who converted to Judaism and became an ardent critic of racial politics. Lester considers himself a victim of victim politics, but his conversion, I argue, is actually a search for a pure victim position within the Cult of True Victimhood. Lester's journey additionally provides a unique perspective on the problems and peculiarities of black-Jewish relations in post–civil rights America, revealing some unexpected consequences of the hegemonic status of the European Holocaust as the venerated American narrative of suffering.

Chapter 5 investigates the relationship between victimhood and blame in several foundational political texts and contexts, from William Ryan's 1971 challenge to the welfare establishment for "blaming the victim," and feminists' efforts to shield rape victims from blame, to criminologists' attempts to gauge what they call "victim precipitation." (The notion that victims bear some responsibility for their victimization underlies "victimology," a subfield of criminology that emerged after the Second War World.) I demonstrate that during the last three decades political debates over victimhood increasingly focused on the psychotherapeutic utility of blaming victims at the expense of addressing the material consequences of victimization or its remedy.

Chapter 6 examines anti-victim discourse in the aftermath of 9/11. The attack on the World Trade Center in 2001 brought forth new groups of victims and, as importantly, gave definitive form to the idea of the nation-state as a victim. Nevertheless, subsequent efforts to assess national and individual responsibility signify neither a rupture nor a displacement of anti-victimism. The rush to bring closure by honoring victims as heroes, the notion that the attack reaffirmed the divide between good and evil, civilization and barbarism, and that the wound at Ground Zero clearly placed the United States on the side of the former—all derive from the convoluted ways we have come to think and talk about victims and victimization.

Through the multiple examples that each chapter engages we will see how anti-victimism has undercut the welfare state, contemporary progressive politics, and the social movements of the 1960s, all of which are cast as incubating a new personality type, the victimist. There is more at stake here than familiar political contestations, disputes over particular victim claims, or the established narrative about the rise of neo-conservativism. Anti-victimism not only produces a "backlash," but categorically denies systemic inequalities and delegitimizes collective action. It is unremittingly privatizing and therapeutic, for it displaces or translates issues of institutional power and social inequity into matters of character. It drives us toward the view that a person must be completely innocent and helpless to qualify as a victim. By investing victimhood with new meanings and rendering it a badge of shame, anti-victimism has made it extremely difficult to address pervasive forms of social injustice that advantage some by subordinating others; instructing us that if we each were self-determining, then no one need be a victim. At the same time, anti-victimists depict a world in which a dominating victim politics victimizes society. This account of victimization has become, paradoxically, the key trope of the anti-victimist discourse.

# 2 Shaming the Victim: The Anti-Victimist Campaign

A TOPICAL CARTOON BY JULES FEIFFER features a young, white man muttering mournfully to himself:

> African Americans are victimized. Native Americans are victimized. Gays and lesbians are victimized. ALL minorities are victimized. All women are victimized. Children are victimized. Senior Citizens are victimized. The physically challenged are victimized. I don't belong to any group that's victimized. Where do I get the right to feel so lousy?[1]

This cartoon concisely illustrates four precepts of a politics I term "anti-victimism." First, claims of victimization pervade American society. Second, virtually everyone can allege to be a victim except for white, able-bodied, heterosexual, post-pubescent–pre-retirement men. Third, group membership determines victim status. Fourth, victimhood entails certain privileges. The joke, of course, is that those who cannot establish an affiliation with any officially acknowledged victim group do not have the right even to feel badly. Beneath the jesting, however, lies a presumption that most victim claims disingenuously cover for little more than general malaise or personal dissatisfaction. As in other expressions of anti-victimism, the lampoon conveys ambivalence toward victims, deriving its poignancy from the murky line dividing victim-envy from victim-hatred.

The humor conveyed in Feiffer's cartoon is absent in most other attacks against so-called victim politics. Roger Connors, director of a neo-liberal lobbying group, the American Alliance for Rights and Responsibility, defines the "culture of victimization" as a "mind set [that constitutes] a profound deformation of our society, a collective form of paranoia." Against the ethos of personal accountability, Connors observes, "there's a widely held view [now] that if something bad happened to you, someone else must be responsible."[2] Likewise, journalist Peter Hamill diagnoses, "We live now in a nation that is sick with what I call victimism." He deems "victimism" the dominant American ideology in the post-communist world. Everybody feels miserable, indulges in self-pity, and blames someone else for his unhappy life, his sorry existence as a "gray, throbbing muscle of resentment." The occasion for this sharp observation was a piece Hamill wrote for *Esquire* magazine about Colin Powell soon after the conclusion of the Gulf War. Accompanying Powell for a visit to his childhood neighborhood in the South Bronx, Hamill extols his subject, "who clearly spent his life refusing to become a victim." The article's title, "A Confederacy of Complainers," marks victimism as doubly un-American: a negation of American masculine power—represented by General Powell—and an echo of another subversion in American history, that of the Confederate South.[3]

The campaigns against the "nation of victims," the "victims' revolution," the "politics of victimization," "victicrats," "victimists," "victimism," "victimology," and other expressions constructed around the word "victim," and used interchangeably, is a prominent feature of contemporary American politics. Since the early 1990s, numerous condemnations targeting the proliferation of groups and individuals who allegedly exploit their self-proclaimed victim status to justify special privileges, to excuse everything from violent crimes to their own personal failings, or even as a banner displayed to capture public attention, have appeared in the daily press, journals, films, television documentaries and talk shows, and dozens of books.[4] In this chapter I examine several of the earliest and most influential efforts to make the supposed rise of victimism the foundation of a comprehensive social critique: Charles Sykes, *A Nation of Victims: The Decay of the American Character* (1992); Robert Hughes, *Culture of Complaint: The Fraying of America* (1993); Shelby Steele, *The Content of Our Character: A New Vision of Race in America* (1990); Alan Dershowitz, *The Abuse Excuse: And Other Cop-Outs, Sob Stories, and Evasions of Responsibility* (1994); and Dinesh D'Souza, *Illiberal Education: The Politics of Race and Sex on Campus* (1991).

These texts were written as popular essays for a large readership; several even became best sellers. Polemical in tone and based mostly on anecdotal data, conceptual rigor is not one of their stronger features. At times I impose an order and consistency lacking in the original texts. Frequently, this has meant draining their lively style and ignoring their entertainment value. My sample, while not exhaustive, is sufficient to demonstrate the variations and permutations of anti-victimism.

This chapter thematically investigates how these critics conceptualize the phenomena they term "victimism"; where they discover its roots and contemporary manifestations; their explanations for what compels individuals and groups to seek victim status; their assessments of the hazards victimism presents to society; and the remedies they offer. There are differences among anti-victimists, both blatant and of nuance, but also substantial similarities that suggest that complaining about the culture of complaint constitutes a discrete political genre, a continuing countersubversive project. The most salient common element shared by these writers, by contrast with most previous uses of the term "victim," is that they employ it pejoratively. "Victim" is deployed to dismiss, ridicule, and condemn rather than to evoke sympathy, empathy, or even pity. Individuals and groups who claim to have been victimized are portrayed as weak, manipulative, self-indulgent, helpless, hopeless dependents.

These books were published just prior to the Republican's victory in the 1994 congressional elections. By the time of Newt Gingrich's Contract with America revolution, the GOP embraced both anti-victimism, especially its attack on the welfare state, and True Victimhood. It vigorously promoted the cause of crime victims and flirted with the then-popular idea of "angry white men," the supposed prime casualties of affirmative action, feminism, and economic downsizing.[5] Nevertheless, most of the anti-victimists whose work I examine here avoid clearly affiliating themselves with any political camp. In line with the tradition of the jeremiad, most cast their arguments as a wholesale critique of a declining American society bereft of its character and moral rudder.

This chapter argues that the anti-victimist literature participates in the phenomenon it criticizes. Most strikingly, while the authors bemoan the proliferation of victim claims, they themselves devise new groups of "real" victims; primarily these are victims of victimism. The literature, moreover, presents the same distorted perspective of society that it attributes to victimists. Both victimists and their critics perceive America as fundamentally and irreconcilably divided between victims and victimizers. But in the critics' depiction roles are often reversed so that the victimist is revealed to be the victimizer, and the alleged victimizer, the genuine victim. The consequences of this inversion are profound, nurturing a general hostility to all claims of victimization, while at the same time elevating an impossibly pure archetype of True Victimhood.

## Sites of Victimism

A primary target of the anti-victimist account is identity politics. Shelby Steele, to give one example, focuses on the dynamic of innocence and guilt that has invaded and denigrated race relations over the last forty years. He claims that African Americans' persistent conception of themselves as victims in the post–civil rights movement era is damaging for both races. Steele identifies the victimist as the black individual who clings to his racial identity, what he calls the "race-holder": "The race-holder whines, or complains indiscriminately, not because he seeks redress but because he seeks the status of victim, a status that excuses him from what he fears. A victim is not responsible for his condition, and by claiming a victim's status the race-holder gives up the sense of personal responsibility he needs to better his condition."[6]

Steele disapproves of racial politics generally, and explicitly denounces social programs such as affirmative action on the grounds that they are bound to institutionalize racial animosity rather than facilitate harmony. He does not attack particular organizations or leaders; instead, locating victimism predominantly in the psychology of racial interactions in America. Both blacks and whites alike, he contends, have a stake in perpetuating blacks' status as victims. Other victim-baiters challenge different permutations of identity politics, for instance so-called victim feminism (see Chapter 3).

The welfare state is also conducive to victimism. Generous programs and complacent administrators encourage individuals to engage in morally suspect behavior, while relying on the public coffers. The parasitical "welfare queen," for instance, victimizes society by exploiting its generosity. To make matters worse, with state support the queen procreates a new generation of victimists who will surely remain a burden on the public.[7] Anti-victimists' attack on the welfare state supplies a new vocabulary for rather conventional stereotypes about the demise of autonomy and individuality brought about by government programs, or previously, by philanthropy.

In addition to welfare, a range of policies conceived as civil rights prompted similar anti-victimist criticism. A case in point is the 1990 Americans with Disabilities Act (ADA). When Congress first debated this legislation and President George H. W. Bush lent his support, ADA was peddled as a nonpartisan initiative to assist deserving Americans, military veterans in particular. Alas, by expanding the definition of impairment and by framing assistance in terms of rights, ADA fell victim to the law of unintended consequences. By the mid-1990s, it

attracted much ire. Conservative writers reported on a range of costly and supposedly superfluous projects, such as investing considerable resources to make
even the remotest post offices wheelchair accessible regardless of the needs
of patrons. Individuals suffering from some of the more esoteric conditions,
who now sought protection under the law, provided another excuse to ridicule
the law. The public was warned that "nearly everyone has a chance to be a victim
now" under the sprawling scope of ADA.[8] Even though recent Supreme Court
rulings dramatically narrowed the application of ADA, television journalist John
Stossel still sardonically muses whether he has found a tool to sue his network.

> What is an "impairment" [under ADA]? . . . Is being stupid a disability? . . .
> Being fat? Who knows? . . . Many businesses settle to avoid [court] costs.
> The ADA requires employers to "accommodate" disabled employees.
> Maybe I can collect some money . . . How about my stuttering? . . . Should
> I sue ABC? It's by no means clear that the law has helped the truly disabled.
> In fact, it's made it *harder* for some to find work.[9]

The campuses of American colleges and universities also figure prominently in the literature. Education is where the anti-victimist onslaught meets
and converges with other conservative concerns, mainly the supposed ascendance of political correctness, the broad application of the affirmative action
rationale, and the prevalence of multiculturalism. Dinesh D'Souza became a
key participant in the debate over higher education curricula and alleged infringements on free speech on campuses. But unlike Allan Bloom's *The Closing
of the American Mind* (1987), in whose footsteps he follows, D'Souza's critique
is formulated against what he defines as "the victims' revolution."

D'Souza's victim revolutionaries can be found among faculty, administrators, and students who claim to represent, or wish to advance, the interests of
minorities or women. Their status was predicated on an avalanche of victim
claims, greatly enhanced by the importation of postmodernism to American
academia. The pro-victimist coalitions on campuses proved to be exceedingly
powerful, generating the transformations D'Souza so adamantly opposes: affirmative action, challenges to the traditional curriculum, Afro-centrism as a project for raising African Americans' self-esteem, codes forbidding hate speech, and
as a consequence of all of these efforts, the loss of academic standards. D'Souza
fears that universities function as a "leading indicator" of changes we can expect
to see in society at large.[10]

Beyond the more obvious realms of contemporary progressive politics, several critics locate victimism in the criminal courts. Alan Dershowitz describes a

recurrent inversion of the judicial system's attitude toward victims and victim-izers. Commenting on celebrity cases such as those of the Menendez brothers, Lorena Bobbitt, and O. J. Simpson, he warns about a pattern in which crimi-nals present themselves as victims, and as such are exonerated by juries, while the victims of crimes become objects of scrutiny and condemnation. According to Dershowitz's account, this shift in judicial policy began with the use of the battered woman's syndrome as a defense, but the triumph of "abuse excuses" in court is linked to a greater transformation in society at large, all of which he views as "evasions of responsibility." [11] Besides the courts, Dershowitz addresses official corruption and misconduct (the "everyone does it excuse") as well as "the political correctness excuse," which he identifies in a host of policy issues from sexual harassment and hate speech to campaigns against pornography. A 1994 caricature by the artist Wiley indicates the popular reach of the thesis that the "abuse excuse" infects the judicial system. The cartoon depicts a classroom during a lesson on modern ethics. The assignment on the blackboard reads:

> DON'T BLAME ME, IT'S: my victim's fault; society's fault; television's fault; the government's fault; the school system's fault; my parent's fault; my vic-tim's parent's fault; my religion's fault; your religion's fault; your race's fault.

As the students dutifully take notes, the professor instructs them to "Choose one for misdemeanors. Any combination of two for felonies." [12]

Several of the critics provide a grand view of victimism as a phenomenon that reaches beyond the actions and the mental state of individuals or specific political groups to encompass a massive transformation of American society. Victimism is a "cultural impulse," a "zeitgeist," a social fashion ("victim chic"), and a distinctive language ("victim-speak"). [13] Charles Sykes and Robert Hughes share a dire view of contemporary America. Sykes's book sweeps through a multitude of examples taken from everyday life involving ordinary people who in the past would not have been considered by others, or by themselves, as dis-advantaged. "Something extraordinary is happening in American society," he declares in the opening pages.

> Crisscrossed by invisible trip wires of emotional, racial, sexual, and psycho-logical grievance, American life is increasingly characterized by the plain-tive insistence, I am a victim. The victim-ization of America is remarkably egalitarian. From the addicts of the South Bronx to the self-styled emo-tional road-kills of Manhattan's Upper East Side, the mantra of the victims is the same: I am not responsible; it's not my fault. [14]

Victimism has spread through American society like a communicable disease (his metaphor is "emotional influenza"), infecting every socioeconomic and ethnic segment of the population.[15] But when he is not bombarding the reader with his arsenal of colorful anecdotes lifted from the daily tabloids, Sykes returns to the permutations of victim politics favored by other critics including feminism, racial politics, and excessive litigiousness.

Hughes also presents a Decline-and-Fall overview of American civilization. As a foreigner, he offers an outsider's gaze at American society, invoking a tradition that goes back to Alexis de Tocqueville. Unlike Sykes, who ignores the political Right, Hughes divides his criticism between the two sides of the political spectrum. In addition to the usual targets on the Left, he observes corresponding phenomena in the pro-life movement, in Christian fundamentalism, and among conservative politicians. If there is political correctness on the Left, he remarks, the Right introduced another form of p.c., "patriotic-correctness," to American public life which is as committed to censorship.[16]

As an art critic, Hughes is especially interested in expressions of victimism in public debates over art exhibitions and public funding for the arts. The Left, he argues, promotes a display of wounds and misery as art and at the same time rejects as prejudiced and offensive any attempt to evaluate this art from a purely aesthetical point of view. The belief that art should serve some moral or political purpose is likewise embraced by the Right in campaigns such as Senator Jesse Helms's and the Christian Right's attack against the National Endowment for the Arts.[17]

## Victims and Victimists

Read together, the anti-victimist books present a great number of cases exhibiting the proliferation of claims by individuals and groups that they have been subjected to one or another disadvantage. They are or were, or sometimes their ancestors or other members of their group are or were, abused, oppressed, persecuted, discriminated against, exploited, marginalized, or otherwise mistreated. The critics also contend that these individuals and groups attempt to benefit from the acknowledgment of their disadvantage, whether in terms of social status, psychological rewards, or more tangible benefits such as government programs or protections, or even by relieving them from certain responsibilities for which they would otherwise be accountable, such as legal liability. However, despite the numerous illustrations, none of the authors offers evidence documenting that these individuals and groups do in fact use the term "victim" to describe their situation or the status and privileges they seek. It is the literature itself, therefore, that attempts to define this phenomenon in terms of victimhood.

Choosing the term "victim" in this context is important. The word "victim" is regularly used to denote an individual wrongly harmed. According to the critics, the victim's innocence is the source of her moral power, the reason she receives deference and assistance from others, and perhaps the basis of her prerogative to blame her victimizer. Used to describe a particular political group or approach (as in victim feminism), or to characterize an entire political culture (as in a nation of victims), the critics deploy "victim" with derision.

They develop a gradual line of attack. First, they maintain that many of the groups and individuals who claim to be victims are impostors; these individuals do not experience discrimination, nor are they deprived by any sensible standard. Second, those who are disadvantaged in some way use their victim status to achieve gains incommensurate with their actual circumstances. Third, apart from the truthfulness or proportionality of the victims' claims, making victimization a central theme of group or individual identity is harmful to the victim and to society in general. Regardless of the innocence of the victim, or the accuracy of his claim, the critics bemoan the hostile and accusatory tone of public discourse. Condemning blaming, as we will see in Chapter 5, is an integral element of the anti-victimist campaign.

Many of the texts derive their poignancy as social critiques by placing within the same rubric a myriad of supposed victimist claims that differ in gravity, if not in kind. Sykes, for instance, devotes much of his book to ridiculing individuals such as the FBI embezzler who gambled away his money and then convinced a court to acknowledge his "compulsive gambling" as a handicap, and the man with a sixty-inch waist who threatened to sue McDonald's under federal equal protection laws for not providing restaurant seats large enough to fit him. He finds these victimists' attempts to model their struggles according to the precedents set by the civil rights movement pathetic and scandalous. At the same time, he approaches contemporary racial politics and feminism with comparable scorn. Combining the serious and the ludicrous, the victim and the victimist, serves not only to dismiss the latter but also to ridicule the former. The ideals of cultural pluralism may be cast as an easier target when the example under scrutiny is Afro-centrism; and feminism can be dismissed altogether if assessed through the "case study" of a woman who thinks that bicycles for two are by definition sexist and an excuse for a public row.[18]

Despite their disparaging use of the term "victim," the critics must concede that real victims do exist. But most are strangely vague about how to identify them. Indeed, the genuine victims who figure most prominently in this literature are victims of victimism. Since victimists allegedly use their privileged status to victimize others, this is a recurrent theme.[19] Victimhood, in D'Souza's view, became a powerful tool that minority activists exploit to intimidate non-minorities: "thus the victim becomes a victimizer while continuing to enjoy superior moral credentials."[20] He argues that as a group, white male students are the primary victims of victimism and suggests that the rise in racial tensions on university campuses is a direct result of the continuing offensive by victim revolutionaries on this demographic. "[W]hites are forced into a defensive position," he explains.[21]

Some of the most vivid examples of victimists-as-victimizers can be found in the annals of the courts. Dershowitz points to a variety of court cases, some quite famous, in which the perpetrator of a crime successfully defended herself by claiming to be a victim—of society at large, of a miserable childhood, of some physical ailment, or, most remarkably, of the people she actually victimized. He contends that this change began outside the courtroom with the rise of a pro-victimist political rhetoric that selectively highlights the plight of some victims at the expense of others. He reminds us, as a counterweight to the media preoccupation with date rape and wife abuse, that there is an "epidemic of rape" among male prisoners, and that husbands also can be the victims of spousal abuse.[22] More momentous still is the possible effect of victimism on our civil liberties, such as the threat posed by Catharine MacKinnon's campaign against pornography. In his typically hyperbolic manner he warns: "READERS BEWARE. PROFESSOR Catharine MacKinnon—the Lorena Bobbitt of academia—is after our erections and orgasms."[23] Dershowitz's discussion of MacKinnon evokes an older conception of feminists as victimizers—the castrating woman.

Campaigns against feminists, such as Dershowitz's, in combination with kindred attacks on other victimizing victimist groups, paved the way for the public preoccupation with the "angry white male" in the mid-1990s. While this literature does not employ this precise phrase, a decidedly anti-victimist rhetoric was exploited by politicians and commentators in their description of the supposed plight of white men in America on the eve and in the wake of the 1994 congressional elections.[24] Beleaguered white men are probably the largest group of victims of victimism identified by anti-victimists, and the campaign to redeem the white, heterosexual male has assumed new dimensions in the aftermath of 9/11, as we will see in Chapter 6.

Victimists also victimize members of their own groups through loyalty tests. Those who fail to comply are accused of betraying their community and are ostracized accordingly. The case of Julius Lester is retold by many of the anti-victimists to demonstrate the mistreatment of those who insist on their individuality, who refuse to subscribe to the rigid and repressive protocol prescribed by victimist groups.[25] Lester, a prominent member of the civil rights movement in the 1960s and cofounder of one of the first Afro-American studies programs at the University of Massachusetts at Amherst, was forced out of his department after voicing views critical of contemporary racial politics. (We will turn to examine Lester's case in greater detail in Chapter 4.) Symptomatically, some of the writers also view themselves as actual or potential victims of victimism. Dershowitz, for instance, portrays himself as a prospective victim braving ridicule and ostracism by breaking ranks with the politically correct.[26] Critics of victim feminism, whose arguments we analyze in the following chapter, depict their plight in similar terms.

## Cynical and Deluded

Contrasting real victims and victimists is only one strategy employed in the literature. Bogus victims themselves may be divided into two general groups: the cynical and the deluded. Both types of victimists seek redress for their alleged victimization, but whereas the cynical victimist is a liar, who exaggerates or invents her victimization, the deluded victimist genuinely believes she is a victim. Poignant examples of cynical victimists appear in different texts to demonstrate the ways in which members of victimist groups abuse their presumed victim status. Marion Barry, Tawana Brawley, and Bernhard Goetz, for instance, are repeatedly used as illustrations.[27] Several of the authors waver between accusing victimists of purposeful deception on the one hand and acknowledging the power of self-delusion on the other. The literature as a whole, however, seems more concerned with deluded victims and, consequently, attempts to find an explanation for this phenomenon in psychology. Hence, victimism is considered not merely a type of public behavior, a political style, but also a mental affliction bordering on neurosis. Depicting victimism as a pathology that pervades an entire culture serves to explain both its proliferation and the growing receptivity of society to victim claims.

Steele provides the most far-reaching account of the psychological incentives that render victimhood so appealing. Victimists cling to their victim status, however dubious, in order to protect their innocence. This is an unconscious reflex, he explains, "fear working on a subterranean level to let us reduce our margin of choice in the name of race."[28] The process is a psychological one, but the benefits reaped are first and foremost moral:

> Victimization is a broad, somewhat sloppy word that one can apply to oneself in the most subjective of ways. And when we do think of ourselves as victims, we are released from responsibility for some difficulty, spared some guilt and accountability. Our innocence is restored because an injustice was done to us. Injustice is what gives the claim of victimization its magic, its power to spray the onus of responsibility on others.[29]

African Americans hold onto their racial identity in the face of greater opportunities, open to them as individuals rather than members of a racial group, because of a profound lack of self-confidence aroused by the possibilities of emancipation, or "integration shock," "the shock of being suddenly accountable on strikingly personal terms."[30] Although Steele concedes that the values and attitudes essential to a free existence were "muted and destabilized by the negative conditioning of oppression," he argues that "since the mid-sixties [African Americans'] weakness in this area has been a far greater detriment to [their] advancement than any remaining racial victimization."[31] We might therefore characterize Steele's view of racial identity as a peculiar variant of the false consciousness argument in which the external victimization is imagined and the false identity built around it is the real oppressive force.[32] As D'Souza puts it in his subsequent book, *The End of Racism* (1995), "One might say that today the most formidable ideological barrier facing blacks is not racism but antiracism."[33]

Innocence is, in Steele's scheme, a moral commodity traded among various segments of American society. But it is a zero-sum game. Victimists wield power by guilt-tripping the powerful. When the powerful succumb to the victimist's demands, it is only to secure their own innocence. The mutually manipulative pursuit of innocence yields destructive results for both the presumed victim and the supposed victimizer. Thus, Steele endeavors to give long-standing arguments about white guilt new theoretical underpinnings. He regards public assistance programs, from President Lyndon Johnson's Great Society to affirmative action policies, as nothing more than a manifestation of whites' preoccupation with their own redemption, not genuine concern for the well-being of society's "victims."[34] Victimism may seem to empower the victim and protect the innocence of the accused, but in reality it fails to secure palpable and enduring benefits for either.

## Therapeutic Culture

The mutual pursuit of innocence is the quest that unites victimists and society at large, according to Steele. Most of the other critics associate this search for a clear conscience with the rise of therapeutic culture. Ironically, while the authors deploy psychological concepts in their analyses and criticisms of the victimist mentality and practices, a central target of their cultural critique is the psychologization of American society. Specifically, they attack the immense influence wielded by the therapeutic professions as well as the recovery movement for encouraging victim claims. According to the critics, therapy inflates expectations for success and promises personal fulfillment, engendering an adolescent culture in which there are no limits beyond the "appetite and ambition of the self." Reprehensible behavior and attitudes are not morally wrong, but "diseased." Condemnation and punishment are not therapeutic tools; the therapeutic response to such conduct is compassion and "emotionality."[35]

The critics' arguments against therapeutic culture are three-pronged. First, they contend that therapy professionals encourage the already ingrained belief that "experts can solve all misfortunes" by therapeutic exercises (of the twelve-step variety), or increasingly by the state (either through government programs, or through extended protections designed by government and upheld by the courts). Second, guided by the principles of therapy, the liberal Left reformulated its relationship to marginal groups. Helping society's underdogs is no longer anchored in a strong ideology but in the therapeutic notion that empathy with the less fortunate brings the helper personal salvation. Finally, and most importantly, the therapeutic and medical professions expanded their definitions of disease to include types of behavior previously considered matters of personal responsibility.

Among the blatantly victimist concepts that critics identify in the recovery movement is that of the "inner child." Focusing on nurturing the inner child shifts attention from other human beings to an imaginary other that is solely the fabrication of the self and has no external referent. D'Souza characterizes victimism as a "collective tantrum."[36] Sykes likewise condemns victimists for "refus[ing] to grow up," remarking that their plaintive wail sounds like a "disappointed adolescent." He blames the youth culture of the 1960s for en-hancing these patterns that infantilize American society, asserting that the pro-tests of the sixties were merely exercises in self-therapy.[37] Hughes identifies the "obsession" with the inner child as part of a collective preoccupation with the unreal, the unborn.[38]

We should keep in mind that anti-victimists elaborated their critique dur-ing a moment when the ascendance of popular therapy in America drew criti-cal attention from many corners. It was also the decade that witnessed fierce debates over "recovered memory" and other aspects of Freud's legacy. In *I'm Dysfunctional, You're Dysfunctional: The Recovery Movement and Other Self-Help Fashions* (1992), for example, Wendy Kaminer examines how the recovery movement made suffering central to the self-conception of its practitioners. Participants in these programs are encouraged to search their personal histories to find abuses that might account for their present misfortunes or unhappiness. This strategy, she maintains, introduces new expansive definitions of abuse and a variety of pseudo-professional terms and concepts that further urge individ-uals to seek psychological refuge in conceiving of themselves as victims. Ac-cording to Kaminer, twelve-step groups have become America's new model of community. But unlike a genuine community, rituals of repetitive testimonies destroy the possibility of a real exchange or conversation. The pseudo-dialogue is scripted: "You can't argue with a testimonial," she points out. "You can only counter it with a testimonial of your own."[39] These practices, which she associ-ates with a misuse of early feminist consciousness-raising activities, on the one hand, and with nineteenth-century Christian revivalism, on the other, have also become common in politics and popular culture, most notably in the culture of confession that permeates television daytime talk shows. "By blurring the dis-tinction between confession and testimony, recovery transforms therapy into a public process too," she contends.[40]

Several of the anti-victimist writers detect a connection between the domi-nance of therapy and the rise of litigiousness.[41] Psychotherapy also significantly impacted criminal trials. Aided by new conceptions of antisocial behavior as disease, defendants may now argue in court that crimes (including murder, rape, and robbery) should be excused because of a variety of syndromes rang-ing from addictions of various kinds to gluttonous junk food consumption and excessive television viewing. Dershowitz offers two explanations for why these "abuse excuse" defenses succeed. First, jurors identify with the defendant's claim of abuse. This identification is aroused and nurtured through a diet of tales of mistreatment fed to the American public on television and in popular magazines. Viewers develop an increased sense of "entitlement based on their own victimization—real, imagined, or exaggerated."[42] Second, the proliferation of such stories not only incline jurors toward identification with the defendant but also lead Americans to believe that abuse is rampant and that formal channels for addressing it are woefully inadequate. Accepting the defendant's abuse excuse helps jurors feel that they are contributing to controlling criminal elements. "It is almost as if we have collectively thrown up our hands in desperation over our inability to solve the problems of crime, poverty, equality, peace and the breakdown of the family," explains Dershowitz. "'We are not responsible' is the cry of frustration."[43]

Central to the authors' critique of therapeutic culture is their observation that it has thwarted the correlation between merit and reward, and between harm and redress. Instead of allocating benefits on the basis of genuine achievements and qualities (e.g., talent, skills, education, hard work), therapeutic culture prescribes that everyone deserves an accolade. Impersonal evaluations are rendered irrelevant. Truthfulness is not a therapeutic concern. Any claim of injury or need is prima facie valid and merits compensation. The belief that self-respect can be conferred, that it need not be earned, is rejected outright by the anti-victimist critics.[44]

## Resurrecting Character

One way to distinguish the real from the bogus victim, the victim from the victimist, might be to scrutinize carefully the content of the victim's claim, its validity, and its correlation to the victim's specific demands. Such a procedure would involve closely examining the harm incurred, the causal chain of events, and the extent of the victim's culpability. In this vein, Kaminer promotes the idea of a "hierarchy of suffering" to arbitrate victim claims. There are many situations in which a sensible calibration is not only necessary but, she believes, blatantly obvious. We can, for instance, distinguish between "holocausts that happen only metaphorically and holocausts that happen in fact."[45] The objective classification of victims, which she contrasts with the relativism of the recovery movement, is ultimately a prerequisite of policy making, since government has finite resources. Sykes, in contrast, maintains that societal compassion, more than governmental reserves, is the limited asset that must be protected from the propagation of excessive victim claims. The danger of victimism, he warns, is "compassion fatigue," a growing indifference in the face of numerous cries for help that cannot be evaluated properly.[46]

However, most of these writers, Sykes included, are not hopeful about the possibility of curbing victimism through a process of evaluation scrutinizing the victim's petition, its validity, and it correlation to her specific demands. They seem to doubt that such assessments will counterbalance the subjectivity of victims' claims and society's susceptibility to them. Recent trends in the courts, where these procedures are supposedly the norm, have provided the most attention-grabbing examples of how testimonies of abuse, however incredible, may obstruct more detached appraisals. Evaluating the veracity of victimists' accusations is further complicated when they are made collectively or in the name of historical injustice. Often the victim's testimony of injury is the only basis upon which to make a judgment. Of course, the courts themselves had already recoiled from adjudicating such claims regarding the scope of injury and the extent of remedy in the case of a set-aside program for municipal contracts, *City of Richmond v. J. A. Croson Co.* (1989):

> To accept Richmond's claim that past societal discrimination alone can serve as the basis for rigid racial preferences would be to open the door to competing claims for "remedial relief" for every disadvantaged group. The dream of a Nation of equal citizens in a society where race is irrelevant to personal opportunity and achievement would be lost in a mosaic of shifting preferences based on inherently unmeasurable claims of past wrongs. [Citing *Bakke*:] Courts would be asked to evaluate the extent of the prejudice and consequent harm suffered by various minority groups. Those whose societal injury is thought to exceed some arbitrary level of intolerability then would be entitled to preferential classification. We think such a result would be contrary both to the letter and the spirit of a constitutional provision whose central command is equality.[47]

In their effort to counter the subjective dimension of victimhood, to judge the victimist, and even to prescribe "solutions," the authors circumvent factual examination altogether and resort instead to appraising the quality of the victim's personality and her manner of grappling with her (perceived) victimization. They employ a model of character that relieves them from the need to differentiate between deluded and cynical victimists as well as between victimists and victims, since the model applies to all. Their ideal is a strong, resilient individual who, regardless of her suffering, refuses to focus on her sense of injustice. The "good" victim, in other words, is a victim who refuses to be a victim.

The comparison of virtuous victims and victimists who cling to their victim status, a variation on the "model minority" argument, is a recurrent tactic in the literature and an essential feature of the Cult of True Victimhood. Narrating stories of good victims and bad ones is a staple of the literature and anti-victimist lore. While titillating and shocking, these "case studies" supposedly carry the weight of important moral lessons. D'Souza, for instance, compares his encounters with two college co-eds. One is a former boat person from Vietnam, a successful student, who does not consider herself disadvantaged. She is cheerful and optimistic, concentrating on the future rather than the past. She tells D'Souza, "The main thing is to focus on what you can do yourself." D'Souza suggests that she was not admitted to the prestigious University of California at Berkeley because of racial quotas, but still she is not resentful. "What do I have to complain about?" she asks. She is, moreover, particularly sympathetic toward the plight of other groups such as the African American students: "They seem so hurt all the time," she remarks. D'Souza contrasts this exemplary victim against an African American student who advocates affirmative action and was likely a beneficiary of such programs in her admission to Berkeley. Although this student could not recall a single incident in which she was personally subjected to racism, she still maintains that racism runs rampant in American society at large and on her campus. "You may be the richest Black person in the world, I may be the son or the daughter of Michael Jackson, but Michael Jackson's ancestors were stripped of their name and their person." "I am oppressed," she declares, "and I will always be oppressed."[48]

Kaminer, to give another example, juxtaposes the self-pity of the middle-class members of the recovery movement with the dignified resourcefulness she observes in a support group for Cambodian refugee women. "Unlike many twelve-steppers I've heard, the Cambodian women don't seem to revel in their victimhood. Their meetings aren't collections of complaints and testimonies about their pain," she recounts. "Sometimes they are sad and serious; sometimes the sadness is an interruption in a long moment of frivolity."[49]

The writers praise the genuine power achieved through self-making or overcoming adversity. "Victimhood may provoke sympathy, but it does not, by itself produce admiration," explains D'Souza. "[W]hat evokes admiration is the spectacle of oppressed victims struggling against their circumstances, heroically, despite the odds. In this way victimhood can pave the way for greatness."[50]

Despite the Nietzschean overtones of their prescription (especially since the adversity to be overcome is a psychological attachment to weakness), ultimately the critics strive to revive a host of virtues associated with the entrepreneurial, male, (Protestant) ethos at the heart of neo-liberalism: individualism, self-advancement, self-restraint, personal responsibility, forward-looking optimism, resourcefulness, and independence. These qualities are strikingly absent from the victimist's frame of mind: she subjects herself to her group's identity and seeks to redress her misfortune through the group rather than through personal effort. Thus, she is dependent on her group, and ultimately on the general public for various government-funded and charitable programs.

In page after page, the critics deride victimists for lacking these qualities. The victimist is portrayed as lazy, lethargic, infantile, and impotent. At the same time, the literature demonizes the victimist, since beyond her apparent weaknesses she is manipulative and dangerous—a symptom of national decay, a paranoiac to be feared. The victimist cleaves to the past, whether personal (childhood experiences) or collective (minorities and feminists). If she has a concern about the future, it is not to improve her circumstances so much as to revenge her past suffering.

Depictions of the victimist as somehow simultaneously impotent and dangerous are reminiscent of previous portrayals of the Other in American history. But if in the past the power of the Other was associated with his masculine virility or, conversely, his conspiratorial skills, the victimist's might and weakness are decidedly that of the stereotypical woman—emotionally incontinent, manipulative, and dependent. Thus, we may characterize the authors' strategies to end victimism as an effort to remasculinize America.

Decaying character is the cornerstone of Sykes's and Steele's assessment of victim politics, and rebuilding character is that of their ultimate solutions.[51] The anti-victimists apply the term to specific practitioners of victimism as well as to racial groups or the nation as a whole. This scope evokes notions of society as the sum of its individuals and of society's strength as the aggregate of its members' moral stature. Therefore, according to their respective designs, fundamental problems of social equality should be addressed not by contending with their root causes, but by mass efforts to reform individuals in order to establish personal virtues vital to good citizenship. The critics do not volunteer details about how such an educational endeavor might be achieved; nor do they specify the precise qualities that should be instilled. Victimism is first and foremost a personal failing. By reintroducing character as a center of national policy they hope to re-atomize society into a mass of responsible individuals.[52]

## Comparative Victimism

None of the writers consider the possibility that a growing demand for attention, and increasing societal and governmental responsiveness, might foster the bonds of community, national or otherwise. Instead they contend that the culture of complaint has fractured society into small groups of victimists, artificially converging around their shared, imagined or real, past or present, victim identities. Members of victimist groups exempt themselves from assuming full responsibility for their individual lives. Rather than focusing on their own efforts, skills and abilities, they regard their personal achievements and (especially) their failures solely in the context of the relationship between their group and its victimizers. They fail to individuate themselves. Blaming others is a telltale symptom of victimism. Victimist groups, the critics maintain, are hostile to society no matter what assistance it has provided them.

Law professor Stephen Carter argues in *Reflections of an Affirmative Action Baby* (1991) that African American activists have promoted identities that are exclusive, dogmatic, and narrowly defined. He advocates a more inclusive group definition. Steele, by contrast, is fundamentally dissatisfied with the notion of black collective identity, whether as a fixed label or as the basis of political affiliation. A stifling "tyranny of identity" manifested in a strict "party line" may be observed in a myriad of other groups defined by a notion of difference, be it gender, race, ethnicity, and so forth; groups who privilege their uniqueness over principles of commonality and cooperation. This is the inevitable fate of any politics founded on victim identity.[53]

"Identity is not the same thing as the fact of membership in a collective; it is, rather, a form of self-definition, facilitated by images of what we wish our membership in the collective to mean," asserts Steele.[54] Contemporary African American identity was formulated during the tumultuous 1960s on the basis of models and values constructed around the most impoverished and disadvantaged segments of black society. African Americans came to see themselves as an "embattled minority." Steele compares this group conception to a national identity crystallized by the experience of war: it is severe, inflexible, and adversarial. Minimizing differences and emphasizing a common experience of oppression proved effective in mobilizing African Americans to fight for their civil rights. Unfortunately, however, the black majority's embrace of this identity continues beyond the civil rights movement, and its victimist undertones have only become stronger. This construction of victim identity—"race as identity"—disguises diversity. It does not account for the ways in which the experiences of African Americans have varied over the last quarter of a century, specifically that a growing number of African Americans joined the ranks of the middle class and share its privileges.[55] African Americans need to shed their "racial mask" and simultaneously "remember and forget that [they are] black."[56] This, Steele claims, is how whites regard their race. "Whites do not have to spend precious time fashioning an identity out of simply being white. . . . [T]heir racial collectivism, to the extent that they feel it, creates no imbalance between the collective and the individual."[57]

The rigidity of victim politics has another effect; it encourages the rise of new victimist groups based on increasingly narrower claims of victimization. In this way victimism reproduces itself. For example, when competing affiliations—such as race, class, and sexuality—seemed to fracture the modern women's movement, some feminists claimed that the focus on victimization fostered hostilities and competitions among and within these groups and undermined women's ability to cooperate in order to achieve common goals. The contests among victim groups vying for public attention are the primary cause, according to the critics, for the deepening cognitive dissonance among victimists, the constantly widening gap between reality and self-perception. A more cynical argument regards victimism simply as a strategy to maximize benefits. In a world of limited resources where victims benefit from their status as victims—either materially or psychologically—there is an incentive to present one's misfortune as greater than any other's.

Victim rivalry is one manifestation of what the authors describe as the paranoid style of victim politics. Instead of leading the practitioners into greater solidarity and empathy with each other, battles between victim groups reveal uncompromising xenophobia and tribalism.[58] The result is a "comparative victimology" that encourages victim groups to regard victim claims voiced by others as a threat to their own victim status. "[T]he politics of victimization . . . turned difference into an existential chasm, which cannot be bridged by shared notions of justice or principles of equity," claims Sykes. "No common language existed for resolving inter-group disputes except the rhetoric of demand and accusation."[59]

Victimist competitions are not an unalterable outcome of identity politics, according to Carter, but an aberration that endangers the possibility of true pluralism. While he regards past injustices as vital to forging a particular group's self-conception as well as alliances among groups, he thinks that victimhood became in effect a meritocratic scale in which the greater the suffering, the higher the place of the sufferers.[60] Most others critics hold, like D'Souza, that comparative victimology is unavoidable, an "inevitable consequence of principles that exalt group equality above individual justice."[61] Victimism cultivates skepticism and a "what's in it for me" attitude, argues Sykes, contributing to the increasing neglect of genuine victims, and facilitating, especially over the last several years, the rise of especially aggressive interest group politics.[62]

Contemporary identity politics replicates victim politics even when these groups do not explicitly employ a victim identity or promote victim claims. The loss of the individual's independence characterizes all such affiliations. It is unclear what form of collectivity might be acceptable to the anti-victimists for only enigmatic alternatives are offered. Steele, perhaps the best example, titles his text "The Content of Our Character" without ever defining to whom the scope of "our" applies.

## Foundations and Legacies

Not surprisingly, the authors concur that victimism as an ideology and practice took shape in the 1960s. They also tacitly agree that the politics of the 1960s had positive aspects, best exemplified by Martin Luther King Jr.'s leadership of the civil rights movement. The critics identify a dividing line between the two sixties: King versus Black Power; liberal universalism versus identity politics particularism; procedural justice versus distributive justice; discriminatory intent versus disparate impact (in judicial doctrines). (In the following chapter, we will see that anti-victim feminists revisit this historical divide.)

Sykes, who is more inclined toward historical analysis than other writers, identifies a specific year, 1965–66, as the moment during which northern white intellectuals and white counterculture youths forged an alliance with Black Power activists, such as Stokely Carmichael. These forces coalesced to replace the universal struggle for civil rights that took place in the South—a movement whose moral edge was epitomized by Martin Luther King's rather middle-class and religious ethos that promoted personal responsibility, self-reliance, and focused on equal opportunity through legal and political rights. Sykes even detects a shift in King's political style. As King moved from his Southern base and attempted to appeal to Northerners, he began using an increasingly accusatory tone toward white society, blaming whites for "'psychological and spiritual genocide' and demanding not merely fairness but 'compensatory treatment' for centuries of victimization."[63] White radicals (both guilt-ridden intellectuals and narcissistic counterculture youth) are responsible for the political transformation; while the black masses, he maintains, remained loyal to King and his traditional politics long after these fell into disfavor with Northern white elites. Therefore, Sykes reasons that it was not black rage so much as the ascendance of left-wing therapeutic politics that facilitated the rise of victimism into a powerful force in American society.

This is a curious and yet necessary shift in focus from black activism to whites' motives. Were Sykes to probe further, he would have to concede that the turbulent 1960s were precisely when the concept of "victim" was embedded with quite different ideological meanings. While in the previous chapter we saw how the politics of suffering has a long, rich, and varied history in America, in black protest movements of the 1960s recognizing the collective victimization of blacks became a rallying point for political recruitment. This consciousness and mobilization spread to other aggrieved groups—women, gays and lesbians, Chicanos and Latinos, and so forth. Contrary to the anti-victimists' reconceptualization of victimhood, at this political moment victimization unquestionably served as the starting point for individual and collective action. It is precisely because the construction of victimhood became so politically potent, so resonant with the experiences of whole groups that it had to be blunted by ideological enemies.

Conceiving of victim politics as a product of misguided elites, the critics make an effort—albeit fleeting and superficial—to identify the intellectual underpinnings of victimism. All of the writers forcefully reject postmodern critical theories, especially the various imports from Paris that over the last quarter of a century left an unmistakable imprint on American intellectual life. D'Souza's and Hughes's derision of French intellectuals such as Foucault and Derrida is inseparable from their views on victimism and victim politics. They regard post-structuralism as providing the theoretical justification for the apocalyptic attack on universalism and on other attempts to give the world an objective meritocratic order.

As disturbed by current academic trends as the critics are, still, they see the work of Foucault, Derrida, and Lacan as merely offering tools to justify and further victimism. Interestingly, while most of the critics identify the radical politics of the 1960s as the origin of victimism, Karl Marx is almost entirely absent from their analyses. (In the aftermath of communism's demise, they might have been searching for a different ideological foe.) Sykes alludes to modern Marxian thinkers (such as the members of the Frankfurt School, Albert Memmi and Frantz Fanon), but when he ventures into the more traditional canon of political thought in search of the originator of victimism, he focuses on Jean Jacques Rousseau.

> [Rousseau was] the first to link the assault on middle class culture with both the championing of the untrammeled self *and* the call for compassion. This trinity of attitudes—hostility toward the bourgeoisie, faith in the self, and the embrace of compassion—was to be the formula for modernity's attitude towards culture, society, and politics.[64]

The Rousseauean "trinity" was further ingrained in the modern sensibility by the early nineteenth-century Romantics.

D'Souza chimes in, albeit some fifteen years later. In his most recent defense of the United States against its critics from within and without, he suggests that Islamic fundamentalists who find American culture immoral may have a point. The unseemly abuses of our treasured freedoms can be traced back to the 1960s, of course, but he proposes that the intellectual architect of such wantonness was Rousseau. In D'Souza's account, Rousseau morphs from being a philosopher who explicated the idea of a "moral freedom" achievable only through a collective decision-making process in pursuit of the "general will," into the preacher of individuals' flight from personal responsibility.[65] Rousseau should be blamed for our present culture of complaint because, unlike other contract theorists who assumed human nature is self-interested, fearful, and often combative (e.g., Hobbes and Locke), he proposed that humans are good in nature but corrupted by civil society. With a few sleights of hand, and a couple of references to neo-Straussian exegesis, D'Souza establishes that Rousseau set the foundation for the idea that we can "blame our suffering and crimes on society."[66]

Targeting Rousseau serves another purpose. Disputing Nietzsche's interpretation of the role of Christianity in exalting the meek over the strong, Sykes adamantly insists that modern victimism originated in Rousseau's attack on middle-class Christianity. Although compassion for sufferers in the nineteenth century borrowed its moral vocabulary from Christianity, it was ultimately a secular sensibility. He enumerates basic tenets of victimist ideology, which he argues are fundamentally opposed to Christian ethos: misfortune confers a special moral character on the downtrodden, reducing pain is society's ultimate obligation to its members, all sufferers are saints, and all suffering is equal.[67] Apart from this defense of Christian traditions, the literature is silent about the role of religion in general and Christianity in particular in shaping the modern notion of victimhood.

## Anti-Victimist Taxonomies

By way of summary, we may classify the anti-victimist critique according to the following three categories: motivation, rewards, and politics. The critics agree that victimism is based on fictitious petitions. Numerous individuals and groups who claim to be victims should not be regarded as such by any sensible, objective standard. At a minimum, there is a profound discrepancy between these plaintiffs' plights and their demands. Some cynically vie for the benefits that victim status bestows. Other victimists suffer from an excessive, endemic pessimism. The victimist may be a whiner, a helpless "crybaby" who makes her complaint the center of her being in the world; or she may be enraged, hate-filled, and vengeful, overflowing with bitterness and unbridled resentment. In more severe cases, the victimist's behavior verges on paranoia. She is so entrenched in her belief that the world (or whites, blacks, men, the "system") is out to get her and her kind, that nothing can quiet her suspicion; even a helping hand is perceived as part of the greater conspiracy.

Another way to group victimists is through the sorts of rewards they seek. First, the victimist may be looking for tangible benefits incongruent with the actual damage inflicted upon her, for instance, monstrous monetary compensation, or remuneration contingent upon elusive claims of historical injustice and group membership. These gains may follow one or some combination of the Weberian trilogy of power, money, and status. Affirmative action programs, to give one example, provide their beneficiaries with a protected trail to secure, financially lucrative, and socially prestigious positions.

A second set of benefits that victimists desire is psychological, which may include attention, sympathy, compassion, pity, and other responses likely to enhance the victimists' damaged self-esteem. The third type of benefit is protection or exemption, although protections anchored in civil rights are not inherently victimist. In fact, the authors usually present the protections against discrimination won by the civil rights movement as examples of legitimate redress. Protections encourage victimism when they endure beyond the circumstances that made them a necessary remedy, or when they generate new groups of victims as in cases of "reverse discrimination." In contrast to protections, exemptions, such as the abuse excuse, are particularly victimist privileges, licensing behavior not otherwise sanctioned. Whether won by manipulating the legal system, by exploiting the presumption of victimization, or simply by seizing these prerogatives, victimists enjoy (or allow themselves) exemptions from social conventions as well as moral and sometimes legal judgments.

Most victimist groups interact with society by making demands. Alternatively, victimists may attempt to achieve their goals by separating themselves. Steele, for example, characterizes the Black Power movement of the late 1960s as the quintessential manifestation of victim politics, despite its militant activism. Sykes also identifies the rise of black victimism with Malcolm X and the Black Panthers. Separatism allows such groups to sustain, or even further cultivate, their victimist self-perception. But separatists pose a problem for the anti-victimists because their aspirations—social and financial self-sufficiency—are what the critics prescribe to cure victimism. Thus, for example, it is unclear where Louis Farrakhan and the Nation of Islam would fit within the victimist taxonomy. On the one hand, in Farrakhan's perception of blacks as eternal victims of white atrocities, he is a typical purveyor of the victimist mentality in both its enraged and paranoid styles. On the other hand, the Nation of Islam's rejection of white assistance and promotion of a host of traditional mores such as accountability, personal responsibility, and self-reliance puts it in a category distinct from most other victimist groups. After all, what finer display of masculine virility and virtue could the anti-victimists have conjured than the 1995 Million Man March?

All of the authors reject separatism and difference, but pursuing sameness does not guarantee an absence of victimism. When the anti-victimists examine fields beyond feminism or racial politics, it is precisely the claim of sameness that they seek to undermine. The claims of organizations such as the National Association for Fat Acceptance to be fighting for rights for "people of size" analogous to those secured by the civil rights movement receives some of the harshest treatment because the critics dismiss the notion that these groups are genuinely victimized, at least not in a way that merits active redress. Likewise, calls for legalizing gay marriage are undermined in part by rejecting the idea that lesbians and gays are currently denied civil rights.[68] Sameness also becomes victimist when the victim demands more than mere equal opportunity or temporary protection to alleviate problems produced by overt discrimination and insists on policies and legislation that will create an equality of results. The ideal of proportional representation in the academy, politics, and the marketplace is tied to a conception of sameness different from that promoted by the civil rights movement, and the critics accordingly reject it.

By their own criteria, there are domains of "victimism" curiously ignored by anti-victimists. Hughes is the only writer to consider the prevalence of victim politics among conservatives. Furthermore, there are other groups that exhibit victimist symptoms but do not fit any of the models delineated by the literature. Consider, for instance, the case of American Jews. Over the last twenty years, the memory of the Holocaust became the most powerful force in galvanizing secular Jewish identity in America, culminating in the establishment of the U.S. Holocaust Memorial Museum on the National Mall.[69] A recent study found that an enduring fear of anti-Semitism is the widest common denominator in forging group affiliation.[70] Arguably, then, Jewish identity may be considered as "victimist" as other collective identities undermined by the critics—it is pessimistic and seemingly incongruent with the socioeconomic success of most American Jews. Not unlike participants in other "victimist" groups, moreover, members of the Jewish establishment (e.g., AIPAC) have used the memory of Jewish victimization during the Holocaust to argue for specific policies.[71] Another significant omission from the anti-victimists' survey, which we will examine in detail in Chapter 5, is the victims' rights movement.

## The Trouble with Victims

In this chapter we explored several of the more prominent articulations of the anti-victimist campaign. The critics aim to dismantle the system of protections and compensations that, they claim, was indiscriminately bestowed upon those who present themselves as victims. They also seek to end the reflexive deferential posture society assumes toward victims and their demands. Such victimist relativism, sustained by norms prescribing excessive "politicized sensitivity," has replaced rational discussion, the authors contend. "To be sensitive (in victim-speak) is not to argue or to reason but to *feel*, to attune one's response to another's sense of aggrievement," Sykes claims. "The greater the wounds, the louder the cries of injustice, the greater the demands for sensitivity—no matter how unreasonable."[72]

By shaming the victim the critics strive to place the onus of responsibility for the victim's fate on the victim herself, as well as to deny her the sort of attention she supposedly has received.[73] However, at the core of the anti-victimist endeavor is not only the victimist and her unreasonable demands but also those forces in society that have provided the victimist's unmitigated benefits, those we might call, employing the self-help jargon, victim-enablers. The anti-victimist literature is decidedly antiestablishment and anti-elitist in its approach. Experts, intellectuals, academics, social bureaucrats, therapy professionals, defense attorneys, middle-class feminists, African American leadership, and other producers and sustainers of "liberal sensibilities" are presented in the literature as the progenitors of victimism.[74]

With few exceptions, the anti-victimists say little of substance about matters of policy, and many of their prescriptions are located in the realm of mood and atmosphere. Clearly the critics are impatient with individuals and groups who simply refuse to be content or quiescent. Sykes, for example, claims to be deeply distressed by the prevalence of pessimism in American society today, and consequently tells us all to just "lighten up." Only Steele is reluctant to claim that a brighter outlook will resolve black victimism. His book is suffused with personal pain, a great agony at departing from the political consensus he detects among African Americans. For although he preaches racial forgetting, his text is not a declaration of liberation as much as an apologia.[75]

The anti-victimist literature records a supposedly novel style in public culture: Americans appear to be less restrained about revealing their despair and deficiencies and, at times, almost eager to admit failure. Miseries and weaknesses that in the past were considered best concealed are frequently displayed publicly. This observation should be fairly obvious to anyone who happens to watch daytime television. The trend has reached into other domains of public life; for instance, the willingness of politicians and celebrities to divulge intimate, and often disturbing, details about their private lives.

Anti-victimist analyses are populated with myriad anecdotes about the loss of inhibitions or, alternatively, reckless individuals who would stop at nothing in order to receive some trifling benefit, or to get themselves off the hook by feigning new diseases, fabricating life stories, and concocting outlandish excuses. Yet, is such behavior unprecedented? Is it a symptom of pervasive weakness and passivity, or actually another manifestation of American entrepreneurialism? The authors do not provide answers to these questions, for ultimately their purpose is to discredit oppositional politics, multiculturalism, and the welfare state. The leap from recounting anecdotes to a sweeping dismissal of political movements renders their arguments particularly weak. Furthermore, their early 1990s prophecies proved false: victim claims have not overwhelmed the United States, the judicial system has not crumbled under the "abuse excuse," American universities did not lose standards of excellence, American art did not digress into a plaintive wail, and citizens have not become lazy, fatalistic, apathetic wards of the federal state. In retrospect, anti-victimism congealed in a moment of moral panic that gripped the country between the fall of the Berlin Wall (1989) and the economic boom of the mid-1990s. During this period, America's role in the post–cold war world and its economic prominence were uncertain, while the forces of the already globalizing economy demanded greater productivity and efficiency. Anti-victimism expressed a longing for lost autonomy, individualism, and especially masculinity in an increasingly corporate and ruthlessly downsizing economy. The desire for rejuvenation sought release through purging the social body of its weaknesses.

While a few of the concerns that fueled anti-victimism in its inception have since dissipated, anti-victimist idioms, modes of argumentation, and political agenda remain entrenched in American public life. Lingering contentions over identity politics and the role of the state continue to nurture similar public reflections on race relations, welfare, and multiculturalism. (John McWhorter's *Losing the Race: Self-Sabotage in Black America* [2000] and John Stossel's *Give Me a Break: How I Exposed Hucksters, Cheats, and Scam Artists and Became the Scourge of the Liberal Media* [2004] come to mind.) American society still grapples with the radical transformations and displacements brought about by the new economy. Anti-victimism should be understood as both an extension of neo-liberalism as well as an attempt to come to terms with its consequences. Most importantly, uncertainties about America's role in the world, its weaknesses, strengths, and foes were rekindled, albeit in a new guise, in the aftermath of 9/11 and, as we shall see in Chapter 6, invested anti-victimism with new force and poignancy.

# 3

# Victims on a Pedestal:
# Anti-"Victim Feminism"
# and Women's Oppression

**THE FILM** *DANGEROUS MINDS* (1995) depicts the "true" story of a former marine, LouAnne Johnson, who as a high school teacher transformed her students from potential criminals and "welfare queens" into responsible future citizens. Hollywood recruited Michelle Pfeiffer to play the role of this teacher engaged in psychological combat; hence her mission, reforming the students' "dangerous minds." In a crucial scene in the movie, the students attempt to excuse their unruly behavior and appeal to their teacher's sense of guilt by attributing their failings to the impoverished conditions of their lives. In response Pfeiffer (as Johnson) firmly declares: "There are no victims in this class!"

Pfeiffer's declaration encapsulates a current popular sentiment against victims and "victimism." Victimhood—politicians and pundits tell us—is a state of mind, and those who choose to view themselves as victims are manipulative, self-indulgent, hopeless dependents. Feminists have been the target of much criticism for allegedly inciting the rise of victimism. As we saw in the previous chapter, anti-victimists blame the modern women's movement for encouraging the proliferation of individuals and groups who attempt to secure their status as victims in order to gain various material and psychological rewards. These critics have been joined by a group of self-described feminists, variously referred to as "third wave," "power," "neo," "post," "revisionist," "dissident," or "post-ideological" feminists.

While these labels designate a variety of critiques and individuals, the coterie of popular writers whom I examine share the conviction that women are no longer oppressed as a group, and that their progress as individuals is now impeded by the women's movement. It is feminism, they claim, that turns women into victims both in theory and in fact. In Katie Roiphe's words, feminists' "conceptual framework"—their language, method, and analysis—"transforms perfectly stable women into hysterical, sobbing victims."[1] No domain of contemporary feminism is beyond the ire of these writers—from the activities of the National Organization of Women (NOW) and the survey research sponsored by the American Association of University Women, to battered women's shelters, women's studies programs and conferences, and other forms of feminist scholarship.

In this chapter I investigate the arguments launched against so-called victim feminism, as detailed in Rene Denfeld's *The New Victorians: A Young Woman's Challenge to the Old Feminist Order* (1995), Christina Hoff Sommers's *Who Stole Feminism? How Women Have Betrayed Women* (1994), Camille Paglia's *Sex, Art, and American Culture* (1992), Katie Roiphe's *The Morning After: Sex, Fear, and Feminism on Campus* (1993), and Naomi Wolf's *Fire with Fire: The New Female Power and How It Will Change the 21st Century* (1993). While attacking victim feminism became quite fashionable in the 1990s—spawning a cottage industry of books, articles, and op-ed pieces—these authors were the first to set the parameters of the critique and provide its most influential specimen.[2]

This group may be too small to categorize in sociological terms; yet a few shared characteristics are discernible. Roiphe, Denfeld, and Wolf regard themselves as spokespersons for a new cadre of feminists, literally daughters of the 1960s second wavers. Their generational claim is enhanced by the biographical fact that Roiphe's and Wolf's mothers reportedly served them as feminist role models. Accordingly, both writers seek to present themselves as what we might call "redstockings babies." All three authors wrote their books when they were in their late twenties, not long after they graduated from college, and campus feminism is an important target in their campaigns.[3] Paglia and Hoff Sommers are college professors themselves and their challenge to their feminist colleagues is even more direct and belligerent. They belong to an older generation of women who witnessed the increasing role of feminists in higher education, flirted with feminism at one point or another, but by and large remained outsiders, or at least inhabited its outer edge. Despite their academic training, they present their manifestos in a popular or "public intellectual" style much like that of Wolf, Roiphe, and Denfeld. As similar as their ideas are (and irrespective of their professed desire to reform the women's movement), these five women do not share official organizational ties, and their public activities revolve around their writings and appearances on the lecture circuit and in the media.

Their challenge to contemporary feminism may be understood as yet another permutation of the long-standing conflict between liberal and radical feminists. But it is their deployment of an anti-victimist rhetoric that this chapter investigates and problematizes. Therefore, I refer to this genre as "anti-'victim-feminism'" (AVF) and to these writers as "AVFers." That they choose to formulate their critique in terms of victimism is, I argue, highly significant. First, it ties their arguments against feminists to the larger anti-victimist enterprise outside feminism that we examined in Chapter 2. Second, AVFers' analyses capitalize on earlier arguments made by many of the same feminists they assail. Much before anti-victimism became the cause célèbre in the early 1990s, feminists were questioning the appropriate use of suffering in defining women's condition and in setting common goals. The following discussion charts key debates among feminists over victimhood, controversies that crossed the liberal/radical divide. Tracing these disputes will lead us back to Betty Friedan's *The Feminine Mystique* (1963), for in this foundational text we will find a powerful description of women's oppression along side great ambivalence about the status of women as victims. In fact, Friedan suggests that suburban homemakers victimize their husbands and sons and enfeeble society at large.

Finally, the declaration "There are no victims in this class" leads to two other, less explicit, disclaimers, both of which expose AVFers' anti-victimism as a rejection of "class." AVFers suggest that feminist politics should be stripped of its affiliation with the Left: it should be separated from questions of economic redistribution and other egalitarian causes (e.g., race, sexuality) and be devoted solely to issues common to all women. Paradoxically, this narrow view of the feminist agenda is paralleled by these writers' hostility toward gender as a classification: women, they maintain, do not constitute a distinct class. In their analyses both egalitarianism and attempts to theorize gender are equated with, or reduced to, victimism. Thus, I argue, in the AVFers' campaign against victim feminism it is not simply (as Pfeiffer's character told her students) that "There are no victims in this class," but also that "There is no class in the class," and finally, that "Women are not a class."

## Anti-"Victim Feminism"

AVFers find contemporary feminism too morose, acrid, and pessimistic. "It used to be fun to be a feminist," Christina Hoff Sommers recalls. "Now . . . it means male-bashing, it means being a victim, and it means being bitter and angry."[4] Certainly feminists needed to struggle to secure women equal rights, to fight sexism, and to win reproductive freedom; but somehow, AVFers maintain, they had fun doing it. More importantly, the battles feminists had to fight have been largely won; now it is time to disarm, to reconcile with men, and to celebrate the hard-earned successes of the second wave. Now individual women may freely indulge in a host of feminine pleasures, including the joys of lipstick, the euphoria of a traditional wedding, the thrill involved in making their workplaces pretty, and even their fantasies of being sexually ravaged by a man.[5]

According to Naomi Wolf's interpretation of recent history, the 1991 Clarence Thomas–Anita Hill congressional hearings set off a revolution in gender relations, a full-scale "genderquake." American women finally have enough money, status, and political clout to alter permanently the imbalance between the sexes. The only obstacles holding women back are the "maladaptive attitudes" promoted by a few, exceptionally influential women—the victim feminists.[6] These radicals, Hoff Sommers charges, have "stolen" feminism and "betrayed" women. Reiterating these sentiments, Camille Paglia asserts that contemporary feminism is consumed by "hysterical moralism and prudery," dogmatism, and a profound fear of the masculine.[7]

Among the AVFers, Wolf provides the most comprehensive description of victim feminism. She contrasts victim feminism to "power feminism," a concept she promulgates as the great hope for future feminism. Victim feminism casts women as "beleaguered, fragile, intuitive angels" and encourages them to "seek power through an identity of powerlessness."[8] Wolf offers a long list of attributes of victim feminism that she detects in a host of feminist activities, institutions, and texts. First, the rejection of overt power: victim feminism prevents women from taking responsibility for the power they have, degrades leadership, and is obsessed with purity and perfection. Second, dogmatism and exclusiveness: victim feminists want all women to share the doctrines of victim feminism; they are judgmental about other women's sexuality and appearances, condemning those who are insufficiently victim-like. Third, social leveling: victim feminism is communal, egalitarian, and suspicious of individualism and of money. Fourth, joylessness: victim feminism requires that women be self-sacrificing; it "fosters resentment" of others' successes and joys, and rejects the pleasures of sex. Fifth, essentialism: victim feminism regards women as inherently better than men, nurturing, closer to nature, noncompetitive, cooperative, and peace loving. Victim feminism "projects aggression, competitiveness, and violence onto 'men' or 'patriarchy,' while its devotees are blind to those qualities in themselves."[9]

The AVFers view themselves as whistle-blowers exposing a great scam. Although victim feminists claim to be victims, and hence powerless, they actually wield a great deal of clout. Victim feminists' anxieties about the direct use of power prompt them to use it deceptively. Their great strength is their skill at manipulating others. Wolf, for example, compares victim feminists to Victorian invalids who relished the control over others that their illness enabled.[10] Focusing on the activities of college-age feminists, Paglia cautions: "Beware of the deep manipulativeness of rich students who were neglected by their parents. They love to turn the campus into hysterical psycho-dramas of sexual transgression."[11] Similarly, Roiphe maintains that on her campus those who claim to be silenced victims actually dominate most conversations. "It is the presumption of silence that gives these women the right to speak, that elevates their words above the competitive noise of the university. Silence is the passkey to the empowering universe of the disempowered. Having been silenced on today's campus is the ultimate source of authority."[12]

Such emotional cunning yields tangible results, as Hoff Sommers warns. Having brainwashed their female devotees into a perpetual state of terror, and armed with wads of "junk science," feminists have duped public officials and spawned a lucrative industry. Now vital resources for a range of more important projects—from enriching libraries and combating violence in schools to medical research on prostate cancer—have been reallocated to programs designed to remedy the victim feminists' fabricated problems. "It's a disaster," an exasperated Hoff Sommers concludes.

> I will give them one thing. They're brilliant work-shoppers, networkers, organizers, moving in, taking over infrastructure. . . . And they know how to work the system. So they will hastily throw together a study designed to show how women are medically neglected or women have a massive loss of self-esteem . . . [a]nd then they move to key senators. . . . What the politicians don't realize is that feminism is a multi-million dollar industry.[13]

Hoff Sommers and, to a lesser extent, Denfeld and Roiphe also attempt to document what they maintain are empirical inaccuracies used to support the claim that women are victimized (by rape, low self-esteem, anorexia, and so forth). However, for these and other AVFers the greatest danger of victim feminism is that it justifies and perpetuates a host of personality disorders that bind women to weakness. Accordingly, much of the AVF literature offers psychological commentary on victim feminists rather than critical analyses of their ideas or political argumentation. Wolf, for example, postulates that women are often unable to seize the power that their new freedom bestows, not because of external constraints, but simply because of a collective ineptitude. In advancing this theory she employs a host of popular psychological concepts, from "psychic exhaustion" to "negative therapeutic reaction" and "trousseau reflexes."[14] Among her other explanations, Wolf includes "power deprivation poisoning syndrome," an exaggerated contempt for power that women supposedly feel because they were socialized to suppress their innate aggression. "In victim feminist's taboos against ego, money, aggression and power," she reveals, "we can see the projection of a blocked set of wishes."[15] To clarify her prognosis, she compares women's attitudes toward money to an eating disorder: "The disorders around money are symptoms of women's 'early power deprivation' and that deprivation affects appetite. . . . [M]any women are financially bulimic."[16] All of these syndromes serve to explain a particular historical pattern: moments of radical change and progress are followed by periods of retreat and regression. The great successes of feminism in the 1960s incurred "light-speed" transformations in women's lives (a sort of feminist future shock). Women's reaction to this stressful change was to cling to the comfort and safety of traditional women's roles.

Within the realm of academic feminism, one manifestation of women's regression in the face of greater opportunities is the credence given to "difference" theories. AVFers construe difference feminists' attempts to invert the cultural devaluation of the feminine as a return to the very notions about female nature that were previously used to relegate women to positions of inferiority. Rene Denfeld argues that in endorsing theories about women's inherent difference from men, feminists replaced action to secure women's equality with passive posturing about women's moral superiority. The popularity of difference theories, she surmises, demonstrates that "feminists have abandoned the idea that women and men should be treated equally, endorsing the Victorian view of women as the guardians of morality."[17] AVFers insist that difference theories have become prescriptions for how women should behave, masquerading as descriptions of how women are.[18]

The term "difference feminism" conventionally is used to demarcate a branch of feminist scholarship that presents women's differences from men—such as their supposed disposition to nurture and preference for cooperation over competition—in a favorable light and seeks to diffuse these qualities into all aspects of political and social life.[19] In the AVFers' lexicon, however, difference feminism is defined either as a retreat to the "private sphere," or as separatism, and often as both.[20] Moreover, they situate under the "difference" umbrella recent campaigns to protect women from sexual harassment, pornography, and marital and date rape. To this they add a slew of new and old clichés about feminists' prudery and (hetero)sexual "phobias." Discrediting the assumptions that women are delicate flowers in need of constant protection, and that women have (heterosexual) sex only when men impose it upon them, is vital to the AVFers' challenge to victim feminism. "By offering protection to women against the leer, the movement against sexual harassment is curtailing her personal power," infers Roiphe. "This protection implies the need to be protected. It paints her as defenseless against even the most trivial of male attentions [and] assumes that she never ogles, leers, or makes sexual innuendoes herself."[21]

By classifying antipornography and antisexual harassment policies—which are matters of continuing controversy among feminists—as examples of difference feminism, and therefore of rampant Victorian prudery, AVFers support their contention that these initiatives ultimately encourage women's weakness. This argument makes at least two important conceptual leaps. First, although protective policies are based on the observation that women may be especially vulnerable to certain types of harm, such judgments need not be founded on any theory of inherent differences between men and women. In fact, men have also successfully used antisexual harassment legislation to protect their interests.[22] Second, theorizing gender differences, problematic as it may be, is not by definition an endorsement of women's frailty.

Paglia achieved much of her notoriety by attacking what she regards as the feminist obsession with rape, especially date rape, a concept she rejects as self-contradictory. But unlike most AVFers, Paglia argues that feminists misled younger generations by teaching them that men and women are the same, and that therefore, it is a woman's right to be able to do, say, and wear whatever she wants. As a consequence, women are unprepared to cope with men's sexuality: "A girl who lets herself get dead drunk at a fraternity party is a fool. A girl who goes upstairs alone with a brother at a fraternity party is an idiot. Feminists call this 'blaming the victim.' I call it common sense."[23] Strikingly, while Paglia seems to be endorsing the exact view of men's and women's sexualities that the other AVFers challenge, she still arrives at the same conclusion: it is feminists who have created the problems of date rape and sexual harassment, either by promoting some false ideal of sexual equality (Paglia) or by retarding women's sexual development with neo-paternalistic legislation (Roiphe, Denfeld, Wolf, Hoff Sommers). Individual women must finally assume responsibility for their sexual behavior. "Whether or not we feel pressured," Roiphe explains, echoing Paglia, "regardless of our level of self-esteem, the responsibility for our actions is still our own."[24]

The expansive view of what may be considered difference feminism is one example of the AVFers' tendency to lump together importantly different (at times contradictory) aspects of feminist theory and practice under the rubric of victimism. Their critique of difference theories, as I will demonstrate shortly, does not deviate much from standard arguments that have been leveled against this branch of feminism since at least the mid-1980s, if not before. The AVFers' arguments actually repeat Catharine MacKinnon's rebuke of difference as a valorization of powerlessness. It is therefore ironic that MacKinnon appears in virtually all AVFers' texts, not to credit her for her earlier analysis, but as the quintessential victim feminist.[25]

AVFers' rejection of difference theories, however, assumes a new edge once it is combined with their antipathy toward contemporary feminism's association with the welfare state, with ideas of social justice and other causes that many feminists commonly embrace (e.g., racial justice, gay rights, affirmative action, environmentalism, and so forth). According to Paglia, radical egalitarianism is a "fantasy," "an Arcadian myth revived and propagated in the past twenty years by feminist politicos."[26] Similarly, Wolf dismisses feminists' critique of market capitalism and skepticism toward institutional politics as a "hangover" from the sixties, a misplaced "infatuation" with Marx. Such ideological rigidity, she asserts, is a "foolish burden" when the market and institutional politics offer women such possibilities for power.[27] In their two-pronged attack on egalitarianism and difference feminism, AVFers imply that just as difference theories serve to excuse women's inability to make use of their liberty, feminists' commitment to social equality likewise offers a political justification for what is ultimately a matter of women's anxieties over competing as individuals.

Beyond matters of ideology, AVFers share an aversion to the practices of the feminist movement, which, they contend, are coercively regulated by intellectual dogmatism. This depiction of a unified and clearly defined feminist "community" may sound strange to those who are familiar with the diffuse nature of contemporary feminism, and feminists' tendencies to shy away from hierarchies, leaders, and even formal institutions. But it is part of the AVFers' complaint that feminism, especially in its academic manifestations, has become a stifling "establishment," and that membership in this collective requires adhering to a strict protocol and a static identity. Paglia turns her attack on identity-as-ideology into a slogan: "Stop imposing the heavy burden of identity on people.

Just let them live and breathe!" She describes the present construction of the feminist collectivity as "a new tyranny of the group, pretending to speak for individuals while it crushes them." She finds it revealing, moreover, that feminists' promote multiculturalism by emphasizing those "tribal cultures [that] suppress individuality. The group rules." [28]

Wolf takes a more guarded approach. She also considers the boundaries delineating "the feminist community" to be too rigid and narrowly drawn but still finds something of value in identifying as a feminist. Wolf premises her assessment on a finding cited by, and central to the arguments of, virtually all AVFers: while most women applaud the achievements of the modern women's movement, few identify themselves as "feminist." [29] Wolf's solution is to offer a new marketing strategy. In order to circumvent the ideological exclusivity of current feminism, the only principle to which all "power feminists" must subscribe is "no hate." Her vision of feminism could thus include pro-life, homophobic, Republican, and other conservative women and men, if only they eschew hatred. [30] Wolf transforms the old feminist maxim that women should define for themselves what it means to be a woman and advocates instead that every feminist decide for herself what feminism means. But in her effort to make feminism more inclusive—what she calls a "populist" movement—Wolf empties feminist politics of its politics. As she writes, "saying 'I'm a feminist' should be like saying 'I'm a human being.'" [31] At the same time, the emphasis she gives to the advancement of women's interests in the marketplace suggests that women's entrepreneurial activities will occupy the center of her future feminism, and that women's problems are ultimately the troubles of the white, heterosexual, American middle class.

Criticizing the supposed therapeutic tendencies of contemporary feminism, AVFers themselves prescribe a therapeutic remedy of the "self esteem" mode. Their solution to the victimist frame of mind is rebuilding individual character. AVFers advance the same array of virtues promoted by the anti-victimists of Chapter 2, virtues traditionally associated with the entrepreneurial, male, Protestant ethic. One way for these women to justify this model would be to deny that these attributes are gendered; and at certain junctures this is precisely what some AVFers do. More often, however, they seem undisturbed by the gender-specificity of their prescriptions. Indeed, their ideals are not merely conventionally "masculine" traits, but actual men's behavior.

Wolf, for instance, instructs feminists to imitate successful businessmen. If women need to join forces in order to fight for a cause, she advises that their "limited cooperation" follow the model of the "Old Boys'" network in creating "alliances based on economic self-interest and economic giving back rather than on a sentimental . . . fantasy of cosmic sisterhood."[32] As a crucial step in the education of future female entrepreneurs, Wolf wants women to discover the benefits of perceiving others as a means to an end.

> [Women] feel they are using people, being insincere. They tend not to per-ceive how much genuine emotion men deploy in their power affiliation, how much love male mentors invest in their protégés, and what a sense of emotional connectedness it gives powerful men to cultivate their power garden and see other men in whom they recognize aspects of themselves pool their resources as well as compete for more.[33]

Among her more specific proposals, she advocates forming investment clubs for women, projecting that "[w]omen's businesses can be the power cells of the twenty-first century."[34] Denfeld, to give another example, has a similarly market-focused vision for future feminist activity.[35]

The ideal liberated woman promoted by these AVFers, it seems, does not transcend specifically "masculine" and "feminine" traits, but rather constructs a hybrid of both. The AVFers offer different archetypes of hybridity. Paglia's cul-tural heroes combine stereotypical feminine and masculine characteristics; Ma-donna is one example.[36] Madonna couples unrestrained sexual energy with the ideals of the entrepreneur: savvy, self-made, financially successful, and hungry for power. Even Justice Clarence Thomas, who, after his defense against Anita Hill's charges became another of Paglia's champions, is described in these terms. Emerging triumphant from his moment of great vulnerability, Thomas meta-morphosed into his own mother. "Giving birth to himself," Paglia enthuses, "Thomas reenacted his own credo of the self-made man."[37]

Wolf's "power feminist" splits her "masculine" and "feminine" selves along the traditional lines dividing the public from the private. In public, which for Wolf encompasses the marketplace and institutional politics, women should be-have as men do: women should be combative, self-interested achievers. Bursting with power, her AVFers are anything but reluctant to use their assets to advance their ambitions and aspirations. They embrace capitalism, indulge in power and pleasure in an unabashed way, and earn money and spend it without re-morse. In their newly constituted private sphere, however, power feminists will revel in things feminine, including reading women's magazines, decorating their homes, decorating themselves, and sexually pleasing their men. Wolf does not claim that all women share the same penchant for these sorts of activities. Yet her argument presumes that women would enthusiastically engage in such behavior if only they were liberated from the feminist super-ego.[38] She also presupposes that there is something particularly feminine about such (private) behavior.

AVFers' assumptions about women's repressed feminine desires, in combination with their diagnoses of women's unique proclivity to be stressed in the face of liberation and possibilities for real power, leads them to promote (unwittingly perhaps) yet another version of difference theory. Like difference feminists, they believe that there are some distinctively female qualities that should be celebrated (though for AVFers it is a matter of desires and consumerism rather than a discrete epistemology or morality). Unlike their predecessors, however, they advance a schizophrenic model that grafts an essentialist masculine ideal onto an equally essentialist feminine one.

## The Cresting of a New Wave?

AVF arrived on the scene in the early part of the 1990s on the tail of a string of prominent public debates over topics such as political correctness, speech codes on campuses, date rape, and sexual harassment. Many of these issues received greater attention during Clarence Thomas's confirmation and the ensuing discussion over sexual harassment in particular and the role of women in public life in general. Although differing in their interpretations of events, the Thomas–Hill confrontation and "the year of the woman" that followed signified, for Wolf, Paglia, and other AVFers, a turning point requiring reflection.[39]

AVFers cultivate ambiguous personal and ideological relationships with feminists and feminism. Paglia, perhaps the most acerbic of the group, appears to relish the uncertainty of her own affiliation, by appearing at times as outsider, at other times as insider, and often as both at the same time. Wolf, to give another example, has been uniquely successful in convincing traditional feminist organizations (such as NOW and *Ms.* Magazine) that she is an "insider critic," despite the great similarities between her ideas and those of the other AVFers. The AVFers' precarious position vis-à-vis feminism renders them a part of the trend commonly called "third wave feminism." Conversely, the third wave designation has been claimed by, or affixed to, a few post-structuralist, post-colonialist feminists, and feminists of color. Declarations about a "new" feminism (under whatever label) should cause pause—not because feminism is not in need of new paradigms, new institutions, and most importantly, new recruits—but because pronouncing a new wave often is merely a generational challenge to some "old guard," an attempt to repackage old ideas under new copyrighted labels, or, most troubling, an either explicit or implicit rejection of modern feminism. For although there seem to be important differences among third wavers (AVFers and others), they all share the conviction that the second wave exhausted itself and ended, whether in triumph or in failure.[40] As Ann Snitow reflects, "Feminist theorists keep renaming this tension, as if new names could advance feminist political work. But at this point new names are likely to tempt us to forget that we have named this split before."[41]

The idea that we are witnessing a "third wave" of feminism suggests a continuity with and simultaneously a break from the past. Virtually all AVFers refer back to some golden age of the women's movement, which in their writings is associated with Betty Friedan's feminism. According to their conception, at a certain point in the 1970s—AVFers vary on precisely when—feminists veered off course: radical feminism supplanted liberal feminism, the puritan antisex campaigns of Catharine MacKinnon and Andrea Dworkin eclipsed the liberated sexual vision espoused by Germaine Greer, and the particularism of identity politics eroded feminists' commitment to liberal universalism. Feminists turned away from the mission of securing equal opportunities for women and sought instead to manipulate equal results.

AVFers' view of the course of the modern women's movement is simplistic and contains numerous misconceptions and omissions. Their formulation of "pure," "equity," or "equality" feminists, in contrast to "radical" or "gender" feminists, is questionable. For instance, Denfeld complains that feminists abandoned "equality feminism," which she defines as the "belief" that "women should have the same opportunities and rights as men." Since this goal supposedly has been achieved for the most part, feminism has little more to offer women. "What they do with those opportunities and rights is their business; the point is that they have them."[42] However, Denfeld, like the other AVFers, ignores that even liberal feminists such as Friedan and Greer (as well as Mary Wollstonecraft and Susan B. Anthony, to mention two women whom Hoff Sommers sees as positive models from previous eras) sought more than equal legal rights for women, as formidable as this goal was; they understood that formal equality would offer women only limited freedom until more fundamental changes in attitudes toward gender occurred.[43] Perhaps most importantly, these revisionist accounts disregard a central tenet of the earlier generation: for these writers, the personal is political.

One curious omission in the AVFers' historical account is their failure to mention that their defiant call for a new feminism is not the first time in the course of the modern movement that self-described feminists have declared, and the media have endorsed, the end of feminism and the beginning of a post-feminist era.[44] In the early 1980s, there was another group of "neo-feminists," that included members of the "old guard," such as Betty Friedan.[45] Much like the AVFers, their theories "simultaneously incorporated, revised, and depoliti-cized many of the fundamental issues advanced by Second Wave feminism," expressing nostalgia for the simplicity of pre-feminist gender relations.[46] But AVFers seek to establish a certain affinity with the Friedan of the 1963 "feminine mystique." They want to ally themselves with modern feminism's inception, not Friedan of the 1981 "second stage." Perhaps the later Friedan is too close in time for comfort.

Both the AVFers and 1980s neo-feminists condemn feminists for pressur-ing women to conform to impossible models. But while the 1990s AVFers target the super-victim, 1980s critics' focus was the "superwoman," who discarded her femininity in her race to compete with men. As Friedan wrote in *The Second Stage* (1981): "Even though we've broken through the feminine mystique enough to demand equal pay on the job, and some choice in our lives, the fact that we come home to that same kind of house, which we may still be trying to run in the same kind of way, makes us doubly burdened now, forced to be superwomen."[47] In her account of the new unarticulated malaise plaguing American women, Friedan did not reduce the problem of feminism to victimism. She mentioned the term "victim" only twice in the entire text.[48] However, when anti-victimism emerges in the 1990s, Friedan is all too ready to jump on the latest bandwagon.[49] In the new 1998 preface to her collection of essays, *It Changed My Life*, she re-casts the arguments she presented in *The Second Stage* in the terms of AVF.

> Sometimes it was all too tempting (apparently it still is) to cast men as monsters and women as victims, when what really mattered was that we were empowering ourselves out of the victim state. . . . We could not simply wallow in victimhood and ignore the complex interrelationship of women and men. . . . I warned against the sexual politics that saw ALL women as an oppressed class and ALL men as sexual oppressors.[50]

## Betty Friedan: Victim Feminist or AVFer?

Does Friedan's newfound AVF amount to a repudiation of her first book? Af-ter all, according to AVFers, a defining characteristic of "victim feminism" is the prevalence of victim talk, and as we shall see, Friedan's *Feminine Mystique* is laden with victim imagery, metaphors, and analogies.[51] The Dell publishing company certainly understood her book in these terms: that her purpose was to reveal that women are victims. Indeed, to entice potential readers, her publisher included the following note on the first page of the 1970 paperback edition:

> Can a majority be treated like a minority? Want a job? You can get one—if you don't mind menial drudgery, at extra-low pay. Want an education? You can get one—if you don't mind being told to take courses that won't tax your brain. Want to think your own thoughts, be your own person, make your own mark on the world? You can try—if you don't mind being called an unnatural monster. No, we're not talking about American Blacks. We're talking about American women of every color and class, <u>all victims</u> of THE FEMININE MYSTIQUE.

How might the author of a book her publisher marketed by proclaiming she revealed that American women "had been sold into virtual slavery," that all women were victimized, now claim she had warned women about the hazards of seeing themselves as victims?

Friedan's self-described purpose in *The Feminine Mystique* is to reveal a problem she observed oppressing some of the most privileged women in America. In the service of market interests, a "feminine mystique" was denying women their personhood, preventing them from actualizing their authentic and whole selves. The effects of this mystique reach beyond these stifled and stunted women to society as a whole. Repressed, depressed, and resentful, these women vent their frustrations on their husbands and children. The cumulative damage, Friedan decrees, has been nothing short of the crippling of an entire nation.

In her analysis of "the problem that has no name," Friedan employs universal terms to refer to those most directly plagued by the mystique, such as "American women," or simply "women," even though the group with whom she is most concerned is white and middle class. (Perhaps Friedan was unaware of her publishers' sales pitch.) Ever since her book was first released, her work has been criticized for this bias. For Friedan, however, finding and exposing profound suffering among affluent women is what makes her study such a great contribution: it is precisely because these women appear to possess every luxury, in contrast to women of other classes, generations, races, and nationalities, that their problem is so difficult to identify and to overcome.

> I do not accept the answer that there is no problem because American women have luxuries that women in other times and lands never dreamed of; part of the strange newness of the problem is that it cannot be under-

stood in terms of the age-old material problems of men: poverty, sickness, hunger, cold. The women who suffer this problem have a hunger that food cannot fill.[52]

Possessing material comforts does not preclude this nameless terror because the shackles entrapping American women are not economic, but psychological, "chains in [a woman's] own mind and spirit."[53] Even when Friedan does, occasionally, acknowledge the devastating economic exploitation, as well as other forms of more subtle discrimination, that working women face, she ultimately dismisses these matters as less important, insisting that few women work for financial reasons. Money is not the point; the psychological freedom that economic independence brings is.[54] Years later, while reflecting upon her role as a "founder" of the movement, Friedan reaffirms this sentiment. The movement succeeded because, regardless of social and economic status, all American women were poor. "What gave us the strength to do what we did, in the name of American women, of women of the world?" Friedan asks rhetorically and then answers definitively. "It was . . . because we were doing it for ourselves. It was not charity for poor others; we, the middle class women who started this, were all poor, in a sense that goes beyond money."[55]

Even though Friedan is championed by the AVFers and, as we have seen, has become a champion of AVF herself, her objective in *The Feminine Mystique* is unquestionably to demonstrate that women are victims. She not only compares women to other victims of all sorts but repeatedly writes that women are "victims." From the opening pages of her text, Friedan describes, in vivid detail, the various ailments that women suffer as a direct consequence of having conformed to the unnatural and unhealthy ideals of the mystique, depicting the mystique as a "disease" or a "sickness."[56] Since women's quest for identity is central to her understanding of women's condition, she not only studies the devastating emotional and physical effects of the mystique but also investigates with whom and with what women identify. Here, too, Friedan presents a parade of victims, from the blind and maimed to those ill with cancer. Friedan, moreover, does not shy away from using dramatic language to illustrate the mystique's crippling impact. To give just two examples, she characterizes the inadequate education women receive at universities as "rape," and compares young wives to "child laborers."[57] Throughout the text, she sprinkles references equating women's situation with that of African Americans (both men and women), comparing, for instance, gender segregation in education and the teaching of "domestic sciences" to women to racial segregation in the South. She also draws upon national, class, and race-specific analogies, such as the Chinese practice of foot binding, the Lowell Mill girls, and Sojourner Truth, to highlight white American middle-class women's oppression.[58] But of all of the rhetorical devices Friedan employs to portray women as victims, the most sustained, vociferous, and revealing is her use of the European Holocaust.

The Holocaust appears in Friedan's text as shorthand for inexpressible evil. She first injects the Holocaust into her analysis by pointing to parallels between the United States of the 1950s and Germany of the 1930s. Comparing the feminine mystique to the cult of Aryan womanhood seems fitting; in both cases women are idealized by reducing them to their biological function as mothers.[59] More surprising, perhaps, is the analogy she draws between women living in the lap of luxury in suburbs throughout America and the millions exterminated in Nazi concentration camps. In a chapter titled "Progressive Dehumanization: The Comfortable Concentration Camp," Friedan equates the psychological, emotional, and physical deterioration nurtured by the feminine mystique to the dehumanizing effects of life in Dachau and Buchenwald.

> [T]he women who "adjust" as housewives . . . are in as much danger as millions who walked to their own death in concentration camps—and millions more who refused to believe them . . . [women's behavior parallels] certain psychological observations made of the behavior of prisoners in Nazi concentration camps . . . walking corpses . . . surrendered human identity . . . indifferent to their deaths . . . adopt[ing] childlike behavior, forced to give up their individuality and merge themselves into an amorphous mass . . . destruction of adult self-respect, of adult frame of reference, the dehumanizing was complete.[60]

The feminine mystique, she proclaims, is nothing less than "genocide," the "mass burial" of American women.[61]

How might we interpret Friedan's use of the Holocaust as a metaphor? The horrifying suggestion that the feminine mystique is an American version of the Final Solution seems rather extreme; it is Friedan at her "victimist" worst. Her reliance on Holocaust victims as an analogy is particularly intriguing when one recalls that Friedan is a Jew herself, and that this biographical detail does not appear in her self-description or her theoretical analysis in any explicit way. In selecting the Holocaust as a point of reference, was she negotiating her own (otherwise effaced) ethnic identity? Or is this another instance of Friedan's unwillingness to address racial and ethnic divisions among American women, here resolved by imagining all women as Jews? Does the Holocaust Jew–suburban housewife comparison allow Friedan to avoid viewing women as class? The ambiguous status of Jewishness as a religion-culture-ethnicity-Otherness that is not obviously racial (in fact, de-racialized in the United States) would make Jews particularly suitable for such an analogy, whereas the enslavement of African Americans was clearly tied to race and class. Perhaps this is why woman-as-Jewish victim became a common rhetorical device to dramatize the atrocities against women in the writings of later feminists, such as Mary Daly, Andrea Dworkin, Catharine MacKinnon, and Susan Brownmiller, notwithstanding the large presence of Jewish women in the modern movement.[62] (We shall revisit the Jew-as-victim trope in the following chapter.)

However, interpreting the Jewish parallel in this way risks anachronistically placing Friedan outside the intellectual milieu of 1950s and early 1960s America, whose concerns and sensibilities are so much part of her book. Heralding the second wave of the American women's movement, *The Feminine Mystique* is an expression of the anxieties of the cold war zeitgeist, with its preoccupation with, if not morbid fear about, the loss of agency and individuality in the face of the silent but deadly might of alienating urban landscapes, mass society, and world communism. Friedan's depiction of the fate of American housewives in the suburbs echoed New York intellectuals' sneers at Stalinist drabness, C. W. Mills's contempt for the "suburban scum," and the attempts of Hannah Arendt and others to theorize totalitarian societies and to contemplate the loss of humanity in an enclosed world where individuals behave as mindless, dehumanized machines.

Much of the tone and imagery of *The Feminine Mystique* resemble the proverbial 1950s science fiction movie of the body-snatching genre. Unseen and amorphous, a strange and alien force has taken over the world, abducted American women and trapped them in houses in the suburbs where methodically, and silently, they have been transformed, robbed of their identities and individual personalities. On the surface everything appears quite normal. Women and men go about their daily tasks, seemingly content, even happy. Closer inspection, however, reveals an eerie hollowness, a queer emptiness, that these people have become robots.[63] In the same vein, the feminine mystique works through "brainwashing." At times she calls it a disease, at others, something resembling a "conspiracy," and still elsewhere, a "seduction."[64] The "problem that had no name" before Friedan named it the "feminine mystique" is clandestine, pervasive, and as dangerous as the love "that dare not speak its name."[65]

By referring to the suburban home as a concentration camp, Friedan wants to suggest that women are imprisoned, robbed of their agency, individuality, and "spirit." But her meaning is revealed only as she begins to retreat from her own metaphor. By the end of the "comfortable concentration camp" chapter, she indicates (perhaps as an afterthought) that her comparison may be a bit extreme. Just like the inmates in Nazi camps, American women are "suffering a slow death of mind and spirit," but they "are not...being readied for mass extermination."[66] Undermining her own analogy, so pivotal to this chapter, Friedan ultimately concedes that "[t]he suburban house is not a German concentration camp, nor are American housewives on their way to the gas chamber." But, she adds, women are trapped. "They must refuse to be nameless, depersonalized, manipulated, and live their own lives again according to a self-chosen purpose."[67]

Friedan's view of the concentration camp owes much, I believe, to Stanley Elkins's conception, in *Slavery: A Problem in American Institutional and Intellectual Life* (1959), of the camp (and the plantation) as a "closed system," a totalizing experience that takes its toll on the psyche of its subjects, mercilessly molding them into subservient, dependent, and complicit "Sambo types."[68] Her depiction of the camps invoked the idea, prevalent in the post–Second World War era, of a "crime against humanity," as opposed to a specific "crime against the Jews." In the spirit of antitotalitarian discourse, as well as 1950s victimology, Friedan views victims and victimizers as somehow "symbiotically" (a word she frequently uses) complicit in a world they created together. (Her view of victims' role in their own victimization parallels the idea of "victim precipitation," as we will see in Chapter 5.) Like the inmates of the camps, American women "walked into, or have been talked into by others" their prisons.[69] Herein lies the paradox of her approach: despite the inescapability of the human condition in a closed-system, an all-encompassing regime, women as individuals, not as a class, must break free.

Because she views the greatest toll of the concentration camp as psychological rather than physical, liberating oneself is a matter of a change in attitude. The feminine mystique is, therefore, first and foremost a psychological problem, a matter of "identity," of "mistaken ideas and misinterpreted facts, of incomplete truths and unreal choices."[70] There are palpable, physical effects on women and on their families as well, but the origin of and solution to the mystique are psychological.[71] This becomes clear in her description of the "sexual sell." On the one hand, women's mystique-driven consumerism enhances the idea that suburban existence is a capitalist plot meant to bolster the economy.

As she writes, "the really crucial function, the really important role that women serve as housewives is to buy more things for the house."[72] On the other hand, women are a vulnerable target because of their own self-induced malaise. Bored and depressed by their empty domestic existence, these women—like clinically "depressed schizophrenics," or soldiers who have endured massive brain damage during combat—compulsively consume, placing their "human existence . . . in danger."[73]

When Friedan finally addresses the issue of complicity, she begins by returning to the concentration camp. "It was said, finally, that not the SS but the prisoners themselves became their own worst enemy," reports Friedan. "They were manipulated to trap themselves; they imprisoned themselves by making the concentration camp the whole world, by blinding themselves to the larger world of the past, their responsibility for the present, and their possibilities for the future."[74] Despite the pervasiveness and intrusiveness of the feminine mystique, she concludes that women should be held responsible for having made choices. Women are thus "victims of a mistaken choice," a "wrong choice," a "kind of suicide."[75] In short, women are their own victims, not victims of men or any institution.

There are "no scapegoats," Friedan declared (approximately three decades before Hollywood scripted Pfeiffer's character to refuse to acknowledge any victims in her class).[76] Women allowed themselves to be seduced; it was a "manipulated complicity." "In the last analysis," Friedan admits, "millions of able women in this free land chose, themselves. . . . The choice—and responsibility—for the race back home was finally their own."[77] Women as a group, therefore, do not have a class interest, despite the fact that her analysis implicitly relies on the premise that women as a group share a common condition.[78] Friedan refused to think of women as a class, especially as an oppressed class battling to overthrow the class of men. Women's liberation is only the first stage in a larger sex-role revolution. Women may be the vanguard, but eventually men will need to join the movement for the complete liberation of both.[79] To think in terms of "women versus men," Friedan cautioned two decades later, forges "too literal an analogy with class warfare [and] racial oppression," an analogy based on "absolute and irrelevant ideologies."[80] Friedan worries that for women to conceive of themselves as a class they would have to sacrifice their individuality to the greater collectivity.

Feminists have criticized Friedan for blaming women for their victimization.[81] That Friedan blamed the victim, however, was not an oversight, or

an incidental and immaterial element of her analysis but, in fact, the crux of
*The Feminine Mystique*. At times, Friedan attempts to circumvent the issue of
blameworthiness altogether, asserting that women can transcend the mystique
without first allocating blame.[82] Eventually, the idea that women are responsible for their own victimization was an inevitable and irresistible conclusion.
By presenting the mystique as a matter of choice, however mistaken that choice
may be, she supports her contention that women have options other than becoming homemakers as well as the agency to choose among them.[83]

Promoting an individualistic, psychological resolution for what is arguably
a structural problem in need of a collective response is only the first of many
features in which Friedan's 1963 work parallels that of the 1990s AVFers, as well
as that of other anti-victimists. Like them, Friedan simultaneously dispenses
psychological advice and attacks the devastating effects of various trends in
psychology. The popularity of psychoanalysis encouraged practitioners and pa-
tients alike to turn from the problems of the world to the problem of the self, reports Friedan, resulting in the infantilization of the entire nation.[84] In formulat-
ing this critique Friedan also relies upon contrasting a glorious past to a pathetic
present. Fearing antagonistic politics that pit one collective against another, she
argues that the feminine mystique was not imposed on women by men, just as
Hughes, Steele, and Sykes conclude that what is really wrong with America is a
culture, a zeitgeist, a ubiquitous degenerative disease that turns individuals into
peons in hostile and overbearing collectivities. But perhaps the most important connection between Friedan and anti-victimism is that she views victims as
victimizers.

According to Friedan, women (supposedly the victims of their own decisions) are themselves becoming victimizers.[85] The feminine mystique has
turned women into "parasites, not only because the things [the woman] needs
for status come ultimately from her husband's work, but because she must
dominate, own him, for the lack of an identity of her own."[86] In this way men
too are casualties of the feminine mystique, as Friedan would explicitly argue in
her subsequent books.[87] Even as she reproaches psychoanalysts for recognizing
that something ailed American women only when they saw it reflected in these
women's sons, she likewise bolsters her argument by detailing the damage these
women have done to their children.[88]

In a linear progression of victimization, overbearing, repressed women, like
"typhoid Marys," first infect their husbands. Then, these "emotionally stunted"
men and women participate in the "dehumanization of their own children."

Their children are psychologically and physically "passive" and "soft," "incapable of effort, the endurance of pain, and frustration, the discipline needed to compete in the baseball field or to get into college."[89] The effects of this cycle of "parasitical suffering," she warned, are taking "a far greater toll on the physical and mental health of our country than any known disease.[90] The end result is nothing short of the "deterioration of the human [and our national] character."[91] Whereas previous generations of Americans exhibited "[s]trength and independence, responsibility and self-confidence, self-discipline and courage," the present generation displays a "vague amorphous 'other-directed personality.'" They are "helpless, apathetic, incapable of handling . . . freedom."[92] Thus, like the anti-victimists, Friedan portrays America as both besieged with victims and as victimized by victims.

## "Victim Feminists" Debate Victimhood

So far I have suggested that the roots of AVF may reach back at least as far as Friedan's 1963 work, but what about those victim feminists' view of women's victim status? Contrary to AVFers' depiction of the period that followed Friedan's moment in the history of the movement, the second wave feminists they attack as victimists were themselves troubled by the uses of victimization in feminist theory and practice. Since the early 1970s, feminists have debated a host of problems that they identified as emanating from politicizing women's oppression, including the association of women with victimhood and powerlessness, the need to balance accounts of past oppression and future liberation, and the risks involved in defining gender or feminist identities around static notions of domination and subjugation. Deliberations among feminists over these issues intertwine, but as we attempt to untangle them a pattern will emerge: each effort to offer an organizing principle for the movement that would depart from a focus on victimization provoked criticism that such attempts remained too victim-oriented themselves.

### Patriarchy

The central insight that men universally and systematically oppress women was first termed "patriarchy" by Kate Millet in *Sexual Politics* (1970).[93] Explaining the mechanisms and ideology of patriarchy became a defining focus of most radical feminists, who viewed it as an important corrective to earlier socialist analyses.[94] But others were less convinced by the supposed explanatory power of patriarchy. Gayle Rubin, for instance, argued that even with the historically specific modifier "capitalism," the concept "patriarchy" collapsed the history of sexual relations into a uniform narrative of oppression, occluding the variety of ways different societies defined gender. She proposed instead the more neutral "sex-gender system."[95] Sheila Rowbotham, to give another example, held that "patriarchy" conceived of women only as acted upon, obscuring how women have defied and resisted male supremacy in the past, and how they might do so in the future. Viewing women's experiences through the prism of patriarchy yields a simplistic dichotomy between a "matriarchal stereotype" and that of a "hopelessly downtrodden victim." Such a conceptual framework implies a "fatalistic submission."[96] Women's victimization appeared infinite and unalterable, or, as Frigga Haug would later write:

> [T]he belief that women are merely victims remains silent about how women could ever be transformed from people who are the subject of actions of others into people who act on their own behalf. Tied hand and foot, they would be forced to remain silent, they would stay where they were and would be unable to raise themselves from their degraded situation, as long as [feminists] retain the conception of women as victims.[97]

The debate over patriarchy may be seen as contributing to a shift in feminist scholarship, especially in the field of women's history, from recording the atrocities of the past to valorizing women's resourcefulness and agency while subjected to male domination.[98]

## Difference Feminism

The ancestry of the dispute over women's "difference" in the modern movement reaches back to a split among radical feminists, between "politicos," women initially politicized through their participation in the New Left and civil rights movement, and cultural "feminists," who joined the women's movement without previous political participation.[99] In part as a reaction to other feminists' disheartening depiction of women as nothing more than victims of patriarchy but also as an effort to move beyond simply asserting women's equality with men, some of the first difference feminists began by investigating the origins of women's differences from men.[100] Others took gender differences for granted and sought to demonstrate that these differences should be viewed as the source of women's liberation, not the basis of their oppression. Thus, at least in its inception, difference feminism was conceived of as a rejection, or an overcoming, of what would later be called "victim feminism."

In reappropriating and revising traditional notions about a distinct female nature, difference feminists sought to define something fundamental that all women shared as women—a women's culture, a different moral voice, a different psychological development from those of men—often at the expense of ignoring the interplay of psychological and cultural factors with social and material ones.[101] The publication of works such as Carol Gilligan's *In a Different Voice* (1982), Mary Belenky's *Women's Ways of Knowing* (1987), and Sara Ruddick's *Maternal Thinking* (1989), to name just a few examples, brought new recruits to feminism. Initially a cause for schisms among radical feminists, and between radical and liberal feminists, in the mid-1980s, "woman's difference," especially interpreted in terms of notions of traditional femininity, remapped the feminist landscape by uniting women from Phyllis Schafly to Betty Friedan. As Alice Echols remarks at the end of her study of the early 1970s split among radical feminists, "The idea that feminism involves the preservation and celebration of femaleness rather than the transformation of gender is no longer unique to cultural feminism."[102]

Ironically, the attempts of some feminists, from "cultural feminists" to "relational feminists," to turn from focusing on women's plight to exploring, accentuating, or even celebrating women's differences from men also provoked warnings that women were accommodating themselves to their oppression. "I have severe reservations about this emphasis [on difference]," Linda Gordon wrote, "because I fear that 'difference' is becoming a substitute, an accommodating, affable, and even lazy substitute, for opposition."[103] Finding a balance between acknowledging the damage women have suffered, while still working to dispel the cultural devaluation of the "female," has always presented feminists with a predicament, as Lynne Segal observed. "Feminist Thought has always confronted intractable dilemmas in its own appraisal of women. . . . Asserting women's strength and value sits awkwardly beside an awareness that many of women's most distinctive experiences and perceptions are products of subordination."[104]

Catharine MacKinnon was among the first to articulate this concern. She derided difference feminists for postulating inherent feminine qualities because these supposedly distinctive female attributes arose under conditions of gender inequality.[105] "For women to affirm difference, when difference means dominance, as it does with gender," she reasoned, "means to affirm the qualities and characteristics of powerlessness."[106] Men have the power to construct gender differences as well as the difference that gender makes. Focusing on difference conceals the fact that gender inequality created gender difference. The real differences between men and women are a product of men's power over women.

> Differences are inequality's post-hoc excuse, its conclusory artifact, its outcome presented as its origin, the damage that is pointed to as the justification for doing the damage after the damage has been done. . . . Distinctions of body or mind or behavior are pointed to as cause rather than effect, without realizing that they are so deeply effect rather than cause that pointing to them at all is an effect.[107]

While warning that women's current condition may be mistaken for their "nature," MacKinnon seems, at times, to leave little room for understanding women outside their oppression. Her argument, therefore, is also vulnerable to the charge that in her attempt to eschew restrictive conceptions of the feminine she implicitly defines women through their victimization, and that her protectionist legal campaigns risk codifying women's subjection into law.[108]

### The Personal Is Political

Concerns over the transformation of "personal politics" were another context for contemplations about the role of victimhood in the women's movement. Rather than serving as an empowering stimulus for change, the idea that "the personal is political" seemed to encourage some women to focus exclusively on their individual experiences of victimization, to behave as if the movement aimed to provide women with a forum to wallow in their personal miseries.[109] The misuse of consciousness-raising and misinterpretation of personal politics catalyzed the formation of the radical feminist group Redstockings. Their 1969 manifesto specified that the sort of group encounters conducted by other feminists were based on a "therapy model of liberation," a turning away from political organizing to personal "moral rearmament." While they viewed consciousness-raising rituals as vital to the development of women's class consciousness, they adamantly opposed psychological explanations of women's subjugation, including the idea of false consciousness. Being "pro-woman" meant shunning all forms of individual accommodation, embracing only collective opposition.[110] The Redstockings were so determined to prevent women from finding individual solutions outside the movement, however, that they tended to depict patriarchal oppression as all-encompassing and unchanging. Thus, much like the difference feminists, the Redstockings criticized the victimist tendencies of certain feminist practices but were themselves criticized for their own monolithic portrayal of women as victims.[111]

There were others who, in the 1970s, also saw feminists "defining all of their personal desires and problems as political," and turning consciousness-raising into therapy. As early as 1973, Charlotte Bunch formulated her critique of these practices by using the term "victim" pejoratively. Like the Redstockings, Bunch observed feminists turning the project of self-understanding into a narcissistic, all-consuming, and ultimately self-defeating enterprise. Moreover, she alleged that the movement had become hospitable to "professional victims." These individuals wore their victimization as a "chip on the shoulder, a cross to bear, or a badge of honor," and "use[d] real oppression as a stepping stone for personal power or a club for personal grudges." The danger Bunch foresaw was that the vital process of learning about the many faces of oppression would instead become a project of "prov[ing] who is best, or wallow[ing] in comparisons, guilt, or navel gazing."[112]

Like critics of difference feminism or patriarchy, Bunch, as well as other writers for the feminist journal *Quest*, such as Beverly Fisher-Manick and Karen Kollias, introduced the diversity of women's experiences to undermine what they considered erroneous views of women's common oppression. They contended that the movement perceived women's conditions only through the experience of the middle class. Feminists were ignoring, for example, the kind of self-reliance and resourcefulness exhibited by working-class women who could not depend on others for help. Paradoxically, subjection could undermine self-worth but also cultivate certain strengths. While working-class women might feel exploited, they did not think of themselves as victims. The victim-image projected by the movement was simply too "degrading."[113]

## Sisterhood

Where these authors emphasized the ways in which class determines women's experiences, ten years later bell hooks would question the homogeneity of women's "sisterhood" from the perspective of race. In *Feminist Theory: From Margin to Center* (1984) hooks argued that feminists' model of sisterhood problematically relied upon women conceiving of themselves as victims. Thinking of women as victims, she held, reinscribes in feminism the sexist view of women as incompetent dependents. Furthermore, a sisterhood forged in victimhood failed to appeal to African American women because they could not "afford" to see themselves as victims. Since the idea that all women are similarly oppressed is fictitious, victimhood could never serve as a foundation for feminist coalition.[114]

In the same vein as Bunch and her colleagues, hooks argued that African American women were strengthened by their particular burden. But beyond the "positive" consequences of adversity, it is important to hooks to demonstrate the comparative severity of her group's oppression. While white women may experience "discrimination," she contends, African American women face racial "oppression." In assuming victim status, white middle-class women "abdicate responsibility" for their role in the oppression of others.[115] Hooks distinguishes between oppression and discrimination not only to expose white women's complicity in the suffering of women of color. Like Marx's view of the proletariat, hooks presumes that oppression bestows a unique perspective on the oppressed; that the standpoint from the "margins" is more comprehensive and revolutionary.

> As a group, black women are in an unusual position in this society, for not only are we collectively at the bottom of the occupational ladder, but our overall social status is lower than that of any other group. Occupying such a position, we bear the brunt of sexist, racist, and classist oppression. At the same time we are the group that has not been socialized to assume the role of exploiter/oppressor in that we are allowed no institutionalized "other" that we can exploit or oppress.[116]

Hooks, therefore, ends up employing the same logic as those she criticized. In place of the universal white man or woman, hooks exalts the "all knowing women of color." Much as the feminists she reproached for amassing a victim sisterhood, hooks also equates victimhood with innocence and purity. She ignores the possibility that the oppressed are capable of reproducing the same oppressive relationships against which they rebel, how the oppressed may have internalized the ways of the oppressor.[117] The problem with such thinking, as Shane Phelan suggests, is that while those on the margins may have a fuller perspective than members of the hegemonic group, theirs is not a total perspective either. "They revive the logic of Hegel's master/slave relation but forget that the slave's superior consciousness is not yet complete. The fact of marginality does not make one an expert on the culture any more than hegemony does. It provides one with access to truth that is invisible to hegemonic groups unless they actively seek it out."[118]

### Oppression-as-Identity

The shift in feminist theories and practices from collective liberation to personal exploration, argued some, encouraged women to valorize their individual (or their groups') victimization.[119] The project of detailing the various manifestations of one's unique experience of oppression contributed to a "hunkering down in one's oppression," an unwillingness or inability to look beyond personal experiences. Victimhood seemed to have become an end in itself. For many, as Jan Clausen noted, suffering transformed into "a mantle of virtue."[120] Much like difference theorists' reappropriation of the idea of women's "difference," these feminists were struggling to sort through what positive attributes, developed under conditions of domination, were worth retaining after liberation. But unlike difference theories, which apotheosized some feminine essence, ignoring the effects of oppression, in this case the experience and site (the socially marked body) of oppression served as the explicit foundation of group identity; personal politics seemed to have become oppression-as-identity politics.

The Combahee River Collective's manifesto illustrates the progression from oppression as the basis of identity to identity as the foundation of a specific politics: "The focusing upon our own oppression is embodied in the concept of identity politics. We believe that the most profound and potentially the most radical politics come directly out of our own identity."[121] Cherríe Moraga and Gloria Anzaldúa depict a similar causal relationship among oppression, identity, and politics, what they call "theory in the flesh."

> A theory in the flesh means one where the physical realities of our lives—our skin color, the land or concrete we grew up on, our sexual longings—all fuse to create a politics born of necessity. Here we attempt to bridge the contradictions in our experience: we are the colored in a white feminist movement. We are the feminists among the people of our culture. We are often the lesbians among the straight. We do this bridging by naming ourselves and by telling our stories in our own words.[122]

"Theories in the flesh" challenged the false universalism of much of previous feminism by emphasizing that black women and Latinas were not simply "white women with color." As importantly, they sought to challenge the idea that gender could be theorized in isolation from race, class, and sexuality, that women of color could neatly distinguish among different aspects of their oppressions, what Elizabeth Spelman ridiculed as "tootsie roll metaphysics," and Kimberle Crenshaw would later conceptualize as "intersectionality."[123] Feminists of color sought to reveal that personal politics had evolved from being a means through which women experienced empowerment by redefining the politics of being female into "the politics of imposing and privileging a few women's personal experience over all women's lives by assuming that these few could be prototypical."[124]

## Coalition of Tears

Some feminists charged that rather than enriching feminists' understanding of the variety of ways in which women are oppressed, oppression-as-identity increasingly served to fragment the movement along lines of discrete experiences of victimization. Claims about unacknowledged universalisms and unrecognized exclusions that in the past were directed outside the movement were, by the early 1980s, leveled within it, especially against heterosexual, white, middle-class feminists. In addition, several fault lines widened among certain groups, such as African American and Jewish women, who allegedly competed for the status of most victimized.[125] Letty Cottin Pogrebin disparaged these contests as "competitions of tears." At the same time, she voiced her concern that the women's movement failed to include anti-Semitism among the litany of "isms" feminists pledged to fight.[126] Like hooks, Pogrebin criticized victim discourse while trying to preserve her group's status as victims.

Minnie Bruce Pratt attributed the infighting among feminists to the problem white women had with acknowledging that they might be both victims and victimizers. Guilt-ridden and threatened, these women sought to secure their victim status by engaging in "cultural impersonation."[127] Audre Lorde offered a similar analysis, but she extended her criticism to include women of color. The problem, as Lorde saw it, was that all women feared and loathed difference, women had "no patterns for relating across [their] human differences as equals."[128] Melanie Kaye/Kantrowitz framed the problem in slightly different terms: feminists argued over whose oppression was most severe because they accepted "the scarcity theory of political struggle," the idea that victims must choose whose victimization is most severe since oppression(s) can only be fought one at a time.[129]

Irrespective of the cause, feminists were once again struggling with the role of victimization in the movement. Is AVF, therefore, merely the latest stage in this debate? Bunch's disdain for "professional victims" certainly reads as though it was written by one of the 1990s AVFers, but only deceptively so. While Bunch was censorious of individuals who, she claimed, exploited the movement for their own personal gratification, the AVFers see victimism in the ideology of women as a collectivity. Similarly, AVFers' analyses of difference feminism resemble earlier criticisms yet significantly departs from them. Like MacKinnon, AVFers point to a chasm between women's reality and feminist consciousness, but their opprobrium works in the opposite direction: difference feminism (like all victim feminism) blinds women, preventing them from seeing beyond their imaginary oppression to their freedom and opportunities. As importantly, the earlier critics, while emphasizing political hazards involved in focusing on women's individual experiences of victimization, still assumed that women had not been fully liberated, that the work of the feminist movement was far from complete. This view has been unaffected by the Thomas–Hill incident; most feminists do not share Wolf's optimism about the ensuing "genderquake."

## Are AVFers the Victims in the Class?

Having established that AVFers revive and distort long-standing debates within feminism, we may now question whether AVFers follow their own anti-victim prescription. Not surprisingly, AVFers, like other anti-victimists, actually participate in the discourse they aim to criticize. Like the victim feminists they ridicule, they too cast women as victims, victims of victim feminism. According to the AVFers, feminists have deluded other women, made them feel guilty for their various cravings, prevented them from taking advantage of their hard-earned freedom, and threatened to return them to an infantile dependency, a Victorian imprisonment. Among their most compelling examples of the disciplinary force of victim feminism are their own experiences of victimization. Paglia claims to have been "tarred with the word neo-conservative"; and Wolf worries about future persecution from the "fem-police." [130] Likewise, Roiphe complains to journalists that she is harassed by feminists, some of whom allegedly hope that she will be raped; and Hoff Sommers alleges that there are "women who wish to excommunicate me from my sex!" [131]

AVFers aver that feminism has lost touch with real women, and even bring the results of survey research to document feminism's growing unpopularity. Paradoxically, they also proclaim that feminists oppress and distort the lives of multitudes of women, while threatening the few brave individuals who dare to dissent. With the publication of *The War Against Boys: How Misguided Feminism Is Harming Our Young Men* (2001), Hoff Sommers accelerated her attack on feminism by identifying another victim group, boys. In the current political climate, however, the cause of victims of victim feminism has even found support in the White House. For example, First Lady Laura Bush launched a new initiative focused on saving "our boys" at the start of the president's second term in office. [132]

AVFers' professed mission is to tell the story of most women's lives, which feminists supposedly have either ignored or misunderstood. But contrary to their presumption to speak on behalf of all women, the AVFers' writing projects the privileged experiences of a few exceptional individuals into an all-encompassing political theory. Wolf's *Fire with Fire*, for instance, follows *The Beauty Myth*, her first best-selling success. The earlier text furnishes an excellent example of victim feminism, depicting male-dominated corporations conspiring to entrap women in restrictive codes of fashion and impossible standards of beauty. In *Fire with Fire*, she attests to her initial ambivalence toward her newly gained power as a sought after celebrity and the rewards that followed.[133] (In light of her previous stance, it is most astonishing that Wolf sees victim feminism as the major obstacle separating women from success, power, and their most tangible expression—money.) But ultimately Wolf chose to embrace the fruits of success, and the new book is a political tract based on this mental breakthrough. Now, women are not victims, but career-oriented go-getters, just like Wolf. Men still may be abusive, but women can also objectify men. Beauty, fashion, and feminine sexuality should be celebrated, however regressive they may seem. Fashion magazines are not fishing nets for greedy businessmen attempting to trap women, but a terrain for women's self-expression, a nucleus of a female community.[134] Wolf finally feels sufficiently secure as a self-fashioned "radical heterosexual" to declare: "[M]ale sexual attention is the sun in which I bloom. The male body is ground and shelter to me, my life long destination. When maligned categorically, I feel as if my homeland is maligned."[135]

Other AVFers' tracts also tend to rely heavily on testimonies of personal experiences as stories of becoming and overcoming. Significantly, their narratives of struggle lead them to a liberation conditioned upon distancing themselves from the women's movement. It is a personal and therapeutic emancipation. Paglia, for example, characterizes her rescue from the feminist clutch as a "classically American" story; describing herself as a "loner riding out of the desert to shoot up the saloon and run the rats out of town."[136] Typical of the AVFers, Paglia mixes and (mis)matches conventional models of women's and men's liberation. It is not that she presents a decidedly masculinist pattern of individual impunity; but that her notion of women as "cowboys" actually inverts the feminist idea of revolutionary liberation. Paglia counsels women to accept that in their relationships with men they are sexual objects. It is only in their relationships with other women that she advocates violent aggression. The idea that women should liberate themselves by "shooting" their feminist alter ego, or doing away with the tyranny of their "feminist elders," invites a Freudian reading of her vision that seems to evoke metaphoric matricide or sorocide. Either by attacking victim feminism or, in a few cases, by embracing it (as in Wolf's first book and in other AVFers' expressions of fear of the "feminist establishment"), victim feminism has been these women's path toward material success and often celebrity status.

That AVFers become implicated in the discourse they intend to undermine epitomizes anti-victimism in all it permutations. Wolf, Hoff Sommers, Paglia, Roiphe, and Denfeld reiterate on feminist turf arguments that were made by Shelby Steele in the context of racial politics, Dinesh D'Souza on political correctness and multiculturalism in the academy, Alan Dershowitz about the prevalence of abuse excuses in criminal proceedings, Robert Hughes and Charles Sykes in their challenges to the "culture of complaint" and the "nation of victims," and conservative politicians' minions in their crusade to eradicate the vestiges of the welfare state. As we saw in the previous chapter, these anti-victimists, like AVFers, view the mass of claims about victimization as exaggerations at best, and most often as evidence of a large-scale psychological disorder. Recall Steele's explanation for the appeal of victimism among African Americans, what he calls "integration shock," and note how closely his methodology parallels Wolf's use of a variety of pop-psychological concepts to assess difference feminism.[137] Like D'Souza, Steele, and Sykes, AVFers advocate individualism and reinvigorated character as the antidote to victimism. In short, there is more than a surface affinity between the arguments and solutions of anti-victimists and those of the AVFers. Most importantly, for the anti-victimists, all victims—women and men—are inflicted by a certain type of "feminine" behavior; they are manipulative, overly sensitive, and treacherously effeminate. This anti-woman subtext of their critique reveals the extent to which AVF, as part of the larger anti-victim movement, undermines feminism.

Feminists have grappled with the tension between defining women's suffering and working for women's liberation throughout most of the modern movement. Indeed, the recent history of feminism may be viewed as a series of renegotiations over what role women's oppressions should play in theorizing what "woman" is and what a women's movement might be. Even post-structuralist feminists, such as Judith Butler, who aim to move beyond "women" as the foundation of feminist collective action, are likewise concerned with the intractability of subjection in the formation of subjects.[138] Irrespective of politics or methodology, it seems, most feminists agree that women's emancipation can be neither properly conceived nor actualized if women are considered nothing more than victims. But as formidable as this problem is, it is unlikely to be resolved by ignoring women's oppression. Women have been and continue to be discriminated against as women, despite their significant advances over the last quarter of a century. The AVFers' efforts to eradicate victim feminism are predicated on denying this reality. Neither AVFers' criticism of the role of victimization in feminism, nor their tendency to embrace the status they claim to attack, are new. What is novel about AVF is proponents' use of this method to deny that women are oppressed, a disadvantaged group, and to reject feminist collectivity.

# 4 Blue Lester: Two Faces of Victimhood

IN MARCH OF 1988, the faculty of the W. E. B DuBois Department of Afro-American Studies at the University of Massachusetts at Amherst unanimously demanded that the administration remove one of its most distinguished members, Professor Julius Lester. The official reason given for this extraordinary request was that Lester had become an "anti-Negro-Negro."[1] In making this demand, Lester's colleagues were reacting to the recent publication of his autobiography. Entitled *Lovesong: On Becoming a Jew* (1988), the book tells the story of Lester's conversion to Judaism as well as detailing his growing alienation from black politics. The faculty's lengthy report concluded "Professor Lester would be infinitely more comfortable at a different location in the University."[2] Elaborating on the written account, one of the authors pointedly remarked that retaining Lester in Afro-American Studies is "like having Yassir Arafat teaching in the Jewish Studies Department."[3] The university eventually complied with the request and transferred Professor Lester to another department.

This bit of academic infighting soon became national news.[4] Journalists reminded their readers that back in the late 1960s, when he was a prominent Black Power activist, Lester gained notoriety as an anti-Semite. The *L.A. Times* maintained that now Lester was himself a victim of anti-Semitism.[5] Despite the administration's intervention, or perhaps because of it, the scandal refused to die. Lester contributed to the prolonged life of this affair by rehashing events and responding to his detractors in published articles and public lectures.[6] More significant still, conservative critics enthusiastically seized upon the story of Lester's excommunication. It is an anecdote repeatedly recited to dramatize the perilous effects of "victim politics."

Lester became the poster-boy for anti-victimism. Dinesh D'Souza's best-selling *Illiberal Education* (1991), for instance, employs Lester's story to illustrate the casualties of what he calls the "victims' revolution."[7] In their respective books, Shelby Steele and Stephen Carter emphasize the Lester debacle specifically to warn other African Americans of the penalties awaiting those who don't follow "the party line."[8] These and other commentators maintain that Lester's great transgression was criticizing blacks for languishing in their victimhood. In fact, Charles Sykes's far-reaching condemnation of the "victim zeitgeist" enfeebling America features Lester's writings as an authoritative account of the rise and proliferation of "victimism."[9] While Lester may seem at first to be just another "multicultural conservative," there is much more to his story that merits careful examination.[10]

## An Exemplary Victim

Julius Lester's trajectory from militant black anti-Semite to Jewish critic of black anti-Semitism is surely exceptional. His conversion is neither part of a mass movement of African Americans becoming Jews, nor emblematic of the experience of most African Americans who are Jews, whether by conversion or by ancestry.[11] The extraordinary nature of his story, however, allows us to probe yet another permutation of victim discourse in contemporary America, its ambiguities and ironies, its power to forge identities, build community, or pit groups against one another.

Paradoxically, Lester occupies two positions within the discourse: one, as an avid opponent of victim politics, the other, as a victim; for Lester is taken to be, and takes himself to be, a victim of victim politics. According to Sykes and the other anti-victimists who retell his story, Lester's treatment by his colleagues vividly demonstrates how those anointed as official victims actually victimize others. Lester concurs, asserting in his autobiography that such victimists are "merely . . . executioner[s] too cowardly to sharpen [their] sword[s]."[12] As we observed in previous chapters, this ambiguity is symptomatic of a larger phenomenon: many critics of victim politics become its practitioners by devising and promoting new groups of worthy victims. And, as this affair makes so clear, the campaign against the proliferation of victimism can be a way for anti-victimists to establish their own status as victims within the Cult of True Victimhood.

Closer examination of the circumstances of Lester's conversion provides additional evidence that his journey was actually a search for a pure victim position. I suggest that Lester is drawn specifically to Judaism and Jewishness because of how Jewish victimization, especially the Holocaust, is commemorated in the United States. The Holocaust has been a recurring reference throughout this book: we noted its role in the current preference for survivorship over victimhood; the anti-victimists in Chapter 2 deploy it as a standard of true victimization; Friedan employed it as a metaphor for women's condition; and, as we'll see in the following chapter, the Holocaust served as an impetus for the elaboration of the science of victims, "victimology." Focusing on Lester's story reveals additional and unexpected consequences of the hegemonic status of the destruction of European Jewry as the venerated American narrative of suffering. Lester appropriates the Holocaust not solely as a symbol of Jewish persecution but also as an account of a private cataclysm, a palpable experience of violence, immolation, and rebirth. His self-understanding has been predicated upon and negotiated through his relationships to Jews, who, at different junctures in his career, he perceived as either treacherous victimizers or innocent victims. In Lester's imagination African Americans also oscillate between the binary positions of victims and victimizers. His case history, therefore, underlines the interplay between two sets of identifications—personal and collective, African American and Jewish—that were forged around victimhood.

Despite Lester's insistence that converting was simply the culmination of his personal quest for God, his autobiographical writings betray a desire for transformation that exceeds an individual search for religion or religious community.[13] Lester justifies his radical transformation from a supposedly existentialist vantage point, claiming that his black identity is inauthentic, while becoming a Jew represents a revelatory moment of authenticity. Furthermore, his conversion seems to be an effort to address what Frantz Fanon termed the "corporeal malediction."[14] Converting, Lester hopes, will liberate him from the racial gaze. Thus, I propose that for Lester becoming a Jew was a racial conversion more than a religious one. Classifying his embrace of Judaism and Jewishness in this way is not to undermine or ridicule his religious conversion, or to condone the appalling way he was treated by his colleagues or by his university, but to highlight how Lester's rebirth as a Jew coexists with the practices of blackface and other forms of what Susan Gubar terms "racechanging."[15]

In Blackface, White Noise, Michael Rogin shows how blackface minstrelsy provided a means for children of Jewish immigrants, as performers and Hollywood moviemakers, to facilitate their inclusion in white America. "The [Jewish] jazz singer," Rogin maintains, "Americanized himself through blackface."[16] By

temporarily putting on black masks Jews accentuated the divide between themselves and blacks, placing themselves on the side of whiteness. Lester's "ethnic transvestism"—his appropriation of Jewish history, Jewish food, music,
and other forms of *Yiddishkeit*—inverts this cultural device.[17] His performance
is fundamentally an act of individuation, not an assimilationist gesture or an
attempt to pass. If Jewish performers wore the black mask to merge into the
white mainstream, Lester dons the *yarmulke* to distinguish himself from blacks
and ultimately to guarantee his double marginality. He achieves this position
by combining two "identities"—African American and Jewish—that have become dramatically opposed in American society. His narrative, then, additionally provides a unique perspective on the problems and peculiarities of black-
Jewish relations in post–civil rights America.

The following analysis is based on Lester's writings, especially his second
autobiography *Lovesong*, which reconfigures his life as inevitably leading to his
conversion. This text affords a view into Lester's emotional state, family relations, bodily sensations, and sexual anxieties, all of which I use in my effort to
understand his remarkable life story. As one reviewer remarked, "Lester almost
invites a reader to psychoanalyze him. . . ."[18] My aim, however, is not to place
Lester on the proverbial couch, but rather to investigate the relationship between the personal and the political in the context of anti-victimism. The highly
personal nature of Lester's public confession may be seen as part of the public style Wendy Kaminer criticized, where intimate experiences function as the
content of politics: "[t]estimony takes the place of conversation," and claims
of abuse and victimization confer political status.[19] Lester denounces politicizing the personal, continually proclaiming his retreat from politics. "[W]hen the
personal becomes political," he cautions, "persons cease to exist."[20] However,
I shall demonstrate that he inundates his readers with titillating intimate details
in order to conceal the political beneath the personal.

## Original Sins

Born in 1939, Lester spent most of his early childhood in Pine Bluff, Arkansas,
until his father, a Methodist minister, received an appointment as the Director of Negro Affairs for the Board of Evangelism of the Methodist Church and
moved the family to Nashville, Tennessee. The Lesters had a devout Christian
home, family life revolving around his father's vocation, and were relatively
affluent. Lester remained in Tennessee for his undergraduate studies at Fisk
University, spending his junior year as an exchange student at San Diego State

College. After earning his B.A., he moved to New York City, where he embarked on a career as a writer. To support himself, he worked as a folk singer, guitar and banjo teacher; he has produced at least two albums of original songs.

A few years after his first marriage in the mid-1960s, Lester emerged as "revolutionary."[21] He made numerous trips to the South, becoming increasingly involved first in the Student Non-Violent Coordinating Committee (SNCC) and later in the Black Power movement. In 1967, SNCC sent him to North Vietnam as their representative. He later traveled to Sweden to report on the tribunal on the war in Vietnam, and accompanied Stokely Carmichael to Cuba. His service as a spokesman for SNCC and speechwriter for Carmichael culminated in his first book, "an anti-white diatribe," *Look Out, Whitey! Black Power's Gon' Get Your Mama* (1968).[22] Thirteen years later, Lester left New York to join the faculty in the Afro-American Studies Department at the University of Massachusetts at Amherst. In 1983, he converted. He presently serves as the spiritual leader for an unaffiliated synagogue in St. Johnsbury, Vermont.

At the time of the 1968 Ocean Hill–Brownsville confrontation, Lester was hosting a weekly broadcast on New York public radio, WBAI. This teachers' strike at a Brooklyn school sparked tensions that pitted black community members and the predominantly Jewish faculty against each other. It was, by all accounts, a pivotal moment in the dissolution of the civil rights alliance between Jews and blacks.[23] As part of his coverage of the events, Lester included a black student's poem that opens with the lines:

> Hey, Jew boy, with that yarmulke on your head / You pale-faced Jew boy—I wish you were dead. . . . I'm sick of hearing about your suffering in Germany / I'm sick about your escape from tyranny / . . . / About the murder of 6 million Jews / Hitler's reign lasted for only fifteen years / For that period of time you shed crocodile tears / My suffering lasted for over 400 years, Jew boy / And the white man only let me play with his toys / Jew boy you took my religion and adopted it for you / But you know that black people were the original Hebrews. . . .[24]

Soon after, Lester gained national repute as "New York Anti-Semite Number 1."[25]

Lester fiercely defended his actions. Airing the poem, he explained during his next broadcast, was an integral part of his responsibility to offer listeners a view of "the black frame of reference, the black psyche, the black mind." His critics mistakenly saw him only as an individual, but he had "no choice but to look upon myself as black."[26] As for the charges of anti-Semitism, Lester countered that American Jews were "borrowing suffering" from the Holocaust, while remaining indifferent to the anguish of blacks.[27] In America, he elaborated, it is African Americans who are the "Jews." "There is no need for black people to wear yellow Stars of David on their sleeves; that Star of David is all over us." Then, going beyond the sentiments expressed in the poem, he clarified that now "it is the Jews who are in the position of being Germans."[28] Even back in 1968, it seems, Lester identified as a "Jew," though at this stage he maintained that Jews had been replaced as the symbol of victimhood: African Americans are the "Jews," and American Jews, the "Germans."

Fifteen years after he equated Jews with Nazis, Lester converted to Judaism. This was a protracted process that began with a growing preoccupation with the Holocaust. His interest in this topic, he claims, was motivated by a fear that African Americans would face the fate of Jews in Europe. But, as he explains in his autobiography, while reading testimonies of survivors, he fell into a depression, consumed by "grief and mourning for the six million murdered Jews," along with "mourning for my own innocence."[29] Images of the Holocaust invaded his dreams, where alarmingly his black body transformed into a Jewish one: "I awake each morning, tired. In the night I have wandered among naked bodies piled atop one another; I shovel bodies into ovens and I am the Jew closing the oven door and the Jew inside; I am smoke and flame spewing from smoke stacks; I am particles of ash. . . ."[30] His grief for the slaughtered Jews blends with guilt, and with memories of himself as a child playing in the dirt. "I see myself kneeling in the dirt of the backyard of the parsonage. . . . I am five years old. I do not know that at that same moment . . . five-year old boys and girls are being killed because they are Jews."[31]

Lester determines that "after Auschwitz . . . it is not possible to be innocent."[32] Even a young black boy living in the segregated South must claim guilt as part of his condition. This epiphany about the universal implications of the European Holocaust is crucial to Lester's break with black politics. He now contends that blacks deny this collective guilt by valorizing their own status as victims to the exclusion of all other victim claims: "through canonizing themselves as victims, blacks relinquished the courage to suffer. . . . Now they languished in the sentimental and self-righteous security of being victims."[33] Lester depicts these feelings as devouring him. "Whatever life we had is swallowed whole and ingested by the metaphor of Auschwitz. It is as if it was always there, as if I knew about it from the instant of conception and the first word I spoke was not 'Momma' but 'Auschwitz.'"[34] Did the horrors of the Holocaust so threaten Lester's victim status that he longed to be born again crying out for "Auschwitz" rather than "Momma"? Or is his fantasy of rebirth an escape from the guilt of his anti-Semitism? One thing is certain: in Lester's mind the Holocaust is the original sin (here conflated with the primal scene) that renders us all guilty from inception.

The decisive public rupture with black politics was occasioned by the Andrew Young affair of 1979—when numerous prominent African Americans claimed that Jews forced President Jimmy Carter to dismiss Young from his office as United Nations Ambassador for having met with members of the Palestine Liberation Organization. "[Blacks'] arrogance," Lester wrote, "is a common fault of oppressed people when they believe their own status as victims gives them the advantage of moral superiority."[35] The black leadership's attacks on Jews, he deduces, reveal "that blacks too can be Germans."[36] Reading his own words he observes, "I have written as if I'm a Jew."[37] It is only when Lester writes as a Jew that he assumes a position outside black politics, for there were previous occasions when he offered public criticism as an "insider."[38] However, Lester maintains that he had little choice in writing what and how he did. To do otherwise, he would be "guilty of murdering those [Jewish] children again."[39]

Jews, as he discovered in the sixties, are capable of being "Germans." In the seventies he realized that the "Jews of America"—that is, blacks—also could be "Germans."[40] Then, in order to be a "Jew," Lester would become a Jew.

## Suffocating in the Womb

Lester's preoccupation with the Holocaust is only one subplot of his conversion story. He also explains his drift from black politics by the need to liberate himself from the "noose of race."[41] His decision to join the civil rights movement, as described some twenty-five years later in *Lovesong*, conveys considerable reluctance. For a long time he resisted the "Siren call of History," but eventually "History claimed me for Itself."[42] While the causal relationship between the two subplots remains ambiguous, the motivating force driving them both is the same: seduction ("siren call," "claimed . . . for itself"), on the one hand, and guilt, sorrow, and shame, on the other, also played a vital role in his decision to convert to Judaism.

In *Lovesong*, Lester provides only scant details about his activities in the civil rights movement because he came to view his years of political activism as a period of personal weakness. Joining the movement, he now writes, was akin to returning to the womb ("the womb-like security that comes when one belongs to a cause"). This womb obliterated his "identity." Such is the nature of collectives, he surmises: they provide a hazardous sanctuary that suffocates individuality.[43] Lester, therefore, sees identity as a process of individuation rather than affiliation, and, by implication, as the victim of identity politics. His use of the womb metaphor, with all of its misogynistic connotations, additionally suggests that Lester conflates the political womb with the biological one. This is only one instance (we shall pursue others) of Lester's tendency to collapse the political into the personal.

In order to relieve himself of the burden of black existence and black memory, Lester immersed himself in what he considered to be a greater historical burden—the plight of two thousand years of Jewish suffering in the Diaspora. Paradoxically, then, to guard his own individuality and separateness, Lester openly criticizes other blacks for maintaining and reinforcing the boundaries between their sorrow and that of others; but instead of embracing the sorrows of the entire universe as he suggests African Americans should, Lester chooses to identify himself with another particularistic grief and alternative community boundaries. Even so, as a black man among an overwhelmingly white community he will always stand out, and thus, Lester can enter into the "womb" of the Jewish collective and still preserve his individuality.

## That Julius Lester

In *Lovesong*, Lester explains that as a youth, the need to relate differently to whites and to blacks required him to lead a disembodied life.

> I chose invisibility and walked as if I did not occupy my body, and talked in the polite tone of a string quartet. I even practiced breathing so that my chest would not rise and fall as I inhaled and exhaled. Nothing could mitigate the ontological terror of being damned in the flesh.[44]

Despite the obvious resonance of DuBois, Ralph Ellison, and Fanon, for Lester the schizophrenic state of black existence in the South later transformed into ambivalence over being pushed to fulfill a role in black politics in which he reportedly was never at ease. With the publication of his first book, *Look Out, Whitey!*, the media anointed Lester "a personal emissary of Black Power."[45] Such a reception caused him great anxiety, confusion, and embarrassment, he later confessed.

This section of *Lovesong* abruptly shifts to the third person. Lester explains that he is not "that Julius Lester" who conceals his doubts about Black Power and revolution by writing in "that black collective voice."[46] Gazing up at his nine books on a shelf above his desk, he feels only shame and regret. These books aren't he; they represent a persona that others wanted him to be. "I have written books that, while not false, are not wholly true. I have lived the life others needed me to live. By doing so I have sold my birthright and I never knew what it was."[47] Lester's period of militancy, he asks us to believe, was simply a blackface performance.

Julius Lester's role in 1960s black politics, whether chosen or imposed, was to express black rage, as a speaker, speechwriter, essayist, and radio personality. This was the time when his vitriolic style and inflated rhetoric first emerged. His political activities (both before and after his conversion) reveal a compulsion to speak out. (This stands in striking contrast to his self-depiction as a shy, aloof, unemotional, and silent person.[48])

What did "that Julius Lester," the black militant, advocate? He repudiated Martin Luther King and SNCC (after he converted to Black Power) for asking blacks to "play the role of the victim" by seeking forgiveness from whites.[49] In contrast to this victim approach, he endorsed violence, disruption, and revenge.[50] Encouraging blacks to abandon the path forged by King, Lester directed them instead to the road paved by "field niggers," Nat Turner and Malcolm X.[51] "You can't do what you've done to blacks and not expect retribution," he explained. "The very act of retribution is liberating, and perhaps it is not an accident that the symbolism of Christianity speaks of being washed in blood as an act of purification."[52] This Lester (the angry black male) held that for blacks to effect change they must be loud and threatening.[53] "I can't ask other blacks . . . to forego the pleasures of hating. A part of me hates also. Sometimes, all of me. . . . I want to drown [whites] in their whiteness."[54] Thus, even as an advocate of the "revolution of the dispossessed," Lester preached some form of anti-victimism, though at this stage in his political metamorphosis black power represents non-victimist politics. Still, in *Lovesong* Lester asks us to regard his forceful public style as literary skill rather than authentic expression:

> Because I can express black anger does not mean I am angry, and it certainly doesn't mean I hate white people. Because I articulate the experiences of many blacks does not mean I am writing autobiographically. I have never been in jail, lived on a Mississippi plantation, picked a boll of cotton, been beaten by a policeman. . . .[55]

He was never enraged; it was all merely a mask, a writer's exercise in using "angry, colloquial black English."[56]

It is difficult to know how to construe Lester's disclaimers. He does not deny the pain he felt growing up black in the South, only the connection between his suffering and detesting whites. The first instance in which Lester alleges to feel connected to his verbal eruptions is when he attacks Jews. It is surprising that Lester does not gloss over this episode of his past, especially since *Lovesong* is unquestionably meant to present a consistent and linear trajectory from his childhood in the South to his conversion in the early 1980s. Nevertheless, he dedicates many pages to describing in detail his collision with Jewish leaders in New York, never offering any strong apology or full retraction. Lester felt that his anger with Jews' paternalism and insensitivity was plainly justified:

> I hear an anger within me, an anger that my suffering as a black person is not understood as I feel the suffering of Jews is. I am angry, too, that Jews, the people I thought most able to understand black suffering, do not understand, do not care, even, to try to understand. Once I see my anger staring at me, I cannot deny that part of my motivation in airing the poem had been to hurt Jews as they had hurt me. If such unspoken anger becomes a comfortable habit, there is no way I can prevent myself from sliding into anti-Semitism as if it were a cool lake at the bottom of a grassy slope.[57]

He distinguishes between a legitimate expression of anger and an anger (unspoken in this case) that becomes second nature and slips into hatred and racism. Such anger, moreover, is somehow feminine—a watery abyss at the base of a moss-covered mound. Perhaps the same female (the "siren's call") that seduced him into entering the black collective womb now threatens to lock him in the unyielding orifice that is black identity.[58]

Lester expected more of Jews than other whites and resented them for not fulfilling his expectations. Paul Berman describes this form of resentment, which he observes among other African Americans, as hatred for those who are neither Other nor brother, but "almost the same"; those whose resemblance "threatens to obliterate everything which is special about me."[59] For Lester, however, the way the pain of each group mirrors that of the other (the anger that stares him back in the face) entails not sibling rivalry as much as an interior rupture between two parts of a single self. (In this configuration Jews are positioned as an inattentive parental authority or alter ego, a construction that correlates well with his charge of Jewish paternalism.[60])

Ten years later, at the height of the Andrew Young controversy, Lester writes the indignant "On the Uses of Suffering" for *The Village Voice* and observes a new congruity between his words and feelings. For the first time, he claims, he writes with "personal conviction," as "a believer."[61] As a convert to Judaism, the person who claims he could not generate real anger at whites because he had not been imprisoned in a Southern jail or shot at from close range now feels free to be angry at the enemies of the Jewish people as though he had personally experienced the Holocaust and two thousand years of pogroms.

## Mirror Images

Lester began writing in earnest while studying among a predominantly white student body at San Diego State College. It was a difficult year, the first time he had not lived in a black community. Lester recalls becoming excessively concerned with his hair during this period. Taming his locks involved lengthy grooming sessions. Despite hours spent in front of a mirror, he found that he could only see himself through others' eyes: "I knew myself as a thought of others, and only in the way they conceived me to be." [62] An inability to see himself as something other than how he was perceived compelled Lester to begin recreating himself through text (just as writing as a Jew would also prove to be a defining moment): "Some instinct told me to write, to put my self on paper where I could see it and touch it, to place it where it could not harm me, as it would if it remained wholly inside, to begin to create a self through words, one which would never again need others to tell it who it was." [63]

With perhaps the exception of his still unpublished novel *Michele*, however, Lester always abandons the self he has created through text. Once he puts his ideas and feelings into a palpable form, they become external to him. More threatening still, others can use his own words to confine and imprison him in a static identity. "I am almost fatally ill with people trying to impose their idea of me on me. I am not an idea, damn it! Anything anyone ventures to say about me will not be true. I will not be pinned by anyone's words, particularly my own." [64] Lester still rages against readers' presumptions. [65]

If initially Lester sought to construct an image in writing that he could not observe in the mirror, he would later remark (often while standing before a mirror) that he could see beyond his own reflection; such moments are revelatory. Staring past his reflection, Lester can see something deeper: "[I]nstead of seeing myself, I saw who I had been. . . ." [66] Similarly, *Lovesong* opens with the declaration that Lester is no longer fooled by his mirror image: "I have become who I am. I am who I always was. I am no longer deceived by the black face which stares at me from the mirror. I am a Jew." [67]

Lester's descriptions of feeling internally divided and disembodied suggest that his newly found Jewish identity may be understood as a response to the specter of double consciousness that W. E. B. DuBois so famously described as the duality of the condition of being Negro and American. "One feels his twoness," wrote DuBois, "an American, a Negro; two souls, two thoughts, two unreconciled strivings; two warring ideals in one dark body, whose dogged strength alone keeps it from being torn asunder."[68] As part of the "talented tenth," Lester's personal struggles may exemplify the particular plight of the black middle class in contemporary America. Nevertheless, his reliance on the metaphor of the mirror directs us not toward DuBois, but toward Fanon's (or Lacan's) formulation. His descriptions are reminiscent of Fanon's depiction of the primal "racial epidermal" trauma that shatters the black man into three— body, race, and history.[69] It appears, moreover, that Lester has never fully resolved the splitting of the mirror stage. He describes experiencing himself on "two levels"; one level always monitoring the other. "I can't integrate the two and it makes Julius seem like a hypocrite, a liar."[70]

The more his prominence grows, the more stifled he feels by this persona; "that Julius Lester" turned the real one into "a prisoner of the black collective."[71] To liberate himself from this "net of blackness," Lester decides to live outside history, "to leap, blindly and joyously, into the void of ahistorical Time which is created only in the leap."[72] Other blacks were clutching to a history of victimization with which they were committing murder:

> Instead of leaping into the void, blacks are jumping to the other side, and in redefining ourselves as blacks, we impose racial definitions on the rest of humanity. Murder is committed when we define others as anything except a variation of ourselves and we of them. And the greater victim of that murder is the murderer. It is we who are the executioners of ourselves, and our paeans to blackness are like the rouge the morticians rub into the cheeks of the dead. Blackness is a cosmetic, obscuring the reality of human existence.[73]

Here Lester restates Nietzsche's famous aphorism that murder "is a detour to suicide."[74] The murderous rage of blacks, he warns, will lead them to exterminate themselves. But Lester's own Zarathustrian ideal of individuality also requires a suicide; Lester's rebirth as Jew occurs only by negating his blackness.[75]

## Triangulating the Black/White Divide

Blacks are the ones who engage in "blackface," according to Julius Lester. They rub their blackness onto their faces, and in doing so, they assume the historical role of whites; they hate, exclude, and murder. The only countermeasure that enables Lester to clean blackness from his face, to remove the "mask" he wore as a political militant, is Jewishness. In order to eradicate one deception (black-face), Lester puts on another (Jewishness). Upon completing his conversion, he therefore asserts that he can finally see beyond his black skin.[76]

Though seeking to transcend blackness, Lester is not simply attempting to become white. His leap is a complex performance that triangulates the black/white divide by making Jewishness a third vertex. Even today American Jews' status as "white" remains uncertain. On the one hand, Jews are often considered to be just another white ethnic group. And, as Rogin observes, Jewishness evolved into whiteness only by "wiping out all differences except black and white."[77] On the other hand, American Jews defy racial classification because it is unclear whether Jewishness is a matter of race, ethnicity, or religion.[78] Bleaching one's epidermal melanin may be impossible (Michael Jackson notwithstanding), but there is a formal route for an individual to convert to Judaism. As importantly, Judaism offers Lester alternative tangible marks of difference to erase blackness, from the *yarmulke* and the *tallit* to his newly circumcised penis.

While ambiguity lingers over precisely how to classify Jews, for Lester, becoming a Jew is jumping to the symbolic "other side." Indeed, his identity play succeeds because it occurs at a historical moment when new antagonisms have overshadowed past empathies between African Americans and American Jews. Many agonize over and mourn this rift, though perhaps the perceived animosity of today is as exaggerated as the supposed romance of years past.[79] Still, in the racial geometry of post-1960s American politics, African Americans and American Jews have come to occupy opposing positions. Lester is well aware of this divide, and reluctantly concedes that blacks may understand his conversion to Judaism as abandonment and betrayal.[80] Furthermore, Lester himself was an active participant in events that deepened the enmity. A crucial part of his role as a militant black was to attack Jews, just as much of his later Jewish self-conception involves criticizing prominent blacks for their anti-Semitism.

By leaping into the void and becoming a Jew (i.e., symbolically non-black) Lester may also suppose he is becoming a better "black," for he imagines that as a black Jew he preserves his role as the eternal outsider, the role he claims other African Americans abandoned. He therefore employs Jewish identity not only for the purpose of making his blackness fade but also because the hybrid of the black Jew will secure for him the status of ultimate pariah, forever hung between two worlds, each of which is itself a pariah status. He becomes an outsider (at least among most African Americans) but at the same time insists upon being a black voice by, for example, writing inspirational novels specifically for young African American readers.[81] His racechange performance thus renders him doubly black, doubly Jewish—Jew and "Jew"—or twice negated.

Lester's craving for distinctiveness merges, once again, the personal with the political. The unique political status of African Americans as the quintessential pariah group does not fulfill his personal ambition for separateness and individuality, but Jewishness does. He connects the essence of being Jewish with separateness and Otherness: "[T]o be like everyone else is to cease to be a Jew. If Jews do not hold to separateness, Jews cease to exist."[82] Jews, it seems, are better Others. Similarly, while black history was too much of a burden to bear (hence his promotion of ahistoricity), Jewish history is something he yearns to call his own. Converting allows him to join "a people who are inseparable from [their] transcendent historical experience." He declares: "I would die from the pain of not belonging to something so vast."[83] Lester's attraction to Jewishness and Jews thus goes beyond rejecting blackness and verges on racial romanticism. He understands Jewishness in terms of tangible physical experiences that have to do not merely with the spirit, but with food and music and "living in the world through small [bodily] actions."[84] "Judaism is not in the knowing," he writes, "it is in the physicality of doing."[85]

In Lester's idealized vision, Jews are an ebullient, colorful people. He pictures himself as part of a world reminiscent of a Chagall painting: ". . . I see myself dancing in the middle of a brick-laid street. A brown yarmulke is on my head and I am dancing . . . in a circle, my arms extended like the wings of an eagle. I am a Chasid and I am grinning and laughing, dancing, around and around and around."[86] Several passages in *Lovesong* echo and invert the fantasies of the late 1950s–early 1960s "White Negroes" (e.g., Jack Kerouac, Norman Podhoretz, and Norman Mailer). But in Lester's narrative the role played in those fantasies by the sexuality of the sensuous black body is replaced with the smells of baking *Challah*, *borsht*, and *gefilte* fish, and the rhythmic, dark tone of jazz becomes the sweet melancholy of Klezmer music and the soul-searching melody of the *Kol Nidre*.[87] The *shtetl* replaces the "jungle."[88]

Circumcision is perhaps the most physical component of Lester's Jewish experience. As he sees it, the final barrier to joining the Jewish community is his foreskin. He envisions being shamed in a synagogue bathroom when someone notices that he is not circumcised: "[S]uddenly the entire congregation rises up and chases me out of the *shul* and down the street, yelling, 'He has a foreskin!'"[89] As this image indicates, Lester is consumed by the idea that others are fixating on his penis. But of course his real illusion is that the Jewish gaze is completely color-blind, that he can be exposed as a convert only by revealing his genitals. In removing his foreskin, he imagines he will be losing his color. After the circumcision Lester claims to feel "whole" as though "something within me has been set free."[90]

Likewise, Lester reports that in the 1960s—much before contemplating conversion, and even before Ocean Hill–Brownsville—he would spend hours watching Hassidic Jews in New York's Riverside Park. Staring at the older ones, he imagines that he can see the blue numbers stenciled on their arms, only to notice later that "I am rubbing my forearm as I stare. It is my suffering and theirs I want to avenge and give voice to—for them and for me."[91] Arguably, this, as so much else in *Lovesong*, should be treated with some skepticism. In his previous autobiography, *All Is Well* (1974), published more than a decade earlier, Lester makes no mention of any interest in the Holocaust or, for that matter, in any Jewish topic or theme. Nevertheless, even as a fantasy about a fantasy, the anecdote is intriguing. The dream of the tattooed arm is a dream of a white arm (the "color" of the arms that were marked in this way). The rubbing may therefore aim not at erasing, but instead at inscribing the numbers and their silent death-camp testimony onto Lester's own body (just as he states blacks rub their blackness on their faces). His fascination with the tattooed forearm additionally signifies the range of ambiguities that govern Lester's relationship to Jews, from his Jew-hating to Jew-becoming days—identification, fantasy, and desire.

Jewish history is as potent as Judaism itself in providing a new burden that will relieve Lester of his own, old one. He compares the "centuries" of black suffering and the "millennia" of Jewish pain, only to find the latter overpowering the former. Thus, the black child who was threatened by lynch mobs in the segregated South believes that he is shamefully privileged when comparing his plight to that of Jewish children in the death camps of Nazi Europe.[92] As importantly, Lester believed he could embrace Jewish victimhood with pride; that, as James Baldwin observed in his essay "Negroes Are Anti-Semitic Because They're Anti-White," and contemporary writers have reiterated in various ways, in America Jews' suffering is privileged over other collective sufferings.[93]

## The Political Is Personal

As we have seen, *Lovesong* deflects attention from the political to the personal. It is not an ordinary autobiography. It was meant not to sum up Lester's career, but rather to tell the story of a spiritual journey culminating in conversion. He includes in this account his childhood memories, family relations, and sexual fantasies in a surplus of detail, suggesting that he regards his conversion in these psychosexual contexts, or prefers his readers to understand it that way. Let us now, therefore, turn to a third subplot of his conversion story, the personal that propels the political.

Lester informs us that his father was a commanding figure. His authority derived not only from his powerful personality (even his mother referred to him as "Reverend Lester") but also from his relatively privileged status as a black minister in the segregated South of the 1940s. The Lesters were different from other black families because they did not depend on whites for their economic survival. Such privilege, however, entailed rigorous obligations, constraints, and a good deal of compunction. Lester remembers his father as always dressed formally. "Anybody can tell that Daddy is a preacher," he contends. "He always dresses in a suit and tie. They are as natural on him as his black skin."[94] Lester and his brother also had to distinguish themselves from other children their age, forgoing all sorts of activities and games. "I cannot do what other kids do. . . . We represent Daddy and he represents God." As a consequence, Lester spent much time alone and was perpetually lonely. "I am a child yearning to be with children," he recalls, "but these wear dirty torn clothes. How am I supposed to play with someone whom dust coats like roach powder?"[95]

Exceptionally high standards of tidiness and cleanliness were instilled in the young Lester, standards he continues to observe. The official reason for such fastidiousness was his father's status, but in a parenthetical remark Lester speculates that "It is almost as if the memories of slavery in our blood demanded perpetual cleanliness as expiation."[96] Nowhere in his writings does Lester explicitly identify the connection, which to the reader may seem obvious, between cleanliness and being white. But years later he comments that he believes he pays homage to his ancestors when working in the dirt in his garden.[97] (Recall also that the mature Lester experiences guilt for playing in the dirt as a child, while Jewish children were exterminated in death camps in Europe.[98])

It was Lester's mother, whom he claims was often mistaken for white, who established and maintained the standards of cleanliness. She never allowed him to be soiled and forbade him to use the filthy "colored" bathrooms.[99] In comparison with the dominant presence of his father, Lester's mother figures very little in his autobiographies. Lester's mother was also his biological link to the Jewish people. A reserved, quiet, strict, and formal woman, she and her mother are described as surrounded by silence. The silence of the two women blends with a mystery, a strange name written in black capital letters on his grandmother's mailbox, ALTSCHUL. He describes one vivid memory of his mother.

> One afternoon we are sitting in the porch swing next to each other. She is telling me about the orchard and her voice is soft like moonlight on a magnolia blossom and I want to melt into her and without thinking, my voice soft like a fuzz on a bee's back, I ask, "Momma? Who is A-L-T-S-C-H-U-L?" [100]

His mother dodged the question; it was his father who informed him that Altschul was the family name of his great-grandfather, a Jewish peddler who, he claimed, did "the Christian thing even if he was a Jew," by marrying an ex-slave. Of course, as Lester would later discover, antimiscegenation laws of the South would have made it virtually impossible for such a union to occur, and, in fact, the two were not officially married. [101]

Lester never met his great-grandfather, and the family stories that he retells in *Lovesong* do not indicate that Adolph Altschul was an observant Jew or educated his children in Judaism. But later in his life, Lester will use his great-grandfather's Jewishness to legitimize his own conversion. [102] Indeed, *Lovesong* includes a sequence of photographs that commence with a picture of Adolph Altschul's tombstone in Pine Bluff, Arkansas, continue with a photo of Altschul's daughter (Lester's maternal grandmother), and end with a facsimile of his great-grandfather's handwritten will and a copy of the notice of his death that appeared in a local newspaper.

## White Mama

Lester's mother referred to her fair skin as a constant burden. She tells young Julius that as a child she was beaten by black children for looking different and ostracized by white people because "we looked white but weren't." [103] Femaleness and whiteness merge in Lester's mind not only because of his light-skinned mother but also because for him his father, and thus masculinity, signified blackness. Lester identifies more with his mother; to relate to his father, especially the "bitterness" he felt toward whites, Lester has to try to imagine "putting [him]self inside his [father's] black skin (which he really is)." [104] Other than family members, *Lovesong* includes virtually no mention of black women but does describe in excruciating detail Lester's enduring attraction to white women. [105]

Lester's attitude toward women, white women in particular, is ambivalent at best. He credits an early encounter with a white girl for having instilled in him a lifelong faith in the humanity of whites.[106] And years later, it is the fear he believes he has aroused in a young white woman that leads him to realize he has become a "captive of blacks" and to decide never again to "let [blacks] use me as a club in their battle against anguish."[107] Perhaps most importantly, his marriages to white women contributed to his growing estrangement from militant racial politics.[108]

While attracted to white women, Lester also fears them. "White women are the deepest terror," he divulges in *Lovesong*. "What a white woman says is truth even when it is a lie. How do I assert my existence if nothing I say is believed as truth, if death has blue eyes, long yellow hair glistening like destiny, and skin as pale as hope?"[109] The title of the book that propelled Julius Lester into notoriety in the heyday of his career in militant black politics in the late 1960s included the warning "Black Power's gon' get your Mama!," and the particulars he provides suggest that we should interpret this declaration as more than a figure of speech.

Lester's dread of white women, at times of all women, typically manifests itself in profound resentment of expressions of female might, especially feminism. He associates women's influence over men with slavery. Informed by a female schoolteacher that his eldest son, Malcolm, is too aggressive and violent, Lester suspects that she is intimidated by Malcolm's "power of the masculine." The incident elicits a long lament about the dire fate awaiting his son growing up in a world where "feminism roams the streets with all the intelligence of a lynch mob."[110] For Malcolm to respect and love his masculinity, he will need to learn to defend himself against the "feminist tyranny." "If he doesn't, he'll find himself hanging from a non-sexist lamp post, crows pecking at his penis."[111] Feminists, specifically their pro-choice politics, also police Lester's organ. "Sometimes I think children cry out from the trunk of my penis to be born and it angers me when I hear women say it is their right to do as they wish with their bodies. How came it to be *theirs*? That body was put in their keeping, but it is not their property."[112] Feminists, according to Lester, are as rational as an enraged mob on a lynching expedition. Women as a group do not even merit classification within the German/Jew dichotomy, so central to his understanding of politics.

The intense anxiety about feminism expressed in *Lovesong* is notably absent from Lester's earlier writings. In several of his articles for the *Guardian*, for instance, Lester not only voiced pro-feminist sentiments but also explicitly criticized those black activists (he did not name them) who ridiculed women's liberation. He reproached detractors for "blaming the victim," and warned them that men would not be liberated until women were as well.[113] How might Lester's decision to become a Jew relate to his antifeminism, to his growing unwillingness to credit feminists with representing legitimate grievances of women or, for that matter, from seeing women as oppressed?

## Another Triangle?

By including an excess of intimate information about his relationship with his parents, Lester averts his readers' attention from the racial triangle—blacks, whites, Jews—to the Oedipal one. He states that his father's death freed him to become himself: "Is that what Freud meant, that a son cannot be himself truly until the father is dead, until the son stands in that void the father leaves and knows that the only other human being who can fill that space is himself?"[114] It is the son's rebellion against his domineering father and his own attraction to his mother that led him, around the time of his father's death, to convert to Judaism (his maternal great-grandfather's religion). Lester feels responsible in part for his father's death, associating his own rejection of Jesus with his father's illness.[115]

Furthermore, the autobiography suggests that the allure of white women may be connected to the whiteness of his own mother and thus to the Jewish element in his ancestry. By choosing Judaism he chooses, by way of displacement, to reunite with his mother, to "melt into her," as he fantasized as a child. Might it be that "Auschwitz" has not replaced "Momma," but instead acquired her? In his Black Power mode Lester "got" Whitey's women by sleeping with them. Now he "gets" his own white Momma by becoming a Jew. Choosing Judaism resolves the double embarrassment embedded in secrecy and the mystery that Lester carries as a burden since childhood: his attraction to his mother, and the Jewish identity of his maternal great-grandfather.

Depicting his conversion as a process of shedding external identities (and, as we saw, skin color) imposed on him, and recovering (by divine wish) an authentic self, may merely serve Lester as an excuse for breaking with other black men, for his rejection of black politics was motivated in part by the tension generated by his various liaisons with white women.[116] In this context, the militancy of black activists functions like a father figure standing in the way of his sleeping with his mother-substitutes. Lester's testimony about the period of his conversion enhances such an interpretation. He writes, "The joy is there each morning when I awake. I not only see it smiling at me like a lover when I open my eyes but it takes me in its arms and strokes my body."[117] Perhaps then,

Lester does not "get" his own white Momma, but some improved version of her. As against his actual, cold, disciplining mother, he claims to have found a warm Jewish one.[118] The text, moreover, is rich with additional allusions to Judaism as a sexual female lover. (He reports, for example, that the sound of a Hebrew feminine noun gives him an erection.)[119] And we should not forget that he characterizes his conversion as a "love song."

## The Woman Within

Lester describes his process of becoming a Jew in terms of descent.[120] "I will not be converting to Judaism," he declares, "I'm becoming, at long last, who I always have been. I am a Jew. I'm only sorry it has taken me 42 years to accept that."[121] Lester takes issue with the concept "convert" as misrepresenting his returning to his "original" Jewish identity, "the name by which God calls me."[122] He is captivated by (and quotes at length) a letter he received from a California rabbi who learned about the conversion from one of Lester's articles. The rabbi suggests that Lester is *gilgul* (Hebrew for reincarnated)—a Jewish soul trapped in a gentile's body. Lester is intrigued but refuses to commit himself to the idea because of its obvious "irrationality."[123] However, in his previous memoir, *All Is Well*, he reports that concealed within his male body lives a female self. Lester never mentions his inner-woman in *Lovesong*. Like his Jewish identity, Lester also attributes his female self (which may be one and the same) to his mother.

When he was a child, his mother informed him that she had actually been hoping for a girl. The young Julius Bernard, who was named after his mother, Julia Beatrice, so identified with her, or at least so desperately wanted to satisfy her yearning for a daughter, that he believed he was female. "I felt myself to be her not as she was in the roles of my father's wife, or my mother, but the woman-her, who existed outside social definitions."[124] Lester christened his female self "Michele."

> I pretended to be a boy . . . all the while envying the girls. . . . Michele was (is?) the real me, and that boy called Julius was the fantasy, a preconceived identity for which I could not be faulted, or held responsible. My sex and name were considered to be me, but my childhood fantasy was an inner language telling me that my definition of who I was was more important than the womb's or the world's.[125]

Michele's primary function was to discipline Julius's organ. While she taught him not to treat women as mere sexual objects, her indifference to his libidinal desires ultimately brought him to hate women. As a youth he wrote a series of short stories (as yet unpublished) whose common plots revolve around young artists so distracted by "a world seething with feminine pulchritude that they became murderers of women."[126] Michele sought to regulate Julius's sexuality in other ways as well, perhaps suppressing homoeroticism. "Michele hated boys . . . and . . . swore that no boy would ever stick it to her."[127] Lester attempts to resolve this tension by considering himself a "male lesbian."[128] Unfortunately, his "third leg" kept tripping him up.

> I particularly hated that thing dropping from the end of my torso like a fat worm, pulsating to an aching hardness as if it lived wholly independently of me. I wanted to cut it off and throw it to a passing dog. I envied Michele, whose organ was invisible to her . . . unable to embarrass her as mine did, protruding against my pants with such rigidity that sometimes it felt like a third leg.[129]

Lester's description of his youthful identity play follows precisely the same lines as his adult conversion. It seems he has never relinquished his childhood fancy that he could transcend the "world's" and the "womb's" definitions. His fantasy is not only that he was female but also that he could become his own mother and give birth to himself. He presents his most significant intellectual influences in these terms. The English Romantic poet Percy Bysshe Shelley, for example, helped him conceive the "embryo of a new identity," which Jean Paul Sartre "midwifed."[130]

## The Kindest Cut

Long before these seminal intellectuals impregnated him, however, Lester had discovered a literary role model in none other than Shakespeare's anti-Semitic caricature of a Jew in *The Merchant of Venice*. Reading the play on Christmas Day, 1951, he found himself infuriated with the way Shylock was mistreated because he was a Jew. It is likely that part of what enraged young Lester was how the trickery of the gentiles replicated the deceptiveness of whites, but Lester proffers that there was more to his intense connection with Shylock. He identified with Shylock rather than black figures such as DuBois, James Weldon Johnson, and Langston Hughes because "they are models of success and I need a model of suffering."[131] Because he can be angry for Shylock, he feels he has permission to begin to feel angry for himself. In this way, Lester projects back to childhood what would become a characteristic of his adult public expressions of rage during his militant days in the 1960s: ventriloquism, donning a mask. Shylock's agony also resonates with Lester because Shylock is a victim mistakenly perceived by others as a victimizer. Decades later during the Ocean Hill–Brownsville teachers' strike, when a Jewish leader of the United Federation of Teachers demanded the suspension of the black teacher who first read the Jew boy poem on Lester's broadcast, Lester retorted: "What does he want, two pounds of flesh?" [132] Jews and Jewish symbols thus serve Lester as both an object of and a vehicle for expressing anger. His evolution from anti-Semite to Jew gives new meaning to Baldwin's reflection that "in the face of one's victim, one sees oneself." [133]

Although proudly reporting, in his first autobiography, *All Is Well*, on all of the books he owned as a child and young adult, he never mentions possessing, or even reading, *The Merchant of Venice*. Since Shylock only appears in *Lovesong*, we may assume that this anti-Semitic characterization of a Jew is somehow crucial to Lester's connection to Judaism and Jews. Leslie Fiedler's interpretation of this Shakespearean drama may be helpful here. Fiedler construes Shylock's insistence on a pound of flesh as a substitute for the mohel's removal of the foreskin. [134] The circumcised penis not only marks the male body as Jewish but also creates a "memory that persists not in the head or heart, but in the blood." [135] The blood that Jewish men share is, according to this reading, not what has passed from parents to children, but the blood spilled during circumcision. By submitting to the knife, Lester can partake in this blood-bond. Sacrificing his foreskin will also connect him to Jews in another way: he will no longer need "to remember that of which [he has] no memory." [136] Like other Jewish men, he will possess a site of memory that can never be "re-membered." Circumcision allows Lester to inscribe Auschwitz on his own flesh. (The Hebrew term for circumcision, *millah*, also means "word.") It will provide him with the wound he shamefully claims he doesn't carry from his childhood or his years working with SNCC in the South. The mohel's cut will, in short, make Lester a true victim. [137]

The source of Lester's ambivalence about his organ may be tied to his childhood experiences, but 1960s racial politics endowed it with new meaning. His hatred of his genitals for marking him as black speaks to concerns raised, for instance, by Frantz Fanon. Fanon depicted the Negrophobe as "no longer aware of the Negro but only of a penis; the Negro is eclipsed. He is turned into penis. He is penis." [138] It may be that Lester finds the idea that black men are defined by their genitals so captivating because it deflects the embarrassment of his desires onto the white man's gaze. Or perhaps Lester is trading in one liability for another. With the rise of Black Power, the black penis was reclaimed as the phallus (in homophobic and misogynist ways). [139] Having participated in that development, Lester had to give his up. At the same time, Lester perceives the circumcised penis as the real phallus, since it gives Jews the authority that he, as a black man, envies. One way or another, inoculating his penis through Jewish circumcision would guard Lester from both his shame and the racialist rendering. Like the blood sign placed over Jewish homes to protect them from the final punishment God inflicted on Pharaoh's Egypt, the "embodied sign" will prevent Lester from being overtaken by his penis.

"Cutting off" his penis (as he fantasized as a child), or just cutting it through circumcision, also assists Lester in liberating himself from the gendering of his body. Lester believes his genitalia make him vulnerable. He contends that it was only because of his marriages to white women that he was able to resist the seductive hatred he observed "stroking at the loins" of other black men.[140] Interracial sex inoculates Lester against his own penis by threatening to eliminate it, for his marriages provoke such rage in black women that they want to "cut off [his] dick." His white wives, however, are also potential castrators, or so Lester imagines in his dreams.[141] Circumcision was therefore a necessary supplementary measure for Lester to become a "Jew." The black penis threatened with castration will now be protected by a partial castration.

Given the amount of attention Lester devotes to the issue, it may be instructive to recall Freud's discussion of the castration complex. According to Freud, the castration complex is "the deepest unconscious root of anti-Semitism; for even in the nursery little boys hear that a Jew has something cut off his penis . . . and this gives them the right to despise Jews. And there is no stronger unconscious root for the sense of superiority over women."[142] Building upon Freud's recoding of anti-Semitism as sexism, Daniel Boyarin attempts to theorize the "Jewish male femme." His conception of the Jewish "sissy" suggests another connection between Lester's feminine and Jewish identities. Boyarin hypothesizes that cross-gender identification may be "constitutive of Jewishness."[143] Becoming a Jew, therefore, may have helped Lester appease his inner female. Then again, even after the conversion and the circumcision, Lester remains preoccupied with castration. In the novel, *All Our Wounds Forgiven* (1994), this vision assumes an interracial, homoerotic, and sadomasochist hue, when a white male sheriff humiliates a black civil rights worker by arousing him with a knife.[144]

## Jesus Envy

Interpreting Lester's conversion to Judaism in psychosexual terms is greatly assisted by Lester's own construction of his life story in *Lovesong* and his insistence on exposing himself, on disrobing in front of the reader, his public.

His autobiographies unfold as verbal stripteases imitating through text Lester's conversions as sheddings of superimposed identities. Both autobiographical unrobings result in nakedness. He offers us so many anecdotes and remarks that promise to shed light on his private life that the reader is sometimes left wondering what this exhibitionism is meant to hide, and from whom. Having considered range of possibilities with respect to his parents, we might add that Lester's relationship with Jesus always had a hint of sibling rivalry.

The young Lester felt uneasy about the images of Christ in his father's church. He held a grudge against Jesus for monopolizing suffering, for preventing others from carrying their own crosses.

> Why should I give my sins to Jesus? They were my sins. It was my task to meditate on them. . . . To carry my cross. To lift my stone. To live with the suffering that comes to me, whether as a consequence of my actions or being born black. To live with the suffering that comes to me because I was born.[145]

It may seem odd that he finds Jesus to be the most objectionable element of Christianity, while his own views on the need to accept suffering and forgive your tormentors seem so Christ-like. But Lester believes that he too is holy. He reports learning this when he was only a boy: ". . . a fear crawls over my flesh like a long-legged spider and I understand in the hollows and crevices and caves of my soul: God has chosen me for himself."[146]

Being pinned is a recurrent trope in Lester's prose. He is pierced by the music of the Jewish prayer of atonement, *Kol Nidre*. "[B]eauty and pain become a piercing that hold me pinioned and I feel old like 'In the beginning,' old as if I was never born and will never die."[147] "In the beginning" holiness was secured for Lester long before Jesus and Christianity intervened, since as Lester tells us in the very beginning of *Lovesong* "I was robed in the mantle of holiness even before the first diaper was pinned on my nakedness."[148] And, as we've seen, Lester complains that his writing also pins him.[149] Stripping off his pinned diaper became a necessary step for Lester to reclaim his rightful holiness. After he stripped for us, too, at the end of *Lovesong*, on the back of the dust jacket, Lester is pictured robed in the Jewish prayer shawl.

Moving in the opposite direction, from Christianity back to Judaism, the child chosen by God for himself ultimately joins the chosen people. At first Lester had difficulty with the concept of chosenness. Such an idea, he explains, "is as repugnant to me as when blacks tell whites they cannot know what it is to be black. It is a statement that negates literature, art and music, nullifies the realm of the imaginative and says it is impossible for human beings to reach out from one loneliness to another and assuage both." [150] Eventually, he comes to embrace it. He continues to reject similar claims made by African Americans, "but Jews," he concludes, "are different." [151] At various junctures, and in blatant contradiction with his ardent advocacy of chosen identifications, Lester asserts that he did not choose to become part of the chosen people. [152]

Lester presents his conversion as a process vital to healing his unbridgeable dividedness and achieving wholeness (holiness). It is therefore intriguing that both of his major autobiographies feature the same anecdote in which he describes a fleeting moment of body/soul unison. He also refers to this episode as his most vivid memory of his years as a civil rights activist:

> May 1966. Lowndes County, Alabama. I go to the outhouse. It is a three-sided tin structure without a roof, and a board over a deep hole. I sit, the warm breeze soft on my exposed buttocks. In the distance a man plows a field. In the tree above me, birds chirp. I am whole again, at peace and at One with God. Time drops away like an oversized garment, and the poverty and the pain and the death all around me vanish as if they have never been. [153]

This paradise, reminiscent of biblical imagery as well as the sort of epiphany that Martin Luther reportedly experienced, unites the "hole in the ground" with holiness, defecation with "wholeness," and identifies anal pleasures as oneness with God. [154] Such an ideal scenario could happen only in the solitude of the outhouse that allows escape from society and human company into the gender and color-blind heavenly nature. For Lester the outhouse is the outsider's sanctuary. He remarks that the pariah's perspective is comparable to the view from the outhouse. [155]

## Trading Places

Despite the chronic inconsistencies in Lester's self-presentation (which he seems to relish as an Emersonian virtue) the preceding analysis points to an underlying coherence in Lester's life story, or at least in his construction of it. As we saw, becoming a Jew is only one among many plots of conversion and self-making in Lester's biography; for instance, his trajectory into the politics of black militancy and his fantasy of possessing an inner female. There is great affinity among these and other decisive points in Lester's private and public life when bursts of aggression give way to moments of guilt and remorse, and fierce tensions are resolved through triangular gestures. Importantly, Lester's sense of identity is grounded in the corporeal. This multilayered physicality is evident in his rejection of his black skin as well as in the bodily desires and sensations that accompany his process of self-fashioning. The primacy of the embodied is also central to his preoccupation both with the violent rupture of the Holocaust, on the one hand, and with his own circumcision, on the other. Through circumcision Lester achieved Jewishness in all of its concrete and metaphoric permutations. It was the palpable apex of his racechange.

But how might we comprehend Lester's conversion in the contexts of antivictimism and the Cult of True Victimhood? What politics does this stream of titillating private anecdotes obscure? Exposing the political concealed by the idiosyncratically personal is not an easy task. After all, Lester is fantastically eccentric and more than a bit of an exhibitionist. The richness of his narrative and the abundant quantity of his prodigious outpouring of prose permit diverse readings. We might, for example, construe Lester's leap into the "void" as an act of defiance against the fixity of identity, a subversive challenge to hierarchical distinctions based on racial, ethnic, and gender stereotypes.[156] There are a few indications of this sort of identity play in his writing; for example, his poem, "Who I Am" (1974):

> I am who I am. / Must I give a name to that? / Must I say / I am black / I am a man / I am a writer? / Those are statements of fact / (the sky is blue. water is wet. snow is cold.) / But what is black? / Not even the color of my true love's hair / (which is red) / What is a man? / The figment of a penis' imagination / What is a writer (doctor/lawyer/Indian chief)? / What do you put in the space of income tax forms / that says OCCUPATION _____ . / So who am I? / I am / who I am / and if that leaves you perplexed, will you accept that / I am you?

In exploring the numerous ways others might define him, Lester rejects them all except for the vague, universalizing "you" in the last line.

Elsewhere Lester insinuates that we should not take him too literally (or even too seriously), that there is much in his writing that is purposefully contrived to mislead. For instance, he alleges that in order to reclaim himself from the public persona he had created by writing *Look Out, Whitey!*, he had to remove his black mask. Doing so, he concludes, requires divulging even more of his inner self through writing: "Because my name was now a public possession, I could no longer allow it to represent someone who did not really exist. Who I was in the interior chambers of my heart had to be exposed for all to see its pulsations. There was no other way to reclaim myself."[157]

What did Lester present of his true, "pulsarating" self? What was the content of this act of self-exposure?—a fictional interview with an interracial couple. He contentedly reports that no one knew for certain whether the interview was fact or fiction.[158] Can it be that Lester is just a trickster playing with his readers' own prejudices about race, gender, and identity?

Compelling as these interpretations may seem in an age that celebrates hybridity and queering, we have observed that Lester subverts neither rigid identities based on presumptions of authenticity, nor the ranking of those identities. Indeed, his conversion thrives on these very distinctions. As opposed to what Stuart Hall describes as "the logic of coupling," Lester reifies a hierarchy of identification, insisting that Jewishness, not blackness, is his authentic identity.[159] In his autobiography he offers two opposing conceptions of identity to support this remarkable assertion. First, he associates identity with interiority, a hidden self that is in need of discovery. Accordingly, he contends he was always a Jew (a claim supported by his Jewish ancestry) but had to struggle to shed his false black mask in order to reclaim his true self, his inner Jew, if you will. Second, he describes his life story as a valiant adventure of self-invention in the Zarathustrian sense, an individual wrestling with grave choices about his Being. Both conceptions are predicated on a robust notion of authenticity. Both are problematic in other ways as well: in one case, identity is opportunistically attached to a remote ancestor; in the other, to notions of extreme individualism, unencumbered will and violence (specifically, the Holocaust and circumcision). More troubling still, Lester deploys these two notions of authenticity to prize Jewishness (whether discovered or chosen) over ordinary blackness. He maintains that as a whole blackness is an inferior and ultimately inauthentic source of identification.

There has been much recent rumination about the black/Jewish divide, especially from the Jewish side of the fence. Lester's story represents both the attraction and the aversion that has characterized the relationship between these two groups. The evolution of black/Jewish relations from presumed fraternity to assumed animosity moves in an apparently opposite path of Lester's trajectory. In this sense he may have fulfilled his ambition to live outside history. At the same time, as I have suggested, his conversion was predicated upon the widening gap between the two groups. *Lovesong* is not a gesture of reconciliation; in many ways it redraws the line, it's a symptom of the divide.

Lester's conversion is indicative of the deep roots that the Holocaust has taken in American collective consciousness. The Americanization of the European Holocaust has coexisted with, if not contributed to, new divisions, competitions, and resentments between African Americans and American Jews. Studies suggest that fear of future anti-Semitism (including anti-Semitism among African Americans) and the Holocaust loom large and may even be constitutive of contemporary Jewish secular identity.[160] Similarly, Peter Novick provides compelling historical evidence indicating that since the 1970s, the Holocaust as a symbol of Jewish suffering has been purposefully recruited to secure and sustain Jewish continuity in the face of secularism, assimilation, and intermarriage. Of course, the European Holocaust could be incorporated into American culture with such force only with the cooperation of non-Jews as well. Such support was forthcoming, Vivian Patraka proposes, because focusing on the European Holocaust as a symbol of oppression and atrocity allows Americans to affirm American democracy (it could never happen here), while occluding the nation's more shameful past (what did occur on this soil).[161] Perhaps this is why, as Stephen Steinberg notes, Americans readily heed the moral dictate to remember and honor the Holocaust but otherwise sermonize racial amnesia.[162] The intensifying commemoration of the Jewish Holocaust in the 1980s and 1990s has contributed to what Novick terms "Holocaust envy." He observes that such ambivalence is most prevalent among African Americans.[163] One way or another, there are indications that the Holocaust has seeped into the imagination of African Americans other than Lester. The Holocaust has become a template of remembering, coloring the memories of other historical injustices.[164]

Employing the Jews of the Holocaust as symbols of victimhood, moreover, is certainly not unique to Lester. However, in contrast to Lester's literal appropriation of Jewish suffering, the Jew more commonly serves as a recognizable signifier to articulate the oppression of other groups. This is the context in which real and metaphoric Jews populate feminists' writings, for example, from Simone de Beauvoir's reference to "Jewish character" and Betty Friedan's comparison of suburban existence in 1950s America to the concentration camps of Nazi Germany to Naomi Wolf's allusion to the Holocaust to emphasize the severity and prevalence of eating disorders among American women.[165] The Jew as a trope has also been used to highlight the political potential of Otherness: whether Hannah Arendt's analysis of the Jew as a "conscious pariah," Isaac Deutscher's "non-Jewish Jew," Jean-Paul Sartre's "authentic Jew," or Jean-François Lyotard's "the jews."[166] As problematic as such constructions may be for, among other things, effacing non-metaphoric Jews, as well as for circumventing the differences among disparate systems of oppression (e.g., sexism, anti-Semitism, and racism), the Jew-as-victim metaphor is employed in these works to facilitate a collective emancipatory project, whereas Lester's "Jew" is formulated as a rejection of precisely this sort of politics.[167]

His conversion coincided with his adoption of a more conservative set of political stances in other ways as well. In Lester's story the anti-Semite becomes a Jew with the same radical ease with which Jews, Nazis, victims, and victimizers trade places. As we have seen, this is a central feature of anti-victim discourse in American politics today. Anti-victimists conceive of a world neatly divided between victims and victimizers, much like the victimists they scorn. The important difference between these two depictions, however, is that anti-victimists want to claim that they are the real victims. Lester is a fine example of this political dynamic.[168]

According to Lester, victimhood, like any other status, is a choice. Just like Lester, blacks, whites, victims, and victimizers can just choose to identify or "nonidentify" with their race and/or condition.[169] Echoing Sartre, Lester asserts that individuals choose who they want to be and how they want to be defined. Such choice includes not only what one's present and future will be but also how to interpret one's history, what will be "definitional."[170] To deny this choice, and attribute it to the past is "bad faith."[171] "We are never so much the victims of another," writes Lester, "as we are victims of ourselves."[172] The womb and the world may try to impose an identity upon you, but only the weak, only the victimist, will allow himself to be defined by others (to be trapped in the womb of identity). There are no excuses, he declares; victims must accept responsibility for their own actions ("the evil they have wrought"), as well as responsibility for what they have suffered on account of others' actions ("the evil they have endured").[173]

Placing Lester's narrative in the context of Sartre's writings suggests that Lester's radical conversion may have been his effort to fulfill the Sartrean idea of a "radical conversion in his being-in-the-world."[174] In Sartre's writings, it seems, Lester found a path to "authenticity," to overcome "seeing himself as others see him."[175] Perhaps, then, interpreting *Anti-Semite and Jew* literally, Lester believed that the only route toward "authentic identity" was Judaism; that to be what Sartre calls an "authentic Jew" he must first become a Jew.

Sartre maintained that the Jew was the creation of the anti-Semite, whose views the Jew internalized; hence the Jew was "overdetermined from within." Building upon Sartre's insights, Fanon saw blacks (unlike Jews) to be "overdetermined from without," perceiving themselves only through the reflection of the white colonizers' gaze. Lester's decision to become a Jew is one expression of his desire to be colorless, to defy others' efforts to impose an identity upon him. In the end, the University of Massachusetts at Amherst accepted his radical conversion and new identity. But instead of relieving Lester from the "noose of race," it simply repositioned him. The administration removed Lester from the Afro-American Studies Department and relocated him in the Near Eastern and Judaic Studies Department. Pointing to the irony of the university's decision is not to endorse it. To the contrary, in reassigning Lester the university, much as the Afro-American Studies Department, relied upon the same assumptions about authenticity and identification that Lester and other anti-victimists promote and that I have sought to destabilize in this chapter.

# 5 Therapeutics of Blame: Blaming Victims and Victims as Blamers

IN THE PAGES OF *COSMOPOLITAN* MAGAZINE journalist Bette Harrison encourages women to abandon what she calls "the blame game." "We may indeed have come from the slums, been married to creeps, or had strict mothers who criticized us in everything we did," she explains, "but blaming robs us of the power to make choices." Harrison cites Wayne Dyer, author of *Your Errone-ous Zones*, who maintains that "[b]laming others, regardless of whether they've caused you harm, is one of the most neurotic things human beings do." Likewise, Barbara Sher, author of *Wishcraft: How to Get What You Really Want*, asserts that blaming has no positive function—"it's inefficient and totally passive."[1] The idea that blaming others for one's misfortunes is itself an expression of weakness, moral or psychological, and a dangerous abdication of personal responsibility, is not confined to women's magazines and self-help books. It has become a staple of contemporary political discourse and, as we observed in the previous chapters, is central to the anti-victimist campaign. In the anti-victimist lexicon "victimism" and "the blame game" function as interchangeable designations of the same social disease: both condemn unproductive, self-indulgent, and dangerously partisan behavior.

This chapter investigates the relationship between victimhood and blame by tracing the curious career of the phrase "blaming the victim," from its earliest use by sociologist William Ryan to challenge prevailing social theories of the late 1960s to the 1990s anti-victimist drive. The blame/victim nexus also takes us to the science of victimology that emerged in the aftermath of the Second World War to gauge "victim precipitation," the works of psychologist Melvin Lerner who documented that individuals in fact do blame victims, feminists' protests against "blaming the rape victim," "self-esteem" programs, media therapists, and finally the victims' rights movement.

Despite divergent political perspectives, participants in the victim debates share much in terms of argumentation and rationale irrespective of whether they are encouraging or discouraging the blaming of victims. Rather than viewing blame in association with other moral or legal attributions, blaming is explained and then opposed or justified in terms of its psychological (and social) recuperative efficacy. As we will see, political causes formulated in terms of victimhood increasingly concentrate on the norms, decorum, and utility of blaming, often at the expense of serious efforts to address the material consequences of victimization or its remedy.

The question of victims' blameworthiness called forth new types of expertise. Indeed, over the last half-century, several scientific disciplines—psychology, sociology, criminology (or victimology)—rendered victims and victimhood their subject. These discourses endeavored to probe victims' culpability, blameworthiness, psychological needs, and frame of mind. In the process they reshaped policies, laws, and public perceptions, spawning a host of other victim professions and professionals: therapists, social workers, advocates, and pundits. The relationship between the sciences of the victim and anti-victimism is thoroughly dialectical. Critics of victim politics assault the social sciences, while still upholding basic formulations that originated in these disciplines. These sciences, in turn, proved deeply ambivalent about victims and claims of victimization. Exploring the role of victimhood in American politics through the lens of blame thus reveals an important dimension in the prehistory of contemporary anti-victimism.

There is a rich literature in philosophy and the law on the meaning of "blame," often in relation to concepts such as "accountability," "culpability," "guilt," "liability," "causality," and "responsibility" (sometimes further qualified by adjectival modifiers such as "functional responsibility," "causal responsibility," "moral responsibility," and so forth).[2] I borrow one distinction from this literature: unlike causal attributions, blaming typically involves a judgment (often assuming intent and an understanding of wrongdoing) of the character of the subject being blamed.[3] Otherwise, the aim of the following discussion is not to define the meaning of blame, but to uncover the rhetorical work of the phrase "blaming the victim"—how each of the users employs it, and why they choose that expression.

## Coining a Phrase

The title of William Ryan's famous 1971 book introduced the phrase "blaming the victim" into public vernacular.[4] In *Blaming the Victim*, Ryan critically examined a host of studies and programs designed during the second half of the 1960s to assist the urban poor, to reduce crime and violence, and to respond to the bursts of social unrest culminating in the 1968 race riots.[5] Most notable among Ryan's targets was the controversial *The Negro Family: The Case for National Action* (1965). In this report author Daniel Patrick Moynihan discerned a causal link between the supposed demise and decay of the black family and poverty in inner cities. He consequently proposed to redress inner-city poverty by restructuring and reinvigorating the family. Ryan demonstrated the inaccurate data and dubious theories at the foundation of such analyses. He showed how vital factors were often neglected, most significantly, economic variables.[6] Nevertheless, Ryan's principal concern was to expose and explain the incentives that led to such distortions and oversights. With great rhetorical flair he labeled Moynihan and other social reformers "victim blamers," arguing that they collude in the oppression of the poor by finding inherent faults within them, while ignoring the social and economic forces that create and perpetuate poverty. Ryan reported that victim blaming infected all aspects of policy analysis and policy making, from academic research to the daily activities of social workers. Victim blaming is endemic, he claimed, to every issue deemed a "social problem," including inadequate health care, escalating crime, poor education, and even ravaged inner-city housing.

Ryan defined "blaming the victim" as an ideology or an ideological process. Building upon Karl Mannheim's theory of ideology and C. W. Mills's critique of the "ideology of social pathology," Ryan understood victim blaming as emerging from "systematically motivated, but unintended, distortions of reality . . . rooted in a class-based interest in maintaining the status quo."[7] Social scientists' propensity to view social problems as "exceptionalistic" rather than "universalistic" is symptomatic of these ideologies. An exceptionalistic approach perceives only the isolated and internal dysfunctions of a specific group. Thus, for example, the Ford Foundation "Gray Areas Report" postulated that the dire conditions of slum housing should be traced not to inadequate funding but to the characteristics of their inhabitants who had not yet "acculturated" to life in major urban centers.[8]

At the core of victim blaming is ascertaining that inequality and the victim's suffering emanate from the victim's difference (or Otherness), often understood in pejorative terms as a malfunction or ineptitude. Ryan mocked this recurrent scholarly tactic as "the art of savage discovery"—the revelation that the victims are savages needing to be civilized. Neglecting the universalistic perspective that, Ryan insisted, would lead to a demand for the fundamental redistribution of power and resources, victim blamers instead identify a cultural pathology as the source of the problem and its removal as the ultimate remedy. "Prescriptions for cure, as written by the Savage Discovery set," Ryan clarified, "are invariably conceived to revamp and revise the victim, never to change the surrounding circumstances. [Victim blamers] want to change [the victim's] attitudes, alter his values, fill up his cultural defects, train him and polish him and woo him from his savage ways."[9]

How different is victim blaming from other types of prejudice? At times, Ryan placed victim blaming within the tradition of racism in America. Although victim blamers attribute the victim's defects to environmental factors, as opposed to inherent or genetic ones, frequently this means merely substituting "liberal, quasi-sociological rationales for unacceptable and blunt racist explanations."[10] More often, however, Ryan maintained that victim blaming is a uniquely liberal ideology that, unlike crude racism, entraps those most inclined to be sympathetic and committed to helping the disadvantaged. Finding conservatives "repugnant," but being even more "allergic to radicals," the victim blamer seeks a moderate response to the inequality he observes. Blaming the victim provides an ingenious middle ground: the middle-class liberal may leave the system that benefits him intact while still seeming to care for those it victimizes. Employing cultural difference theories (read as dysfunctions) allows victim blamers to "absolve" themselves of their "sins" of complicity in injustice.[11]

Social pathology theories tend to rely heavily on the alleged psychological impairments of victims (often associated with a deficient mentality or character). Ryan blamed "Freudianism":

> It sometimes appears that [American liberals] worry more about the resolution of Negro Oedipus complexes than they do about black men getting decent jobs, black babies being bitten by rats, [and] black teenagers being pushed out of school with the equivalent of a fifth-grade education.[12]

While he ridiculed others' reliance on Sigmund Freud's doctrines, I will show how Ryan also recruited basic ideas of psychoanalysis to explain victim blaming; indeed, I suggest that Ryan pathologized the social pathologists.

The phrase "blaming the victim" rings with indignation. It is rhetorically powerful because it conveys, simply and concisely through the juxtaposition of two seemingly contradictory terms, behavior that is patently wrong—blaming the blameless (i.e., misattributing responsibility, or more simply, a mistaken judgment). Ascribing blame to the injured party, rather than simply a bystander, amplifies the gravity of this transgression. Although a commonly used expression rarely requiring explication, Ryan's phrase is still somewhat puzzling. Is "blaming the victim" an ideology, as Ryan writes, or does it refer to an ordinary activity—the practice of blaming—as most of his examples suggest? Or is the expression used as a metaphor or an approximation?

The structure of the idiom enhances these ambiguities; that "blaming the victim" contains a definite article (the) and appears in the singular form (victim) regardless of context.[13] There is also a certain incongruity between Ryan's Marxian orientation and his employment of terms such as "victim" and "blame" that elide class distinctions, insinuate innocence and culpability, and in the case of "victim," are laden with religious undertones. Ryan did not explain his choice of words. Perhaps he adopted the term "victim" to refer to the urban poor because, unlike the working class, their relations to production less easily define them. Nevertheless, the most confounding aspect of the way Ryan employed "blaming the victim" is that he seemed not to use it literally. Oddly enough, "victim blaming" does not entail blaming the victim.

First, it is important to remember that in contrast to the contemporary pejorative use of "victim," which links victimhood to passivity and helplessness, Ryan did not equate victims' condition with a lack of agency, inaction, or dependence. Structural economic and political inequality, rather than some deficiency of character, renders those with whom Ryan was concerned "victims." Second, there is the complication of what he means by blame. Moral philosophers distinguish attributions of causality and responsibility from blame. Blame, they maintain, concludes a sequence of judgments and involves an evaluation of moral stature.[14] While social scientists' employment of cultural pathologies (such as the "culture of poverty") would seem to amount to such a judgment, Ryan maintains that identifying distinctive cultural traits does not constitute, in itself, "blaming the victim."

Revisiting Ryan's work reminds us of the distance traversed by the American Left over the last quarter of a century, for he was categorically antagonistic to the idea of cultural difference.[15] Cultural difference theories, he repeatedly asserted, rely on "stigmas of social origin." Blaming occurs only when such ideas are recruited to explain certain "failures" of the poor: insufficient education, criminality, crumbling families, lack of hygiene, and poverty itself.

In other words, the blaming in "blaming the victim" is not moral condemnation but a causal attribution. The victim blamer actually pities victims for their dire circumstances, but understands these circumstances in cultural rather than economic terms. He professes great sympathy for the poor, and Ryan believed these feelings were "quite genuine."[16] Moreover, victim blamers do not judge victims or hold them responsible for their condition in any explicit way. They deploy cultural difference theories for precisely the opposite purpose—to diffuse judgment, regarding both the victims' and the victim blamers' complicity in sustaining social injustice.

Consider, for example, the 1966 Equality of Educational Opportunity study sponsored by the U.S. Office of Education (otherwise known as the Coleman Report). James Coleman did not attribute the poor performance of black students in inner-city schools to some innate inferiority or even laziness. Instead, he pointed to the correlation between students' achievement and motivation (gauged by whether the student expressed a desire to go to college) and family backgrounds (measured by one factor: whether there was an encyclopedia in the student's home). Not surprisingly, he concluded that black students, whose families typically did not own encyclopedias, are "culturally deprived." The problem, Coleman surmised, is this "functional inferiority"—poorly educated parents, an absence of books, and family's disinterest in education—all "attributable to the depressing and stultifying effects of living in poverty."[17]

Perhaps, therefore, Ryan misused the concept by conflating blame, a moral judgment, with causality.[18] At times, Ryan seems to employ "blaming the victim" inconsistently, or at least does not consider the multiple meanings of his charge. Twenty years after his work first appeared in print, Ryan opaquely remarked that he might have used the phrase "glibly."[19] Alternatively, it is possible that Ryan selected the phrase, with all its moral weight, primarily for its rhetorical effect. The potency of "blaming the victim" as a retort has been repeatedly demonstrated since Ryan published his book; it has become a hardened trope, an epithet.[20] Regardless of Ryan's intent, we should explore other ways to account for its place in his work, if only because of the importance this expression has assumed in American public discourse.

If victim blamers are not blaming, what then are they doing? At certain points in Ryan's text "blaming the victim" refers to a greater act of aggression than simply making a judgment. While the victim blamer may not hold the victim responsible, he does seek to reform her and expects the victim to make an effort to change. These attempts to modify the victim's behavior and attitudes may amount to punishing the victim both by perpetuating inequality—for, according to Ryan, none of the victim blamers' plans would substantially improve the victim's circumstances—and by forcing the victim to alter her ways.

The text suggests a more far-reaching idea: victim blaming itself turns the poor into victims. The intellectual process or ideology is what "victimizes" them. From this perspective, the poor become victims in two distinct ways. First, striving to deflect their own responsibility (to victims, to their culture, or, as we will see, to other agents), victim blamers scapegoat the poor. They render themselves blameless by designating "victims," for scapegoat is the original meaning of the term.[21] Second, ultimate responsibility is further deflected, especially through the idea of cultural deprivation, from the victim to a narrowly defined host of social and historical factors. Victim blamers regard the victim's plight as an inevitable product of a long tradition of cultural dysfunctions (as a "victim of circumstance"), often inherited from previous generations. In this way, victim blaming deprives the poor of their agency precisely because it does not blame them, but blames unalterable circumstances instead. Does Ryan's theory more accurately describes "making the victim" rather than "blaming the victim"? Attempting to adjust the phrase "blaming the victim" by finding some literal meaning (such as replacing "blaming" with "punishing," "making," or "attributing causal responsibility") actually misses the point. We have already established that the apparent affinity between Ryan's subject matter and the phrase he uses to encapsulate it hides a complex relationship between the signifier and the signified; there is an incongruity between the practices he portrays and the label he assigns. Nevertheless, this tension opens new possibilities for interpretation.

For Ryan, victim blaming is not simply a mistaken attribution; it is a product of psychological strife. He described this conflict, rather sparsely, in terms of a "sub-conscious reconciliation" of opposing self-interests and humanitarian "impulses."[22] "Blaming the victim" is part of a larger ideological structure that facilitates and justifies class inequalities and, at the same time, is rooted in a collective unconscious. There are hints in the text that "blaming the victim" resembles a psychological complex, especially since it involves deflections, or displacements, leading to unintended results. Therefore, "blaming the victim" may be the diagnostic term referring to the unconscious roots, the desire, or the complex, rather than to its myriad effects. Capturing, understanding, and bringing these repressed desires to collective consciousness (by calling the desire by its real name) is essential for a healthy resolution of the conflict. The shock value of the expression and its consequent therapeutic effect derives not from its accuracy in describing a specific practice, but from naming the victim blamer's motives and feelings of which he is not aware. It is part of the potential therapeutic effect. Indeed, in a presentation before the annual meeting of the American Psychological Association in the late 1990s, Ryan passionately called for psychologists to accept their roles in bringing about social change. One activity these professionals might pursue, he proposed (perhaps tongue in cheek), is "ideology-therapy."[23] Could it be that the enticing phrase "blaming the victim" was a first step in a prospective ideology-therapy?

Ryan's examples of victim blaming support this rather unconventional interpretation. Victim-blaming theories usually focus on poor African Americans and trace supposed pathologies to the "heritage of slavery." Moynihan, Coleman, Kerner and their cohort ultimately attribute blame for the contemporary endemic suffering of African Americans on some real or metaphoric American ancestors or fathers. As Ryan writes, the only class of people whom victim blamers fault (rather than pathologize) is "that long-dead ancestor of ours, the villainous slave master."[24] Ryan's text, therefore, suggests that the mechanism of deflecting responsibility may intersect with that of a famous Freudian formulation, despite Ryan's own reservations about applying psychoanalytic theories to social problems. Victim blamers, it seems, accomplish two tasks—symbolically killing their forefathers while concurrently burying their own guilty consciences.

A contemporary example further illustrates Ryan's point. We can see how discussions of past injustices may serve to avoid addressing the inequalities of today in the proposal to offer an official federal apology for slavery. The idea for such a gesture originated in Congress. Not surprisingly, given his reputation for contrition, then-President Bill Clinton reacted favorably. Doubtful that Congress would eventually approve a formal apology, Clinton decided to act independently and offered his own expression of regret during his state visit to Africa. Apologizing for slavery in the very same year that government gutted the federal welfare system seems (if we apply Ryan's ideas accurately) a ripe example of victim blaming.[25]

## The Just-World Hypothesis

Ryan's analysis of liberals' predilection to scapegoat victims parallels social psychologist Melvin Lerner's just-world hypothesis. Beginning his studies in the mid-1960s, Lerner established that ordinary Americans are strongly inclined to blame victims. He presented the participants in his experiment groups with several scenarios of extreme misfortune such as serious accidents and violent crimes. Participants tended to fault either the victim's behavior or character, which, Lerner hypothesized, allowed them to rationalize the sequence of events. He described this reaction as an expression of individuals' need to believe in a just world.

We embrace a "fundamental delusion" that life is predicable. Accordingly, we apply a structure of principles about deservedness. Blaming victims allows us to restore order by accounting for what is otherwise inexplicable; it is a control fantasy. Lerner also observed that the more we identify with the victim, or the more implicated we feel in the victim's plight, the more likely we are to blame the victim. Identification for Lerner encompasses personal relationships, the perception of a shared vulnerability, or attachments to people who embody some virtue or value we respect. Thus, for example, women tend to find greater fault with raped women than do men; and both are more likely to blame a Catholic nun than a topless dancer for having been raped.[26]

Lerner's findings seem counterintuitive. The notion that we might be more responsive and attentive to the needs of the less fortunate if only we could imagine ourselves in their circumstances has guided numerous political thinkers. It is at the foundation of Hannah Arendt's notion of "representative thinking" and John Rawls's "veil of ignorance," to give just two examples.[27] Nevertheless, Lerner insists that we are especially "eager to find fault with those we care about, to blame them for the things that happen to them." We might reorder reality, just so that we do not need to view them as victims. If we cannot find such a justification, "we try to run away." When all else fails, we conclude that an injustice did not actually occur.[28]

Like Ryan, Lerner turned to Freudian psychology to explicate his findings. He reasoned that victim blaming was rooted in the child having learned to delay gratification. In order to sustain a calculus that balances restraints on current pleasures with the allure of more desirable outcomes in the future, individuals enter what Lerner calls a "personal contract" that guarantees rewards for additional efforts and for postponing satisfaction. Since the tension between present and future gratifications never entirely subsides, individuals are deeply invested in the rationality of deservedness and find it hard to accept evidence that they (or anybody else) may be denied what they deserve or not deserve what they get.[29]

Both Ryan and Lerner point to a psychological dynamic by which a basic empathy with victims ironically propels individuals to derogate victims and justify their suffering. The two differ in that Ryan's blamers are entrenched American elites who self-servingly find fault with the poor rather than capitalism, whereas Lerner assigns seemingly more benign motives to the participants in his experiments. It is their confidence in the fundamental fairness of life— rather than the material benefits they derive from the social, economic, and political hierarchy—that leads them to scapegoat victims. Their faith in justice paradoxically produces and sustains injustice. This difference notwithstanding, another form of self-interest motivates the belief in a just world: the individual's need to sustain the rationale of the "personal contract."

Ryan's and Lerner's theories provide complimentary explanations of the psychological investments that motivate victim blaming. As compelling as their studies may be, they cannot help us explain the recent preoccupation with victims in American politics, or the specific permutations of anti-victimism. Anti-victimism, in other words, is not simply blaming the victim. Furthermore, it is important to understand Ryan's and Lerner's work as part of the elaboration of the modern science of victimhood. Their respective projects contributed to the reconfiguration of the relationship between victimhood and blame, which, as we shall see, ultimately informed modern anti-victimism.

## Blaming the Rape Victim

In the mid-1970s, feminists adopted "blaming the victim" as a slogan for their work on behalf of rape victims. Initially true to Ryan's approach, they identified a universal principle of (gender) inequality in society as facilitating both victimization (victim making) and victim blaming. They also argued, following Ryan, that because a social problem, in this case rape, was viewed exclusively in exceptionalistic terms, advocates and detractors alike tended to attribute the source of the trouble to the victim's psychological inadequacies and character failings, if not her own conduct.[30]

Accordingly, feminists held that patriarchy manifests itself first in the pervasive threat of rape and then in the act itself. Patriarchal systems socialize men to be sexually aggressive, in some sense prospective offenders, and women to be potential victims—fearful and sexually passive, alluring but unavailable.[31] "Women are trained to be rape victims," Susan Brownmiller asserted. "To simply learn the word 'rape' is to take instructions in the power relationship between males and females."[32] The "pathology of oppression," Germaine Greer added, "prevents women from fighting back and defending themselves against rape."[33] Rather conveniently, as Susan Griffin observed, the myth about female sexuality is that women want to be raped and actually provoke it. Men think that "[l]urking beneath [women's] modest female exterior is a subconscious desire to be ravished."[34] Rape victims are thus cast as the seducers and their rapists as innocents simply acting out their natural biological drives.

By viewing myths about rape as manifestations of victim-blaming ideology, feminists could elucidate precisely how the severity of the crime, as well as the offender's culpability, tended to be diminished. Not only is the victim considered blameworthy, but she is ultimately held accountable for the actions of her victimizer.[35] Just as Ryan's victim blamers secured their privilege by deflecting their complicity, so too men avert their responsibility for rape, first, by projecting their desires onto women, and then by refusing to acknowledge how the "mass psychology of rape" serves men's "class interest" by preserving male domination.[36]

Another application of the phrase "blaming the rape victim" characterized the entire experience to which rape victims were subjected after the crime—in their encounters with the police, physicians, social workers, and prosecutors, and especially in the courtroom. Such ordeals were called a "second rape," as much a violation and as humiliating as the first one.[37] As in Ryan's text, "blaming the victim" at times referred to behavior and practices that amount to punishing the rape victim. The victim's travails in court, where victims were frequently accused of being responsible for their victimization, presented especially poignant examples of victim blaming. Before the advent of rape shield laws, a typical defense strategy was to question the victim's actions, motives, and character, in an attempt to establish consent. The victim may have been raped, but the defense would argue that the act was somehow justifiable or excusable. By shifting blame from the offender to the victim, defense attorneys constructed a deserving victim or a "legitimate victim." "If the impression of a 'legitimate victim' is created, then part of the burden of guilt is relieved from the perpetrator, and some crimes, like rape . . . can emerge as without either victims or offenders."[38] Even after new legal limits on the admissibility of the victim's sexual history, many states still allow the defense to introduce other evidence intended to undermine the victim's testimony; for example, evidence of prior consensual sex with the accused.[39]

Some legal scholars reason that the rape victim's status remains precarious because the discourse of heterosexuality still normalizes men's predatory behavior, shifting blame back to female victims.[40] One study, for example, found that raped females were seen as victims only if the female was either a child or shown to be comparably incompetent, as in the case of mentally challenged women. If, however, the victim was sufficiently mature and competent to have given consent, the defense, and often the jury, tended to assume consent was given.[41] Compounding matters further, rape is still understood, first and foremost, as an act of sex, rather than of violence. Sexually experienced women, therefore, have a more difficult time proving their victimization. Woefully few can be convinced that sex workers, for instance, can also be raped. The law may now prohibit attorneys from probing into the victim's character and sexual practices, but research consistently demonstrates that jurors, and some judges, still take such issues into account.[42] In their groundbreaking survey of 115 rape cases, Ann Wobert Burgess and Lynda Lytle Holmstrom found that "girls or women are seen by the public as 'asking for it,' 'fantasizing about it,' or 'just plain lying.'" Explicitly applying Ryan's analysis, they ask: "If one comes to believe that rape is the female's fault, then who can find any fault with the rapist or with the male-dominated society?"[43]

Despite increasing sensitivity among authorities and advances in legal regulations governing what may occur in the courtroom, rape victims continue to be blamed, because preventing rape is still assumed to be women's responsibility. The codes regulating women's behavior—don't go out alone late at night, don't dress or behave in ways that might be construed as sexually provocative, and so forth—perpetuate victim blaming by asking women to adjust their activities rather than transforming the conditions that put women at risk. Instructing women to engage in such self-protective conduct relies on the a priori assumption that women have a causal responsibility for rape, according to Susan Brownmiller.

> [T]o impose a special burden of caution on women is no solution at all. There can be no private solutions to the problem of rape. . . . [T]o accept a special burden of self-protection is to reinforce the concept that women must live and move about in fear and can never achieve the personal freedom, independence and self-assurance of men. . . . [Such advice views] rape as a woman's problem, rather than a societal problem resulting from a distorted masculine philosophy of aggression.[44]

Scrutinizing the victim's sexual history (to suggest that sex was consensual, despite the victim's testimony to the contrary, or that the defendant reasonably assumed the victim had consented, even if she did not) may be construed as judging the victim's character (as in the attempt to demonstrate that the victim is promiscuous). But even without such explicit evaluative judgments, attributing causal or functional responsibility to the victim may be considered victim blaming, in part, because it may lead to an acquittal. As we have seen, Ryan also employed a similarly expansive notion of blame to denote a variety of attributions other than blame.

However, in applying "blaming the victim" to rape, the phrase acquired new meanings. In the first place, feminists sought to establish the status of raped women as victims. While it is a fundamental tenet of American criminal law that the accused is presumed innocent until proved guilty, in the case of rape trials, scrutiny turns to the victim and typically the inverse is true: the accuser is assumed guilty until proved innocent. Laws are designed to question the victim's veracity, to test her innocence as much as to evaluate the perpetrator's guilt. In other criminal proceedings, the victim's integrity is rarely part of the process of determining the guilt of the accused. When it comes to rape, by contrast, prosecutors worry about the possibility of false charges, though decades of research has shown that only a fraction of rape victims ever report the crime.[45]

Even when those who applied the critique of blaming the rape victim promoted a universalistic explanation, as had Ryan, their work focused on victims of a specific crime. The concreteness of the crime—which is then relived in the police station and courtroom, where women are treated with contempt and disbelief—adds an urgent quality and human face to the offense of "blaming the rape victim," an attribute virtually absent in Ryan's criticism of social scientists, intellectual processes, and the blaming of social groups. Furthermore, the issue of consent, or perhaps simply the fact that the assault assumes a sexual form, makes rape a unique crime. More than any other criminal proceeding, rape trials facilitate an adversarial confrontation between alleged victims and victimizers, contributing to excessive scrutiny of the victim.

Another complication in litigating rape cases is that the crime of rape was originally conceived of as a violation men performed against other men. While the woman's body is the site of violence, men were presumed to be the victims of the rape—the raped victim's husband, father, and so forth, or conversely, a man falsely accused. Rape laws were therefore crafted to protect men as possessors of women. Indeed, well into the late 1970s, rape victims were not even referred to as "victims"; the term employed by authorities and in the courts was "prosecutrix." Thus, while Ryan's decision to employ the term "victim" may be unclear, the designation "victim" in "blaming the [rape] victim" was essential to the charge. The rape victim's legal standing as a "victim" continues to be greatly disputed.[46]

The campaign on behalf of rape victims marked a new approach toward victims of crime, whose most fundamental principle was that prosecuting offenders does not exhaust the assistance society should extend to victims. Acknowledging victims' vulnerabilities led to a variety of programs and services devised to help victims overcome their injuries, injuries that were increasingly understood as including psychological harm. Ideas about the victim's fragile emotional state and consequent need for assistance added further dimensions to the idea of "blaming the victim." Where emphasis falls on emotional trauma suffered by victims, the victim's perceptions tend to govern what counts as "blaming." For rape victims more than for Ryan's, "blaming the victim" is not merely futile and wrong; it is downright harmful.

Rape victims' tendency to blame themselves, regardless of their actual contribution, augments the damage incurred by "blaming the rape victim."[47] Holmstrom and Burgess first explored this dimension of the rape victim's emotional state in their 1974 study of what they termed "rape trauma syndrome" (RTS). Diagnosing and publicizing RTS was a vital step in advancing the public's understanding of the psychological impact of rape as well as in helping victims recover from the experience. They also found several distinctive behavioral traits typical of rape victims, conduct they took to establish that rape is different from other forms of harm. Subsequent research documented that, unlike most victims of assault, rape victims frequently do not immediately report the crime and tend to minimize the injury they endured, behavior that previously led authorities to conclude that complaints were unfounded.[48] Other studies confirmed that the crime of rape has a uniquely devastating impact on the victim: the violation "attacks the whole person, affecting the victim's physical, psychological and social identity."[49] In the aggregate, these projects marked the beginning of a trend: scholars researching the psychological impact of victimization also began to advocate comprehensive victim services.

Feminists' concern with the direct psychological effects of blaming rape victims departs from Ryan's analysis. While Ryan provided a psychological reading of the victim blamer, he did not consider the impact blaming the victim might have on the victim's psychological state. The shift from the psyche of the victim blamer to that of the victim entailed a different therapeutic approach. In the case of rape victims, one step involved shielding victims from critical judgment, even their own.

## Victim Precipitation

The principles that guided rape victim advocacy in the 1970s also informed much of the social sciences during the period, especially the science of victimology. Vulnerable populations had been the subject of examination since the advent of the modern social sciences, but only at the middle of the twentieth century did the concept of victimhood become an organizing principle for scientific observation and policy recommendation. Importantly, the idea of a science dedicated to studying victims first emerged in the context of research into the crime of rape. As early as 1937, the barrister Benjamin Mendelsohn, one of the founders of the discipline, began collecting data on rape victims for his law practice. Upon concluding his study three years later, he became convinced of the need for a field of research distinct from criminology, in which the victim would be the focus of investigation. Such a science would, according to Mendelsohn, uncover and aggregate "the whole of the socio-bio-psychological traits common to all victims, [traits] which society wishes to prevent and fight, no matter what their determinants are."[50] As a first step in this grand endeavor, Mendelsohn classified and calibrated the scope of "victimity" (a term he coined) by generating a scale of victim culpability that ranged from "complete innocence" to "ignorant guilt" and "false victimization."[51]

Although Mendelsohn explicitly sought to establish an interdisciplinary science of all victims, not merely victims of crime, his own work and that of sociologist Hans von Hentig, credited as another founder of the field for his *The Criminal and His Victim* (1948), firmly rooted victimology in the paradigms of criminology. Like Mendelsohn, von Hentig emphasized the reciprocity between the "doer and sufferer," proposing that "it may be the case that the criminal is victimized," for the victim may tempt the perpetrator. (Reportedly, his work was profoundly influenced by Franz Werfel's 1920 novel, *The Murdered One is Guilty*.) "If there are born criminals," von Hentig contended, "it is evident that there are born victims, self-loathing and self-destroying through the medium of the pliable outsider."[52] Allegedly marked by an inherent vulnerability and weakness, von Hentig saw women as a group as the best illustration of born victims. In the 1940s, von Hentig introduced the concept of "victim precipitation," suggesting that the victim may be responsible for the act of victimization as much as the victimizer. He justified the study of victim precipitation in the following manner:

> The reality of life . . . presents a scale of graduated inter-activities between perpetrator and victim which elude the formal boundaries, set up by our statues and the artificial abstractions of legal science, that should be heeded by a prevention-minded social science. By separating in time the fatally "harmonizing" parties, the formation of an explosive social compound can be averted. Remaining would be a potential perpetrator without a victim and a potential victim without a partner to whom he or she could turn to be victimized.[53]

The idea that criminals and victims are "partners in crime" or, in Mendelsohn's words, a "penal couple," guided research in the following decades.[54] Whereas Mendelsohn conceived of this discipline from his work with rape victims, the paradigm of "victim precipitation" was first systematically employed in a study of homicide; specifically in cases where the victim seemed suicidal and researchers consequently hypothesized the offenders' guilt might be diminished.[55] Victim precipitation as applied in these early projects presupposed that the criminal picks his target based on particular traits or clues provided by the prospective victim, "dispositional factors" in addition to "physical or social characteristics." The victim was, in a sense, always already a victim: "he or she is perceived by the offender to be performing the role of victim and is, therefore, an appropriate target."[56]

Victimologists also credit Stephen Schafer's 1968 work as instrumental in establishing another classification for the study of victims. His *The Victim and His Criminal* (inverting the title of von Hentig's famous work) proposed categorizing victims according to their responsibility rather than simply their risk factors. Too often in the analysis of crime and law, argued Schafer, the issue of criminal causality occludes the question of victims' responsibility. "Many crimes don't just happen to be committed—the victim's negligence, precipitative actions or provocations can contribute to the genesis of the crime." Accordingly, he proposed a continuum of victims' roles and "functional responsibility." His normative prescription was that "[t]he victim's functional responsibility is to do nothing that will provoke others to injure him, and to actively seek to prevent criminals from harming him."[57]

The experience of the Second World War and the expansion of national and international law and jurisprudence to include novel categories of crimes, most notably "crimes against humanity," fueled a new interest in victims *qua* victims. Efforts to define and protect potential victims came in many forms, including a Universal Declaration of Human Rights and new organizations such as the World Health Organization and UNESCO. Only in the 1970s, however, was victimology formally organized as a discipline. The first International Symposium on Victimology was held in 1973, and *Victimology: An International Journal* began publication three years later. Falling far short of Mendelsohn's conception of victimology as "the reverse of criminology," victimologists' studies often tended to replicate those of criminologists. Both disciplines sought to assess causality and legal and moral responsibility by focusing on the individual victim or offender. Adopting this individualistic perspective, victimologists and criminologists alike tended to emphasize the offender's perspective and in doing so, to mitigate the offender's guilt. In its application, the idea of victim precipitation seemed to mean, as victimologist Menachem Amir put it, that "in a way the victim is always the cause of the crime." [58]

Amir's own study, *Patterns in Forcible Rape* (1971), provides a good illustration of what critics found objectionable in the victim precipitation paradigm. Amir sought to offer a "situational" examination of rape. Rather than investigating the psychology of the actors, as most previous studies had, Amir aimed instead to define the "modus operandi of the crime and the situations in which it is most likely to occur." [59] The only psychological dimension that he considered was the extent to which past traumas might have been a factor in offenders' behavior. He mentioned the psychological impact of rape on the victim only in passing, in a footnote.

Amir's findings disrupted established theories about rape. Most importantly, he documented that "sex offenders do not constitute a unique clinical or psycho-pathological type; nor are they as a group invariably more disturbed than the control groups to which they were compared." [60] Whereas most scholars had viewed the rapist as emotionally unstable, and often himself the victim of a woman—the rape victim, his mother, sister, or wife—Amir offered evidence that rapists did not deviate from the general male population. By normalizing the rapist, his research provided considerable support for feminists' contention that rapes were not isolated, aberrant acts, but part of a larger structure of male supremacy. At the same time, having found that rape was, in a sense, "normal" male behavior, Amir concluded that the only course of action to reduce rapes was for women to modify their behavior. This conclusion led some to charge that Amir engaged in blaming victims. Weis and Borges, for instance, pointedly described Amir's work, and the notion of victim precipitation itself, as "the personification and embodiment of the rape mythology cleverly stated in academic-scientific terms."[61]

The paradigm of "victim precipitation" remained the norm until the mid-1970s, when victimologists' scholarly focus moved from victims' complicity in the crimes they suffered to the material and psychological needs of victims. Accompanying victimology's rise as an established discipline was the institution and expansion of federal and state assistance programs for victims, including victim compensation programs, formal restitution programs (to allow offenders to repay their victims), victim-witness programs, and the National Organization of Victim Assistance. A major force driving the renewed political and academic interest in victims during this period was the women's movement, especially its work on behalf of rape victims. As one victimologist remarked,

> Interest in [and research about] rape victims . . . has probably contributed more to creating and sustaining a new consciousness of victims than any other single issue within the criminal justice system. The need to understand the reality of the rape victim's plight has provided stimulus for research programs, service policies and public education that may eventually improve the condition for all victims.[62]

It was not until the late 1970s, however, that victimological research began to consider the "victim's perspective." The women's movement influenced this new concern with researching and addressing the victim's subjectivity. "One of the major contributions of the women's movement to victimology itself," explained Jacqueline Scherer, was "to illuminate the political dimension of victimhood, namely, the power to define or redefine an offense with subsequent effects for victims."[63]

Critics both within and outside the discipline began to condemn victimologists for focusing their professional gaze on victims' culpability, for "hav[ing] turned victimology into the art of blaming the victim."[64] Accordingly, these critics encouraged a radical shift in emphasis. Stripped of its former claim to scientific neutrality, victimology was now recruited for the purpose of victim-advocacy, what Andrew Karmen terms "victim-defending," and Ezzat Fattah provocatively characterizes as "affirmative action for victims."[65]

The discipline underwent tremendous change. Even those who still worked within its foundational assumptions embraced new sensibilities. In his opening remarks at the 1973 victimology symposium, Israel Drapkin implored fellow practitioners to make certain not to repeat past mistakes, the "common pitfall," which he described as "overdo[ing] the emphasis on the role of the victim and reach[ing] the opposite conclusion, namely, that the victim is the real criminal and the criminal a mere victim of his victim."[66] To underscore his empathy toward victims and personal connection to victimhood he alluded to the historical persecution of Jews and made much of the location of the meeting in Jerusalem.[67]

Naming themselves "radical victimologists," some practitioners sought to expand the profession's mission to assist the "victims of police force, the victims of war, the victims of the correctional system, the victims of state violence, the victims of oppression of any sort."[68] Radical victimologists hold that the systematic oppression of social groups ("social victims") is comparable to victimization in crimes and can thus be understood through the perpetrator-victim-action triad. Social victimization remains "neglected as a field of study and research," as Emilio Viano complains.[69]

Anne McLeer, furthermore, seeks to "reclaim the idea of 'woman as victim,'" to "save the language of the victim."[70] She insists that no other terminology allows women effectively to describe their oppression and name their oppressors. Going even further, she proposes that the idea of victim precipitation— now much criticized—actually prevents victim blaming. Victim precipitation is central to establishing "the subjectivity of the victim," meaning that in examining victim precipitation, researchers are forced to consider the victim's experience, the victim's "subject position."

> Viewing the [victim] as a victim (in the victimological understanding of the term) of an oppressive system does not void that subjectivity of agency; instead, in tandem with the understanding of the agency of the [victim] as a "subject-in-pain," it can bring into focus the criminality of the practice.[71]

The paradigm may have been misapplied in the past, but McLeer insists that the concept need not presuppose either intentionality on the part of the victim or an attribution of blame.

## Blaming Themselves

The therapeutic dimension of "blaming the victim," seen so clearly in the concern with the psychological state of the rape victim, should also be considered in light of the general ascendance of therapy over the last few decades. This trend encompasses the proliferation of therapeutic experts as well as the ubiquity of popular forms of therapy, such as the recovery movement and various twelve-step programs. Most significant for our purposes is the increasing popularity of therapeutic strategies among those who work on behalf of oppressed social groups (often viewed as "social victims").[72]

Even as criminal law shifted from a rehabilitative or restorative model of justice to an increasingly retributive one, rehabilitation became a guiding principle for a variety of programs that offer methods for improving "self-esteem" in individuals and groups considered, by others or by themselves, to be victims because of their oppression or marginalization. One stunning example of the application of therapeutic assumptions and strategies to social, political, and economic problems was a bipartisan initiative in California. Originally conceived by Democratic State Assemblyman John Vasconcellos, Assembly Bill 3659 was soon signed into law by Republican Governor George Deukmejian in 1986, and the California Task Force to Promote Self-Esteem and Personal and Social Responsibility was formed. As the name of the task force suggests, the aims of this project blended traditional notions of self-sufficiency, individual perfectibility, and individual will with therapeutic ideals about "positive thinking." The diverse cultural contexts to which author Vasconcellos pointed—"the social action movements of the 1960s, the personal growth movement of the 1970s, and the entrepreneurial spirit of the 1980s"—also indicate an unusual amalgamation, a governmental enterprise contrived to respond to social problems by repairing each individual's sense of self.[73]

The premise that led to the formation of this group of researchers was that low self-esteem was "a primary causal factor" behind a range of social problems, such as "crime and violence, alcohol abuse, drug abuse, teenage pregnancy, child and spousal abuse, chronic welfare dependency, and failure to achieve in school." California state legislators reasoned that since such behavior was clearly "self-destructive," programs enhancing self-esteem should aid in prevention. In other words, individuals could be inoculated against their cultural pathologies if only the task force produced the proper "social vaccine."[74] The first mission of the task force was to validate legislators' intuitive sense, their feelings "based on [their] own personal experiences and . . . observations of others." Studies were designed to investigate whether low self-esteem not only correlated to deviant behavior but was the "causally prior factor in individuals seeking out types of behavior that become social problems."[75] Additionally, the task force instructed researchers to explore methods to enhance the self-esteem of individuals and groups who engage in self-destructive behavior.

Even before research commenced, the task force received national attention, inspiring elected federal officials to pursue consonant programs on a nationwide scale. Rhode Island Senator Claiborne Pell was so impressed with the idea of the task force that he, along with Kansas Senator Nancy Kassebaum, recommended a similar federal program, the National Commission on Human Resource Development. Congress did not pass their proposal. Undeterred, Pell started his own private organization, the Human Potential Foundation.

Members of the California task force conceived of their mission in incredibly magnificent terms. Comparing their efforts to discovering "the secret of the atom" in the 1940s, and to penetrating "the reaches and mysteries of outer space" in the 1960s, the project's organizers declared that the task force aimed at nothing less than "unlock[ing] the secret of healthy human development ... plumb[ing] the reaches of inner space."[76] Embarrassingly meager results followed the grandiose rhetoric. As it turned out, researchers found little evidence that self-esteem was in fact an independent variable in the causes of deviant behavior. Not even the hypothesis that self-esteem is high among those with achievements and correspondingly low among those without could be verified.[77] Blindly optimistic, the studies collected and presented in the book *The Social Importance of Self-Esteem* (1989) conclude that perhaps more research should be done with different definitions and measurements of self-esteem. When Ryan condemned liberal social scientists and elected officials in the late 1960s for blaming the victim, it is unlikely that he could have imagined such an extraordinary enterprise as the California task force. Since the bipartisan task force is representative of a larger trend, it seems that victim blaming is an ideology not easily relinquished.

Just as the task force approached social problems through repairing the individual's character, some manifestations of identity politics also have been justified in terms of improving the self-regard of particular groups. Afro-centric curricula, for instance, often are defended as a key method for raising African American students' self-esteem.[78] Afro-centric history functions, as Mary Lefkowitz suggests, like other nationalistic allegories; the point of the narrative is to provide simultaneously a basis for group pride and an explanation for group suffering and marginalization. While Lefkowitz disparages this approach, arguing that these stories only misinform, others demur. Professor of psychology and black studies, Halford Fairchild, for example, claims to observe "transforming effect[s]" among his African Americans students. Developing pride in their heritage, he reports, compels students to achieve more themselves.[79] Likewise, in the California state-funded HAWK Federation Youth Development and Training Program, Professor Wade Nobles employs Afro-centric pedagogy to address "simultaneously the problems of substance abuse . . . gang violence, academic failure . . . low aspirations and poor self-esteem."[80] In teaching Afro-centric curricula, as in similar endeavors for other traditionally marginalized groups, the radical notion of "empowerment," once understood as requiring direct action to seize power, is reconceptualized in psychotherapeutic terms. Improving collective self-regard ("maternal thinking," "black is beautiful," "gay pride") is presented as a prerequisite to achieving tangible power, at times as a goal in itself.[81]

The argument for augmenting self-esteem may be seen both as a reaction to victim blaming, as well as an instance of "blaming the victim." In the first case, a history of victimization enhanced by victim blaming (i.e., various theories that pathologized the Other) is challenged (perhaps even overcome) either by discouraging victims from blaming themselves for their victimization (self-esteem), or by inverting cultural devaluations that perpetuate oppression (celebration of difference). At the same time, these efforts often participate in what Ryan identified as victim blaming by implicitly or explicitly accepting that these groups are victimized because they suffer from some mental deficiency (low self-esteem), and that their inability to empower themselves materially may be attributed, completely or in part, to this psychological inadequacy. (The critics of difference feminism whose arguments we examined in Chapter 3 offered a comparable analysis of the trap of difference theories.) Whether such programs succeed and how that success is defined and measured is beyond the scope of this chapter. What is pertinent to our present discussion is how benign the Moynihan Report seems in comparison to its contemporary progeny. The victim blaming Ryan condemned has been inverted as "self-help," so that the problem he identified has become the very core of empowering those victimized by oppression.

## Shaming and Re-Blaming

Drawing as much from self-help literature as from other sources, a therapeutic understanding of victimhood is also evident in anti-victimism. Anti-victimists frequently expose victimists not by their self-presentation as "victims" (since few readily accept the designation), but by their tendency to blame others—often society as a whole—for their plight. Regardless of what an individual may have endured (that is, even if she really is a victim), blaming, whining, complaining, and other public displays of weakness are considered aesthetically repulsive and socially harmful. Indeed, these critics often seem more concerned with the accusatory, antagonistic quality of those who make their pain public, than with any questionable innocence or fabrications of crimes.

William Ryan holds a prominent place among those attacked for contributing to the rise and spread of victimism. Charles Sykes explicitly criticizes Ryan's book for setting the tone and providing the content of victimism. "For Ryan, being a victim . . . meant never having to say you're sorry or suffering the consequences of your misdeed . . . there was always someone else to blame." According to Sykes, Ryan's work encouraged a dramatic transformation in sensibilities from sympathizing with victims to shielding victims from any sort of critical judgment, moral or otherwise. "[Ryan's] *Blaming the Victim* not only gave victim politics its rhetorical theme but elaborated in great detail the doctrine that victims should not be held responsible for their conduct or their choices."[82] The penumbra of protections attached to victim status, Sykes says, now extends beyond the incident of victimization by, for instance, allowing those who have secured their status as victims to commit offenses, including actual crimes, without being subjected to punishment. (Recall Dershowitz's discussion of the abuse excuse in Chapter 2.)

Much has been made of the preface to the second edition of *Blaming the Victim*, where Ryan suggests that all but the richest 5 to 10 percent of Americans may one day become victims.[83] Ryan's revised and expansive notion of the potential class of victims is not, as critics allege, a promotion of victimism.[84] He does not propose that everyone think of themselves as victims, rather he warns that few Americans are economically secure. Sykes confuses Ryan's argument with later, therapy-inspired, protections of victims. He also misconstrues the differences between Ryan and Moynihan (as well as other liberal reformers); the social studies that Ryan challenged did not advocate personal responsibility so much as government action on behalf of the poor. Equally inaccurate is Sykes's view of Ryan as preoccupied with exposing racism. Ryan regarded economic inequality or capitalism, not racism, as the invidious force to be fought, and distinguished (albeit not always clearly) victim blaming from racism. Sykes's misunderstanding of "blaming the victim" as a form of racism (or some other "ism") suggests that after Ryan the expression acquired an additional meaning: accusing someone of blaming the victim may also be a way to denounce his latent prejudices.

Most of the anti-victimist literature is written as though in response to Ryan's legacy, although only Sykes mentions Ryan by name. What is surprising, however, is the extent to which the anti-victimists' and Ryan's analyses share basic formulations and tactics. The critics' depiction of the victimist is the mirror image of Ryan's victim blamer. Where the victim blamer cleanses himself of his responsibility to engage in radical change to end inequality, the victimist exempts herself from responsibility for her own misfortunes. Victim blamers and victimists seem to suffer from the same psychological malfunction—a distorted perception of reality that results in deflecting responsibility onto others.

Not unlike Ryan the anti-victimists are particularly interested in the psychological dimensions of victimism as a pathology that pervades society. The anti-victimist diagnosis, as we have seen, is reminiscent of the Nietzschean critique of slave morality, especially Nietzsche's discussion of *ressentiment* in the *Genealogy of Morals*. Nietzsche regards *ressentiment* as an unhealthy reaction, a state of mind in which individuals are incapable of acting on the basis of positive values and are instead confined to "imaginary revenge" and other such negative compensations. Sufferers are compelled to discover or invent some external cause of their misery, a "guilty agent" to blame.

> The suffering are one and all dreadfully eager and inventive in discovering occasions for painful affects; they enjoy being mistrustful and dwelling on nasty deeds and imaginary slights; they scour the entrails of their past and present for obscure and questionable occurrences that offer them the opportunity to revel in tormenting suspicions . . . they make evildoers out of their friends, wives and children, and whoever stands closest to them. "I suffer: someone must be to blame for it"—thus thinks every sickly sheep.[85]

Symptomatically, those consumed by *ressentiment* adopt a moral scale in which weakness, passivity, and suffering are virtues.

Steele's analysis of race-holding in an "era of blame" is remarkably similar to Nietzsche's depiction of *ressentiment,* though Steele never directly employs the concept.[86] (Perhaps referring to African American's "slave morality" was a bit too much, even for Steele.) The term "ressentiment" does appear in Sykes's work to characterize the victimist's mentality and behavior, though he relies solely on Max Scheler's discussion in *Ressentiment* (1915). According to Sykes, inflated expectations of success—which he attributes to the rise of therapy in the early 1960s—unleashed great jealousy, spite, and hatred. Thus, victimists do not merely deflect responsibility onto others, they seethe with envy of more successful individuals and groups, and seek revenge for their miserable plight.[87]

As in Ryan's and the rape victim advocates' use of the term "blaming," a fine line separates the deflecting of responsibility from other forms of aggression.

There are additional similarities between Ryan's and the anti-victimists' analyses. Ryan worried that attributing cultural differences to the poor perpetuates inequality. From a different perspective, the anti-victimists voice a related concern: valorizing cultural differences perpetuates antagonisms in society and the weakness of "victim" groups, even when they are given special privileges and protections. Likewise, anti-victimists challenge not only the victimist but also the forces in society that they believe encourage and sustain victimism by equipping those who engage in socially deviant behavior with excuses, justifications, protections, and exemptions. Ryan and the anti-victimists seem to share contempt for the modern "scientific" welfare state and the elites and experts who supposedly control it.

Blaming others is what the anti-victimists criticize in victimists, but their remedy for victimism is more blaming. They endeavor to invert the imperative against blaming the victim. Camille Paglia, for example, explicitly (and defiantly) conceives of her project as re-blaming victims. Others followed suit, not only in enthusiastically blaming victims but also in blaming those "who told us we could not blame the victim." [88] Thus, anti-victimists, like Ryan, employ "victim" as a tool to incite, with a therapeutic purpose in mind. The anti-victimists' ambition to blame victims resonates with the greater conservative call for reintroducing morality into American public life in general, and into policy making in particular. Morality and personal accountability are prescribed as the antidote for moral relativism. This moral "softness," conservatives claim, is promoted by liberals and their welfare state, where moral failures (e.g., criminality, welfare abuse, illegitimacy, and so forth) do not entail any punishment and, even more importantly, do not prevent individuals from squeezing as much as they can from the reservoir of public resources and sympathy. Recall, however, that the anti-victimists' solution is not reinstituting objective, quantitative standards for evaluating victim claims (as against the depraved relativism of the welfare state and its minions), but instead resurrecting a qualitative measure for personal health: strong character. What could be clearer than renaming welfare reform in 1996 the Personal Responsibility and Work Opportunity Act?

Ultimately, anti-victimists deploy a moral language to repackage therapeutic ideas. Character building and "personal responsibility" actually serve to repair the individual rather than to address claims of injustice (just like the California task force). The notion that each individual should take responsibility for himself promotes the same self-aggrandizing illusion that anti-victimist critics claim therapeutic practices have encouraged. Indeed, long passages in the anti-victimist literature read like popularized versions of the idea of a "locus of control," especially in its most rudimentary form, which draws a binary opposition between "external" and "internal" psychological loci.[89]

Another dimension of the anti-victimist campaign that brings it closer to therapeutic culture is its tendency to promote its own coterie of advice-dispensing professionals and experts. Of course, there are the anti-victimists themselves: members of think tanks, lecturers on the circuit, academics, pundits, and so forth. Conversely, many popular therapeutic experts have embraced the anti-victimist ethos. For instance, the host of one of the most popular American radio talk shows, Dr. Laura Schlessinger, specializes in verbally flogging listeners out of their victimist ways. The *U.S. News & World Report* cover story on her success, "No Whining," recounts her aptitude.

> She is as skilled as a surgeon in locating the heart of a caller's problem, as unbending as an officer in pushing away excuses and justifications. "Guilt is good," she declares. She bans the term self-esteem and laments the "Age of the Victim" where "nothing is anybody's fault." In her version of morality, willpower is paramount. Not only do people have "freedom" over their feelings, and urges, she declares, but they are morally obligated to exercise that freedom.[90]

Beyond her haranguing of willing listeners, Dr. Laura's show serves the same purpose as dozens of other comparable programs that offer moral judgment under the guise of guidance. Her authority derives from her expertise in family matters, not moral reasoning, and she offers her listeners (in addition to their share of entertainment) specific solutions concerning their particular problems in a manner quite similar to that of other hosts of call-in shows and television therapists, such as Dr. Phil.

## Victims as Blamers

In our examination of the relationship between victimhood and blame so far, we have observed a lingering concern with blame, initially regarding the blaming of victims and subsequently with victims as blamers. With all of the antipathy toward blaming, it is rather astonishing that during this same period the victims' rights movement (VRM) gained momentum and unprecedented legislative ground, especially in its quest to provide an official forum for victims to engage actively in blaming.[91] The VRM fuses the sensibilities of both the anti-victimists and the anti-victim-blamers. Frequently viewed as an integral part of conservatives' "war against crime," the political roots of this movement are actually an amalgam.[92] Feminists' efforts on behalf of victims of sexual abuse (rape, spousal abuse, incest, and so forth) increased public awareness about the need to establish support programs for victims and to amend laws and criminal proceedings to incorporate victims' needs. These pioneering campaigns prepared the way for the early stages of the victims' rights movement. In the 1990s, by contrast, the VRM adopted a stronger law-and-order focus, promoting the idea that the swift and severe punishment of victimizers is the best remedy for the causes and effects of victimization.

The VRM sponsors, among other things, securing victims a greater part in the prosecution of criminals, a role that supporters defend as a matter of rights.[93] The movement's major triumph to date, in this context, is the victim impact statement (VIS). These statements provide a formal context in criminal trials, after the defendant has been found guilty and before sentencing, for victims or their families (defined by the movement and courts as "secondary victims") to describe in detail the pain and suffering they endured. When VIS are introduced and in what form (e.g., testimony in court, written statement, videotaped presentation) varies greatly, but all state and federal criminal courts have adopted some form of this procedure.

VIS are justified by both retributive and therapeutic rationales. Since victims' rights proponents contend that the judicial system is geared unfairly toward the interests of criminal defendants, they promote impact statements as a vital measure to restore justice, by forcing "the court to refocus its attention, at least momentarily, on the human cost of the crime."[94] No longer construed primarily as a violation of societal regulations, the VRM upholds a conception of criminality as an interaction between two individuals (though victimization may have secondary consequences).[95]

Although impact statements endow victims of crimes with a new tool to indict their victimizers, these testimonials paradoxically shift attention to the moral stature of the victim, amounting to another form of blaming the victim. According to legal scholar Susan Bandes, VIS "detract the jury from its duty to consider the individual defendant."[96] When the question of the constitutionality of impact statements came before the Supreme Court in *Booth v. Maryland* (1987) and *South Carolina v. Gathers* (1989), the possibility that they might impermissibly challenge the victim's innocence guided the decisions to reject VIS in capital sentencing hearings. Justice Powell, writing for the majority in *Booth*, worried that the only way for the defense to rebut VIS would be to conduct a "'mini-trial' on the victim's character," which certainly resembles the sort of counterdenunciation that victim advocates considered victim blaming in the case of rape.[97] Individualizing victimization by wrenching criminal law from a collective focus, however, is precisely what dissenters in *Booth* sought: "[J]ust as the murderer should be considered as an individual, so too the victim is an individual whose death represents a unique loss to society and in particular to his family."[98] By arguing that previous holdings "unfairly weighted the scales," the justification for VIS relies upon a problematic parity between the defendant and the victim.

Overturning *Booth* and *Gathers*, in *Payne v. Tennessee* (1991) the Court established that impact statements provide pertinent information. VIS, the majority reasoned, would elucidate the "uniqueness" of the life lost in or abruptly altered by a crime.[99] Studies confirm, however, what the dissenters (those in the majority in *Booth*) feared: despite the seemingly benign intent, these statements encourage jurors and judges to gauge sentencing according to the "worth" of the victim compared to that of the perpetrator, to evaluate whether the victim was "a sterling member of the community [or] someone of questionable character."[100] VIS critics hold that justice therefore depends upon the victims' "eloquence, financial position, or family's presence . . . [rather than] the severity of the crime."[101] After all, murdered thieves or raped sex workers are not likely to benefit from family or friends testifying on their behalf.

VIS consequently contributes to True Victimhood by facilitating ranking of victims. Impact statements entrench the conception of true victims as entirely innocent, even beyond the facts of the crime. Of course, not all victims were treated equally before the advent of impact statements. The state pursued some crimes with greater vigor and the identity of the victim (including her purity and innocence) certainly influenced prosecutorial decisions. However, VIS accentuate differences among victims in new and troubling ways. The statements' purpose may have been to account for the specific plight of the victim and to allow the victim to condemn her victimizer, but VIS can lead to undermining the victim; at least in those cases in which the victim does not conform to some chaste stereotype of absolute innocence.[102] In staging a conflict between individual victims and victimizers, impact statements encourage a comparison of their respective backgrounds, worth, innocence, and power of articulation. VIS thus partakes in the dissolution of the social bond, which is at the foundation of the criminal justice system. It also blurs the division between criminal law and tort.

The personal accounts presented in VIS, interpreted by both proponents and opponents as acts of blaming, are defended as rituals that help victims recover emotionally.[103] The victim's public testimony, as well as her opportunity to blame her victimizer, are meant to make her feel empowered, to heal her wounded psyche. In this way the VRM resembles other groups in the recovery movement where naming and accusing your victimizer is thought to be an integral part of the process of emotional healing. However, some opponents reject VIS precisely on these grounds. They argue that VIS actually retard recovery. Law professor Lynne Henderson, for example, warns that by emphasizing "innocence as a prerequisite to being a 'real' victim" VIS "make it very difficult for a victim to avoid displacing the criminal event from her experience."[104]

The therapeutic underpinnings of the victim's public avowal are also at the core of extra-judicial activities, such as victim impact panels (sponsored by groups such as Mothers Against Drunk Drivers) and Take Back the Night gatherings (where victims of sexual abuse are encouraged to testify about their experiences). The prevalence of such forums as well as the admission of VIS in criminal proceedings suggest a transformation in victim advocacy over the course of the last thirty years or so, from sheltering victims from blame to the therapeutics of victims-as-blamers.[105]

The designation "victims' rights movement" emulates the model set by civil rights groups in the 1960s, though it is unclear whether this particular movement is meant to supplement or supplant its predecessors—a rights movement to end all other rights movements. After all, oppositional politics is unquestionably a primary target of anti-victimism, as we have seen in the previous chapters. In their conception, progressive politics replicates victimism even if it does not employ victim talk or pursue "victimist" ends. Embracing the cause of crime victims, as defined by the VRM, facilitates anti-victimists' effort to turn charges of injustice into evaluations of the individual's worthiness.[106] Such a hierarchy of victims conforms to the principles of the Cult of True Victimhood. Reifying a juridical model of criminal victimhood diminishes and domesticates victim claims by limiting remedies to actions by a therapeutic/retributive state intervening in a conflict between two individuals.

## From Victim to Survivor

Others may debate the value of specific therapeutic techniques developed to help victims of particular hardships—sexual assault, natural disasters, and other such experiences. The purpose of excavating the genealogy of "blaming the victim" is not to condemn therapy per se, but rather to chart how psychologizing tactics growingly substitute for politics. When therapeutic logic infuses public debates about collective suffering and systematic inequality, it tends to preserve the social status quo, as others have argued before.[107] Without the perspective of structural inequality, attention shifts from evaluating actual social circumstances to focusing on individual character. The struggle for power becomes instead an exercise in self-help. Moreover, in the *en masse* application of therapy we can clearly detect the discursive fingerprints of anti-victimism. The fact of victimization itself now marks the victim as deficient. No longer simply descriptive, "victim" serves as a derogatory evaluation, if not outright condemnation.

Victimhood is a transitory state from which the victimized are expected to ascend. Left untreated, it threatens to lock individuals in abject paralysis. Here, popular therapy (as well as more sophisticated writings about trauma) draws from Freud's famous distinction between a healthy process of mourning through which the individual accepts the fact of loss, on the one hand, and a debilitating state of melancholy, on the other.[108] Even victim advocates now suggest abandoning the term. Many trauma counselors, for instance, prefer "survivor."[109] The desire to bestow dignity on victims by highlighting their agency—having endured, having made it through—may fuel the current preference for the designation (much like other self-esteem projects). "Survivor" denotes the victim's journey, her progress up from victimhood. Where the victim is immersed in the past, pessimistic, melancholic, and fatalistic; the survivor is forward-looking, energetic, functional, and optimistic.

"Survivor" commonly refers to those who continue living in the face of death (such as passengers who did not perish in a shipwreck or the living family members of a deceased relative). Victimhood, by contrast, stands for death—actual death or symbolically social death. Another pairing in ordinary language juxtaposes the victim to the victor, emphasizing a reversal of fortune, a victory, and by implication renders the victim vanquished or simply a loser. (Common in testimonials about religious conversions, the victim/victor construct evokes triumph in the struggle between good and evil.) Survivorship is more ambiguous. By relegating victimhood to the past, it refers to victimization without the stain of victimhood. Is "survivor," therefore, just a more acceptable way to claim victim status?

One unexpected response to this question comes from the comedy of Larry David. In "The Survivor" episode (2004) of his HBO sitcom *Curb Your Enthusi-*

*asm*, he stages a contentious dinner table debate between a Holocaust survivor and one of the participants of the immensely successful CBS "reality" game show *Survivor*. The two quarrel fiercely over the gravity of their respective experiences. This scene makes a poignant commentary on contemporary survivor discourse, although its political edge is open to contending interpretations. On the one hand, the joke partakes in anti-victimism by mocking the audacity of the idea that overcoming any hardship—including those encountered by a person who "plays himself" on a largely prescripted television show—amounts to surviving the ordeal of the concentration camps. On the other hand, the comedic incident rejects the victimist/anti-victimist dichotomy altogether by suggesting that the two claims actually have much in common, both participate in the Cult of True Victimhood.

Therapeutics and anti-victimism inflect the contemporary conception of survivorship, as do two archetypes of victimization—the crime of rape and the Holocaust of the Jews in Europe. The subject position "survivor" now connotes assuming personal responsibility. For some this responsibility amounts to giving testimony about what they endured; for most others, it demands prevailing against the sorrows of victimization to become a self-sustaining member of society (and the marketplace). The valorization and lionization of survivorship in politics, popular culture, popular psychology, and religion is quite new, as is its contemporary coupling with victimhood in expressions such as "victim/survivor" or "from victim to survivor."[110] Against the tide of popular sentiment, intellectuals such as the late novelist and Holocaust survivor Primo Levi, emphatically reject the celebration of survivorship. Survivors of the Holocaust realize, according to Levi, that the best among those sent to the Nazi camps perished, and that those who survived did so by resorting to means that were ignoble, petty, and often outright cruel.[111]

The therapeutic victim/survivor pairing is ubiquitous much beyond the actual use of the term "victim." Again, mass culture provides a fertile field for the articulation of the anti-victimist credo, and the immensely successful film *Forrest Gump* (1994) furnishes a fine example. The film depicts three models of coping with adversity. The protagonist, Forrest, has mental (75 IQ) as well as physical disabilities. The added burdens he endures because of human ill will recall the historical abuse of blacks in the South. (For instance, early in the film he is chased and stoned by a gang of boys in a truck adorned with the Confederate flag, and later he befriends and then literally replaces his African American "double" Benjamin Buford "Bubba" Blue.)

Forrest's odyssey intersects with that of his childhood friend (and later mother of his child), Jenny Curran. A victim of sexual abuse as a youth, Jenny remains trapped in a cycle of recurrent victimization: abusive partners, risky politics, drug use, and finally AIDS. (Indeed, the film equates sixties counter-culture radicalism with abuse: violence against women and self-destruction.) In contrast to Jenny's eternal victimhood, Forrest accepts his lot in life. He is the happy, big-hearted optimist. "My mama always said you got to put the past be-hind you before you can move on," Gump explains. Where Jenny is ambitious, Forrest is completely innocent, bereft of any desire for fame and riches. Almost despite himself, he becomes a star football player, a war hero, a pop icon, and a very rich man. A survivor of the tumultuous 1960s, he lives to narrate his story to passersby and the movie's audience; Jenny dies.

To further the survivor motif, the film introduces a third victim type, Lieu-tenant Dan Taylor. After losing both legs in war, he is morose: "I'm nothing but a goddamned cripple! A legless freak!" Immersed in self-pity, he leads the life of the stereotypical Vietnam vet dropout—drunkenness, prostitutes, and squalor—eventually becoming a ward of the state: "I'm living off the gov-ernment tit. Sucking it dry." Reuniting with Gump in the South, however, he eventually conquers his resentment, makes peace with God, and becomes an immensely successful businessman. With such unambiguous heroization of survivorship, it is no wonder that Newt Gingrich employed *Forrest Gump*'s por-trayal of the excesses of the 1960s in his 1994 Contract with America campaign; and Bob Dole announced his 1996 candidacy for the presidency by endorsing *Forrest Gump*'s message that the American Dream is within everybody's reach regardless of the hardships they face.[112]

## "An Unfortunate Phrase"?

The victim-blame genealogy reveals how, despite its innovations, the contem-porary anti-victimist discourse has roots in the sciences of victimhood and their permutations in popular and political discourse. If in its early phases victim science sought to modify prospective victims' behavior as a means to prevent crime, including crimes against humanity, since the 1970s, repairing the victim after victimization became the primary goal. A host of recuperative practices have been elaborated for precisely that purpose. Efforts to assist victims of all kinds increasingly focused on the psychological harm resulting from victimiza-tion. Concurrently, blaming has been given a psychological reading: at times seen as an unjustifiably aggressive act rooted in some collective "neurosis," at others, as a therapy. The causes of victimization were also gradually understood in psycho-pathological terms. Whereas Ryan's work belongs to a tradition of social criticism that conceives of inequality in universal terms of exploitation based on economic interest, many post-1960s progressives identify cultural manifestations of irrational hatreds—racism, misogyny, homophobia, and other similar prejudices—as universal forces of inequality. We may find similar thinking in the conservative counterpathology, "victimism." Importantly, victimism is a "universalistic" pathology as against the "exceptionalistic" pathologies that Ryan challenged (e.g., culture of poverty, criminality, illegitimacy).

Another pattern that emerges from our discussion is how central the crime of rape has been to changing views about the nature of criminal victimization. Rape was the subject of most of the foundational studies in victimology, and feminists' work on behalf of rape victims in the 1970s altered the direction of research in this field. Feminist-sponsored services for rape victims also heralded the advent of victim advocacy, paved the way for significant pro-victim legislation, as well as for the rise of a victims' rights movement, and growing attentiveness to the "victim's perspective."

Although Ryan coined the phrase, current understanding and use of "blaming the victim" more closely resembles its application to rape victims. In many ways rape has become a paradigmatic crime whose lessons extend beyond victims of crime. The ambiguity about intentions and events that is characteristic of many rape cases offers an intriguing analogy to the uncertainty and suspicion that anti-victimism injected into the process of evaluating victim claims. More than any other criminal victim, victims of rape must demonstrate that they were in fact victims and not willing participants. It is a crime still easily dismissed. Similarly, the Cult of True Victimhood requires victims to prove that they were subjected to intentional and severe wrongdoing, which they were entirely helpless to prevent.

While anti-victimists refer to issues of crime to undermine collective claims of social victimization, victim-defenders also borrow from the language of criminality to conceptualize social injustice. This emphasis on blame grants jurisprudential doctrines and concepts, if not the courts themselves, a role in negotiating what otherwise would be considered matters of social policy.[113] Significantly, the influence of legal paradigms in victim discourse mixes and mismatches doctrines from criminal law and tort. The VRM, for instance, imports practices taken from civil law into criminal proceedings in the guise of constitutional rights. The allegations about the blame game, moreover, echo a now familiar complaint about the increasing litigiousness of Americans. By criminalizing offensive behavior and strengthening police powers (e.g., more officers and prisons, tougher sentencing), the courts became an alternative to the welfare state.

The notion of "blaming the victim" and the concept of victim (or victimism) mirror each other. Both function in contemporary public debates as an insult that simultaneously names a pathology and makes a moral judgment. This fusion of diagnostics and moral evaluations runs throughout victim discourse. Ryan argued that pathologizing the poor ("culture of poverty") concealed moral judgments ("blame"), which were themselves based on other pathologies (the subconscious compromise called "blaming the victim"). Likewise, when anti-victimists object to victimists' immoral behavior (blaming society), they uncover a pathology ("victimism") and propose a therapy (re-blaming, strengthening individual character), which they present as a moral imperative (reintroducing morality to policy making).

Ryan made a structural argument that foreshadowed anti-victimism in at least two ways. First, he attacked psychology but then resorted to psychological explanations himself to explain the behavior he condemned (i.e., he undermined blaming the victim by blaming the victim blamers). Second, he denounced the liberal welfare state. But whereas he assails it as a therapeutic state in the service of class redistribution, anti-victimists do so for the service of individual morality (which turns out to be therapeutic). Moreover, when Ryan published *Blaming the Victim*, there was a tacit agreement between him and those he criticized that something should be done to help the poor. Today, the poor are seen as merely a criminal class. Herbert Gans suggests that the designation "underclass," a classification that includes both the unemployed and the unemployable (such as ex-convicts), undermined the already problematic distinction between the deserving and undeserving poor by collapsing them all into the category of dangerous victimizers.[114]

Importantly, while Ryan did employ the term "victim" to designate the poor, and thus shifted his focus from the productive class to those outside it, he is still attached to the old Marxian solution. For Ryan, victim status is a class status. (There is a victim in the class.) Indeed, in a recent interview Ryan described his uneasiness with the current use of his charge to apply to individual victims. Asked to reflect upon the legacy of the phrase he authored, he expressed great frustration with appropriations and applications of "blaming the victim" for purposes he never foresaw, including its use on behalf of rape victims. Perhaps, he said, he had chosen his words badly and coined "an unfortunate phrase."

> [F]rom the beginning, it was used in ways that I didn't mean to use it. . . . What I had in mind was the process by which problems that . . . have to do with the social structure . . . get defined as having the cause of the problem in the people who are enmeshed in the problem. But I didn't mean that in any individual sense. . . . [Blaming the victim] doesn't have to do with attributing particular characteristics to individual persons. It has rather to do with the analytic process.[115]

Toward the end of the interview, Ryan suggests that "blaming the victim" may have itself become a victim-blaming ideology. Despite his promotion of ideology-therapy only two years earlier, he now proposes that psychology is no longer a discipline that can grapple with issues of social injustice, for "psychology has become the science of understanding individual differences, which leads to the kinds of ideological distortions that support inequality." More forcefully still, he adds, "I think we can blame psychology for a lot of things that have happened that are bad."[116]

# 6

# 9-1-1: The Nation as Victim

IN THE AFTERMATH OF 9/11, political leaders and commentators alike proclaimed that "the world would never be the same." Nevertheless, many contributors to the litany of reflections exploited the attack on America merely to settle old scores. Thus, in his offering to post-9/11 punditry, *What's So Great about America* (2002), Dinesh D'Souza renewed his assault on those here and abroad who wrongly view themselves as America's victims. Launching his tome with "two cheers for colonialism," he opines that foreigners who hate America today are in effect envious of its astounding success. Bashing the United States is nothing more than "a way to salvage pride."[1] D'Souza then swiftly proceeds to his recognizable targets, America's detractors at home, the harbingers of victim politics:

> The foreign critique of America would not be so formidable if Americans were united in resisting and responding to it. Patriotism, then, would be an easy matter of "us" versus "them." But in truth there are large and influential sectors of American life that agree with many of the denunciations that come from abroad.[2]

As in the 1990s, D'Souza claims to observe ample indications of insidious moral and cultural decay. The cry of 9/11 beckons us to rally around the flag. Americans should cease complaining lest they assist their nation's foes.[3] The United States has worked wonderfully for immigrants, as he can attest from personal experience. Despite old abuses (he mentions slavery as an example), the country affords great opportunities. Blinded by multiculturalism, minorities stubbornly refuse to acknowledge this reality. Instead, "[m]ulticulturalists seek to fill white Americans with an overpowering sense of guilt and blame so that they accept responsibility of minorities in America and poor people in the rest of the world."[4] The recently reinvigorated campaign for reparations for slavery epitomizes the worst of multiculturalists' exercises in guilt-tripping.[5] Even while conceding that vestiges of racism may still exist, D'Souza finds it astonishing that African Americans willingly assume the victim mantle. Of Jesse Jackson, he writes, "I found the concept of this rich, successful man . . . identifying himself as a victim of oppression a bit puzzling and amusing."[6]

Beyond his consternation and amusement, D'Souza sees a genuine problem: African Americans (as well as Native Americans) lack patriotism. To become patriots, these groups would need to discard their "profitable narrative of victimization."[7] D'Souza advises minorities to heed the examples of the "greatest generation" or that of contemporary immigrants who boldly face the future, recognizing education and entrepreneurship to be the vehicles of success in this country, rather than dwelling on the past and its hardships.

> Only now are those Americans who grew up during the 1960s coming to appreciate the virtues—indeed the indispensability—of this older, sturdier culture of courage, nobility and sacrifice . . . confident, self-reliant, tolerant, generous, future oriented—is a vast improvement over the wretched, servile, fatalistic and intolerant human being that traditional societies have always produced and that Islamic societies produce now.[8]

William Bennett, another veteran of the battles over victimhood, also detects in 9/11 glaring evidence of pervasive national weakness. In his *Why We Fight: Moral Clarity and the War on Terrorism* (2001), Bennett takes aim at those who "blame America first." Their "pernicious . . . jejune pacifism and . . . reflexive anti-Americanism" rendered the nation soft, leaving her vulnerable to evildoers.[9] Maintaining a critical posture in the face of the evil that unleashed 9/11 "is worse than irresponsible, it is a species of a deep perversity."[10] Unfortunately, these assaults found the country unprepared morally and intellectually, immersed in uncertainty and relativism. Who is responsible for the laxity that undermined America? The usual suspects: academic post-structuralists, self-indulgent pacifists, busybody feminists—in short, the "victimology-mongers."[11] These groups diluted the country's military resolve, depleted its arsenal, undermined Americans' freedom (to carry guns) and invaded private homes to interfere with the manner in which American parents raise their children (boys in particular). In other words, on September 11, 2001, we paid dearly for the feminization of

America. Fortunately, we now have "George W. Bush, a 'cowboy' president like Ronald Reagan, to revive the language of good and evil."[12]

In the 1990s Bennett's allies responded to victims' exasperated demands with "get over it," but in the wake of 9/11 he espouses "the morality of anger." Both individual and national character are at stake and, as it turns out, the morality of anger entails "the morality of military action."[13] The true foundation of the antiwar party is a pertinacious hostility to America that trivializes the 9/11 atrocities as a mere crime against international law. However, Bennett detects an unseen benefit beneath the rubble: the attack was a "necessary and salutary thing" for it brings us back to "what matters." The war against terror compels us finally to abolish relativism in all of its forms, restore masculine confidence in American civilization, and secure moral certitude. We must, therefore, recognize that even as we fight for freedom abroad, the real combat will have to occur on the homeland, in our schools and universities. Bennett issues a clarion call for reviving the culture wars.

One might think that the 9/11 attack and its numerous victims would curb the anti-victimist sentiment and ideology. However, as this chapter demonstrates, America's response to 9/11 remains firmly rooted in the anti-victimism of the 1990s, with its Janus-faced dynamics: enmity toward victims and the Cult of True Victimhood. The post-9/11 rendition of anti-victim discourse features Manichean rhetoric, political demonology, increasing hostility toward collectives, and a plethora of gendered archetypes that encompass victimizers, victims, and "rescuers." In the following discussion I examine anti-victimism in public debates after 9/11 by focusing on three themes: the conception of victimization, the identity of the victimizer, and the logic of America's response. This chapter contends that even as President George W. Bush and his supporters promote the notion of the United States as an innocent victim of a radical evil force, charging their critics with "blaming the victim," they remain so uneasy with victimhood to the point of obscuring, evading, and often simply denying victimization.

## America's Holocaust

September 11 marked the end of America's "holiday from history," journalist Charles Krauthammer declared. He additionally cautioned, "Year One of the new era, 2002, passed rather peaceably. Year Two will not: 2003 could be as cataclysmic as 1914 or 1939."[14] Other commentators correspondingly drew upon historical models to find meaning in the midst of incomprehensible ruin. As in

Krauthammer's reflections, many precedents came from the iconic arsenal of the Second World War. Japan's attack on Pearl Harbor provided one standard of a surprise attack that engendered a collective sense of violation, indignation, and national determination. By badging the World Trade Center site "ground zero" Americans unwittingly also aligned themselves with the victims of the devastation their country wrought on Hiroshima and Nagasaki. (The irony is even greater when we recall that this designation emerged from the only time that the deadliest of "weapons of mass destruction" were put to use.) Still, the most poignant reference used to anchor the attack historically is probably the annihilation of European Jews at the hands of the Nazis.

During the 1980s and 1990s, American culture became increasingly preoccupied with the fate of the Jews in Europe (as we saw in Chapter 4). On September 11, 2001, genocidal horror arrived closer to home. In their self-described "manual for victory," Richard Perle, one of the architects of the Pentagon's strategy against Saddam Hussein, and David Frum ominously advise, "terrorism remains the great evil of our time . . . our generation's great cause. . . . There is no middle way for Americans: It is victory or Holocaust." [15] Urging us further, Jonah Goldberg, editor of *National Review Online*, stresses that the destruction of the World Trade Center should provoke the same moral outrage and military response prompted by the mass killings in Europe's concentration camps. To have this sort of impact, he instructs the media to stop sanitizing and editing images, for example, the sight of individuals falling to their death from the towers in lower Manhattan. [16] Even Elie Wiesel lent his authority as America's most honored camp survivor to legitimate the analogy between America's "war on terror" and the Holocaust. He consequently endorsed the administration's operations abroad. [17]

While President Bush has not explicitly equated 9/11 with the Holocaust, he has classified al-Qaeda as the "heir of all of the murderous ideologies of the 20th century . . . fascism, Nazism and totalitarianism." [18] (Of course, others in his administration, as well as his father, George H. W. Bush, directly compared Saddam Hussein to Adolph Hitler. [19]) The president drew another implicit line connecting the struggles of the 1930s and 1940s and the post-9/11 landscape by pronouncing that the "war on terror" is nothing less than a battle "to save civilization" from an enemy whose "goal is remaking the world and imposing its radical beliefs on people everywhere. . . ." [20] Vice President Dick Cheney used the occasion of the sixty-year commemoration ceremony at Auschwitz to advance this comparison, at least by insinuation: "The story of the camps reminds us that evil is real and must be confronted."[21] On a more optimistic note, he added that he found hope for American citizens in the story of individuals who survived the "terror" of Nazism.[22]

The survivor motif further links Holocaust memory with post-9/11 political culture. Thus, to give an example, the *United in Memory Quilt Project* promotes a more expansive conception of survivorship by defining its mission as "honoring the victims—comforting the world." The project's healing message conceives of the entire nation (indeed, virtually anyone who watched the events on television anywhere in the world) as mournful survivors and consequently in need of repair.

> Whether we have loved ones who were maimed or killed in the terrorist attack on America, or whether our sadness comes from a heartfelt identification with and compassion for these innocent victims, we are part of a grieving process that is both personal and national. Our lives will never be the same.[23]

Their Web site accordingly dispenses specific advice for the nonspecific visitor: "Don't underestimate your need to grieve," "Be kind to yourself," "Breathe," "Say no to persistent negative thoughts," and so forth. The quilt project appropriates its commemorative template from the *AIDS Quilt Project*, which in turn was inspired by the principles that guided the Vietnam Veterans War Memorial in Washington, DC.[24] The memory of 9/11 is founded on a mnemonic palimpsest whose layers feature much of the twentieth-century experience of war, plague, and genocide.

## The Victim Is Less Than a Man

Another model for framing and representing the events of 9/11 has been the crime of rape. In recent decades, the experience of rape has become, much like the European Holocaust, a paradigm of victimhood, often at great remove from actual violated bodies (see Chapter 5). Indeed, in the aftermath of attack, public reflections metaphorically dressed the nation in a skirt. "Gendered images and narratives migrated from embodied subjects to discursive constructions of the nation," Mary Hawkesworth observes. "The US was stripped of its sense of invulnerability. The impregnable fortress was breached. America joined the ranks of the violated."[25] America's new poet laureate, Billy Collins, unambiguously depicts the attack as the day the United States "lost our virginity."[26] The language of sexual violation genders the victim as less than a man—wounded, exposed, weak, dominated, invaded, in a word, penetrable. Within this conception, victimization emasculates or feminizes the victim by constituting a loss that indicates a prior lack.[27]

Metaphors and similes of rape appeared in public conversations not only to denote the violation but also to respond to real and imaginary critics who blame America for bringing the events upon itself. After 9/11 conservatives, who had previously prescribed more victim blaming, fully appropriated "blaming the victim" as a reproach. A LexisNexis search confirms that since Ryan coined the phrase in 1971, it has been in great public use, reaching a peak in the mid-1980s, and then gradually waning. While applied to a range of policy areas—rape, poverty, affirmative action, and even the Israeli/Palestinian conflict—those associated with the political Left most often used the expression. September 11, 2001, reversed this trend. As of 9/12, "blaming the victim" is commonly uttered to undermine calls to probe the conditions that may have facilitated the attack, as well as any stance critical of the Bush administration's policies. Consider, for example, the unremitting condemnation of Noam Chomsky's "chicken coming home to roost" remark (which he borrowed from an infamous slight made by Malcolm X in reaction to President John F. Kennedy's assassination). One reviewer sneered over the Internet: "I imagine [Chomsky] would blame a woman for getting raped too."[28] Carrying the imaginary of a sexually violated nation further, Newsweek journalist Jonathan Alter scoffed, "the same people always urging us to not blame the victim in rape cases are now saying Uncle Sam wore a short skirt and asked for it."[29]

Chomsky became the emblem of America's blamers. Christopher Hitchens went as far as to compare Chomsky's reaction to Jerry Falwell's diatribe about how depraved and decadent New Yorkers finally met God's wrath.[30] Perhaps there is some validity to this comparison, for both Chomsky and Falwell conjure a universe in which cataclysmic events exact justice on aggressors, though in the latter case historical justice is divine and in the former, ironic. At the same time, Chomsky sought to distinguish between the victimization of those who perished or were wounded and the manner in which the United States government precipitated the attack through its policies and actions. America is not an "innocent victim," he asserted, employing a problematic coupling from the victim debates and leaving open the question as to whether it is a victim at all.[31]

The charge "blaming the victim" identifies and chides two errors in a single phrase: finding the victim blameworthy enacts a second victimization and reduces the blameworthiness of the victimizer. In the 1970s and 1980s, those who made such indictments increasingly focused on the damage of re-victimizing victims. When applied to 9/11, administration defenders accentuate the victimizer's diminished guilt. As Alter emphatically warns in the title of his article— "Blame America at Your Peril"—the real danger in questioning the nation's innocence is how such inquiries supply "ammunition to America's enemies." We may be at liberty to do so, but "terrorists are taught how to use America's freedom as a weapon against us."[32]

## When Woman Is a Victim . . .

Discussions about victimization drifted from metaphoric rape to actual women's bodies and psyches, as Bush's war machine ramped up. The administration repackaged the war in Afghanistan (and to a lesser degree the subsequent war in Iraq) as a momentous struggle for the emancipation of women. Suddenly, conservatives of all stripes were versed in the entire feminist vocabulary— reproving "misogyny," "gender apartheid," and even "the feminization of poverty."[33] In another historic first, the first lady substituted for her husband during the president's Saturday morning radio address to christen the new crusade on behalf of third-world women. When Mrs. Bush announced, "the brutal oppression of women is a central goal of the terrorists," she became the female face of the administration's war against al-Qaeda and the Taliban. A narrow target to be certain, but the implications, she explained, are global. "Our hearts break for the women and children in Afghanistan, but also because in Afghanistan we see the world the terrorists would like to impose on the rest of us. . . . The fight against terrorism is also a fight for the rights and dignity of women."[34]

After allowing his spouse a temporary place at the bully pulpit, the president soon signed the Afghan Women and Children Relief Act (AWCRA), a gesture that helped redefine America's mission as less to protect itself than to wage battle for its values and mores.[35] Deputy Chief of Staff Karl Rove clarified: America was at war with "organizations that have totally disrespected the rights of individuals and make women objects of scorn and derision."[36] These brutes apparently encountered swift defeat, since one month later Bush used his State of the Union address to pronounce another "mission accomplished": "Last time we met in this chamber mothers and daughters in Afghanistan were captives in their own homes. . . . Today women are free."[37]

Laura Bush's appeal harked back to a late-nineteenth-century discourse that championed colonialism as a tool for introducing progress to underdeveloped societies, whose ill treatment of their womenfolk evidenced their backwardness. The notion of a bestial enemy torturing helpless women served as a powerful rallying cry for war at the turn of the twentieth century as well; whether in the guise of "the rape of Belgium" at the hands of German troops at the beginning of the First World War or—nearer to our shores—the sort of titillating atrocities that the Hearst papers reported from Cuba in the late 1890s. The contemporary outpouring of official empathy for the oppressed women of the world gave credence to Washington's peddling of its new Middle East mission as a "war for freedom."

The White House's commitment to women's "rights and dignity," however, remains exclusively reserved for women in Afghanistan. Less than a year after Bush's self-congratulatory announcement about the AWCRA, for instance, he refused to sign the international treaty prohibiting discrimination against women, the Convention on the Elimination of All Forms of Discrimination against Women (CEDAW). Often the attention solicited for the cruelties veiled women abroad endure seemed primarily to veil the realities of Bush's antifeminism or antiwomanism at home. Talking the feminist talk and having female ventriloquists—including mascot figures such as Karen Hughes and Condoleezza Rice—only assisted the deception. Zillah Eisenstein labels these highly visible official spokeswomen "gender decoys" for a new imperialism in female garb, "lur[ing] us into a fantasy of gender equity rather than depravity." [38] There are other examples in which George W. Bush's administration appropriated feminist causes and cloaked its programs in feminist rhetoric for ends incommensurate with feminism, such as in the case of the Violence Against Women Act of 1994. As with VAWA, what began as a feminist call to expose the Taliban's mistreatment of women became instead a way to substitute one model of paternalism for another.[39]

The administration's conception of Middle Eastern women as victims abides by the rationales of both the cult of true womanhood and its contemporary progeny, the Cult of True Victimhood. (Although by distilling the feminine into virtuous helplessness, this rhetoric may be applied to disempowered Iraqi men as well as to oppressed Afghan women.) Cynthia Enloe offers the neologism "womenandchildren" to denote the condensed singularity of this view of victimhood as entirely powerless and desperately needing rescue.[40] Associating women with victimhood in this way supports a triangulated gendered logic in which two masculine types—the dominator and the savior—act upon the feminized victim. While a more benign form of power, masculine protectionism is simply the flipside of masculine domination, as Iris Young theorizes; both sustain relations of subordination. "[T]his relationship carries an implicit deal: forgo freedom, due process, and the right to hold leaders accountable, and in return we will make sure that you are safe."[41] "[Since 9/11 g]ender symbolism is invoked in very old and familiar ways, anathema to feminist values and objectives," Mary Hawkesworth correspondingly argues. "Discourses of women fighting for rights have been supplanted by discussions of 'feminizing processes' that trade on a notion of the feminine as weak, vulnerable, and at risk, in need of rescue and protection."[42] Feminist scholars recognize how this construction of women's oppression has displaced arguments for the empowerment of all women with campaigns for particular women's rescue, and in doing so upheld inequality (whether patriarchal or colonial). As we will see, however, the gendering of victims and victimizers in post-9/11 anti-victimism plays out in additional, unfamiliar, and at times, opposing ways.

## . . . Perpetrators Are Victimists

Post-9/11 anti-victimist discourse produces a range of feminine, feminized, or unmasculine personae. Having considered the violated virtuous victim, we shall turn to another, the sexually ambiguous, treacherous perpetrator. In American public discourse, the individuals who stood behind the attack came to represent an ideology (the ephemeral "Terrorism"), immorality, and also a pathology. "We are fighting against men with blind hatred—and armed with lethal weapons—who are capable of any atrocity. They wear no uniform; they respect no law of warfare or morality."[43] The threat is best understood through the extreme, violent negation our enemies pose to the very essence of civilization—the equally opaque "freedom" or "liberty" that stands for the foundation of the American political system as well as the capitalist marketplace. "This is not . . . just America's fight. And what is a stake is not just America's freedom," proclaims Bush. "This is the world's fight. This is civilization's fight. This is the fight of all who believe in progress and pluralism, tolerance and freedom."[44] Negotiations, or for that matter any other kind of communication or exchange, with the enemy are unthinkable. "No act of ours invited the rage of the killers—and no concession, bribe, or act of appeasement would change or limit their plans for murder," he explains.[45] The terrorist is pure evil, devoid of any redeeming quality, or as one critic put it, "a wild-card moral anarchist beyond our comprehension."[46]

America's nemesis is also variously described as sick—maniacal, murderous, deviant, even homosexual.[47] "Their grievance is rooted in psychology," Thomas Friedman elucidates, "not politics."[48] Probing deeper, terrorist expert Jerrold Post diagnoses "negative childhood experiences" and "low self esteem" among the many pathologies that afflict terrorists.[49] Of course, such observations borrow only the diagnostic tools of therapy to dissect terrorists' troubled psyches; there is no rehabilitation program. Drawing upon Foucault's conception of the figure of the monstrous, Jasbir Puar and Amit Rai find great affinity between post-9/11 portrayals of terrorists and those of sexual monsters of previous centuries. "The construction of the pathologized psyche of the terrorist monster enables the practices of normalization, which in today's context often means an aggressive heterosexual patriotism."[50]

Suicide bombing constituted the paradigmatic encounter between terror and freedom, evil and innocence, exemplifying terror's irrational, fanatical drive and, ultimately, the character weakness of its perpetrators. Though brutal and terrifying, our enemies are nonetheless not real men, but cowards. "[A] coward is less than a man, one who does things underhandedly and either refuses to fight or plays dirty when he engages in a fight. The coward is not man enough to say it to your face."[51] Comedian-turned-pundit Bill Maher almost paid with his career for broaching the possibility that flying airplanes into buildings was not necessarily an act of cowardice.[52] As punishment for contesting the official line about of our enemy's deficient manhood, Maher lost his show. White House Press Secretary Ari Fleischer used the incident to advise the public that "[t]here are reminders to all Americans that they need to watch what they do, and this is not a time for remarks like that; there never is."[53]

Like the victimist at the center of the 1990s controversies over the welfare state and multiculturalism, our adversary's criminality is multifold, encompassing his bestial aggression, seething resentment, as well as his unconscionable ingratitude. In this regard, it is telling that a new coinage surfaced: Islamic or terrorist "welfare queens." Already raced and gendered for not properly responding to society's generosity—indeed, for accepting or even needing it in the first place—the Muslim "queen" is ever more menacing. Welfare is the elixir of terrorism, or so the argument goes. *Slate* blogger Mickey Kaus, for example, points to the fact that Zacarias Moussaoui, the French North African charged with conspiracy in connection with 9/11, reportedly turned radical while receiving welfare benefits in London. Reviewing cases of other individuals with ties to terror networks in Europe, including Muslim clerics, Kaus deciphers the independent variable—all were recipients of state support, at one time or another.

> [T]here's a good argument that "welfare benefits + ethnic antagonism" is the universal recipe for an underclass with an angry, oppositional culture. The social logic is simple: . . . relatively generous welfare benefits enable those in the ethnic ghetto to stay there, stay unemployed, and seethe. Without government subsidies, they would have to overcome the prejudice against them and integrate into the mainstream working culture. Work, in this sense, is anti-terrorist medicine.[54]

That Muhammad Atta and other perpetrators fraternized with the West, were schooled in Western culture, and lived in the United States while preparing the attack, only amplifies their crime and their deceit. These individuals clearly abused their welcome. The connection between welfare and terrorism became an issue again after the 2005 summer bombing in London, when investigators learned that at least one of the suspects resided in public housing.[55]

President Bush cemented the connection between the battle over the welfare state and the "war against terror" by analyzing the motives of the terrorists in a manner remarkably similar to the 1990s derogations of "victim politics." Speaking about the al-Qaeda organization at a ceremony honoring the National Endowment for Democracy, he expounded that the militant network "thrives like a parasite, on the suffering and frustration of others." Muslim radicals built "a cult of victimization, in which someone else is always to blame and violence is always the solution. They exploit resentful and disillusioned young men and women, recruiting them through radical mosques as the pawns of terror."[56] In other words, Bush maintains the Middle East "blame game" gave rise to the ultimate victimists who, under the victim mantle, now victimize us.

Finally, the antiterror campaign conjures another feminized archetype—the wimpy American leftist. Liberals, progressives, as well as anyone else who publicly expresses hesitation about the administration's policies and rhetoric are deemed dangerously soft on terror, accommodating of the enemy, and as undermining America's fortitude in a time of war. Bush and his allies attempt to stifle and derail public discussions about 9/11 and the subsequent wars by alleging that investigations and criticism only facilitate future attacks. When Democratic Senator Richard Durbin expressed his outrage at the brutal treatment of prisoners of war, Rove chastised him for being unpatriotic and unmanly. According to Rove, "Al Jazeera now broadcasts [Durbin's performance] . . . to the world" as a recruiting device.[57] The ad hominem attack on Durbin served as an example in a longer tirade during which Rove admonished the effeminate Left for preaching tolerance and understanding, dispensing psychological salves, and preparing to litigate.

> Conservatives saw the savagery of the 9/11 attacks and prepared for war; liberals saw the savagery of the 9/11 attacks and wanted to prepare indictments and offer therapy and understanding for our attackers. In the wake of 9/11, conservatives believed that it was time to unleash the might and power of the US military against the Taliban; in the wake of 9/11, liberals believed it was time to submit a petition. . . .[58]

Lynne Cheney, the vice president's wife and former head of the National Endowment for the Humanities, voiced similar criticism of educators who, after the attack on the World Trade Center and the Pentagon, called for greater broadmindedness toward and more study of other cultures in American schools. Such a perspective, she scoffs, "implies that the events of September 11 were our fault, that it was our failure to understand Islam that led to so many deaths and so much destruction. And this is not the case."[59] In contrast to the Left's misguided sensitivity, conservatives confronted the enemy with the mental mettle and military force to defeat him. Real men knew "[i]t was a moment to summon our national will and to brandish steel."[60]

## The Cult of True Innocence

George Bush's conception of the offenders—even those who were not verifiably part of the 9/11 attacks but were soon baptized as "helpers and enablers" of terror—is inseparable from his construction of America as a victim. The White House elaborates a crude Manichean world whose building blocks come only in two contrasting shades: good and evil, light and dark, bondage and freedom, us and them. Bush's millennial rhetoric undergirds a paranoid public culture that emerged in the wake of 9/11 and may qualify as another phase in the history of American demonology. Michael Rogin's remarks in his 1988 analysis of the dynamics of political repression in the United States now seem prophetic:

> [I]nternational terrorism not only permits the American government to sponsor its own acts of surveillance and state terror. By merging savages (from the first moment in American political demonology), revolutionaries (from the second), and Soviet agents (from the third), the theory of international terrorism also encapsulates and brings up to date the entire history of American counter-subversion.[61]

Twelve years after the demise of communism, America found renewed certitude as it faced, once again, a monumental foe. As in previous demonological moments, America's enemy is conceived of as ruthless, omnipotent and omni-present, largely external, but very likely among us as well. Hence the president reported during the first anniversary of the attack, "[t]his threat hides within many nations, including my own." [62]

As in the most visceral moments of the cold war, the "war on terror" rhetoric presents the United States and freedom as synonyms. "Freedom and fear, justice and cruelty, have always been at war, and we know that God is not neutral be-tween them." [63] In order to protect its vaunted liberties, however, leaders called upon their citizens to cede freedom. Americans were asked to accept the dra-conian measures of the Patriot Act, to turn a blind eye to infringements of hu-man rights in prisons and detention centers in Guantanamo, Iraq, Afghanistan, and other undisclosed locations, and, as we have seen, to refrain from criticiz-ing the administration. The battle between good and evil knows neither borders nor boundaries. Like a metastatic cancer, Terror's passion must be isolated and eradicated: "The only way to defeat terrorism as a threat to our way of life is to stop it, eliminate it and destroy it where it grows." [64]

Antiterror demonology extended and further entrenched 1990s anti-victim-ism with its own set of Manichean dichotomies and penchant for vilification. While in the past the supposedly anti-victimist Right flirted with the much-dreaded victim politics (disseminating ideas such as crime victims' rights, the fetus as a victim, and the beleaguered white male), the attack on America opened the door for a full embrace. Bush portrays the United States as perpetually at risk, as either an actual or a potential innocent victim. Even more devastating attacks, officials repeatedly caution, are inevitable, indeed imminent. Noth-ing is left to nuance, as in the famous 2004 Republican campaign television ad that depicted America surrounded by a pack of wolves awaiting the opportune moment to slaughter its prey. "Americans should not expect one battle, but a lengthy campaign, unlike any other we have ever seen . . . hug your children. I know many citizens have fears. . . . Be calm and resolute, even in the face of a continuing threat." [65]

Like other anti-victimists, Bush becomes a practitioner of victim politics. Journalist Renana Brooks, who titles her article "A Nation of Victims" (which ironically is also the title of Charles Sykes's anti-victimist harangue), makes the case that Bush fosters a "victim mentality" among the citizenry through his careful deployment of fear. Borrowing from the language of the battered wom-en's syndrome, she avers that the public now displays symptoms of "learned helplessness." But how could it be otherwise, she concedes, after tallying a total of "forty-four consecutive statements referring to the crisis and citing a multitude of possible catastrophic repercussions" in a single major policy speech Bush gave on Iraq in 2003.[66]

On some occasions, Bush directly tied post-9/11 politics and pre-9/11 anti-victimist causes. In a public address supporting a victims' rights amendment to the federal constitution, for instance, he fuses the "war on terror" and the drive for a constitutional amendment.

> We seek justice for victims. We seek justice for their families. And for justice to prevail in our struggle for freedom, we must rout out terrorist threats wherever they exist. . . . And while the war goes on . . . we will continue to work for justice at home, including justice for the victims of violent crime. . . . Victims of violent crime have important rights that deserve protection in our Constitution.[67]

In a reciprocal gesture, victims' rights groups added homeland security to their list of causes and informational links along with child abductions and sexual abuse.[68]

Bush's battle between good and evil reinforces the stark opposition of blameworthiness and blamelessness as these concepts were shaped and reshaped in the 1990s debates over victimhood. Bush insists upon the unqualified innocence of the United States. (This aspect of America's victim status transcends historical and gender analogies, even as it gestures toward them.) America's innocence, in this regard, is comprehensive. It is the innocence of the righteous, of course, but encompasses a much greater terrain. The administration refuses to acknowledge any wrongdoing, negligence, or mistake in the events that led to 9/11, as though admitting any failing or flaw would belittle America's moral standing. Conflating causality and blame, the White House was reluctant, and sometimes overtly refused, to study seriously the circumstances of 9/11. Illinois Republican Congressman Ray LaHood borrowed from the anti-victimist lexicon when he maintained that instituting an investigative body would be little more than "another one of those blame game commissions that . . . is just looking to lay blame on an administration or a director of an agency." [69]

Only after public pressure for investigation became too strong to resist did the administration relent. Still, it impeded the probe in numerous ways—failing to turn over documents in a timely manner, denying necessary funds, placing restrictions on access to official papers, refusing to allow the president to testify under oath or alone, and, as New York Senator Charles Schumer has claimed, even intimidating witnesses. Once it was blatantly obvious that no weapons of mass destruction (WMDs) existed, however, the administration freely spread the blame around. When authorities finally began to concede that they might have been mistaken, personal pronouns took a plural form. "If everyone was wrong about WMDs, then no one—especially not Bush—is to blame now," journalist David Corn remarks.[70]

Such obstructionism served transparent political needs. Exposing official ineptitude either by the CIA, FBI, or other federal agencies might call the administration's competence into doubt and raise questions of the what-did-the-president-know-and-when-did-he-know-it sort; questions that were ultimately raised, and never fully answered. Investigation could exact a political price. As importantly, the study of the events that led to 9/11 (or a reasoned inquiry into the motives of Bin Ladin and his men) stood against the vision of the conflict as a millennial struggle between complete and extreme innocence and radical blameworthiness. In other words, America could not retain its status as a victim if any causal link between its behavior and the attack could be established. It thus upheld the notion that the only true victim is the thoroughly innocent one.

Numerous commentators point to 9/11 as the date America lost its innocence. Bush stated as much himself, though he presents our innocence as only diminished: "We are a different country than we were on September 10, sadder and less innocent, stronger and more united."[71] But perhaps the opposite is true: the events of September 2001 enabled America to regain its innocence. After all, America lost its innocence several times before—Pearl Harbor; Vietnam; the assassinations of John F. Kennedy, Martin Luther King Jr., Robert F. Kennedy; and Watergate; and more recently Oklahoma City and Columbine. At most of these tragic junctures, claiming a lost purity depended upon a highly selective collective memory.[72] A different historical amnesia afflicts the nation since 9/11. The violation created the possibility to reclaim virtue and to engage in new transgressions. As Judith Butler suggests:

> In order to condemn these acts as inexcusable, absolutely wrong, in order to sustain the affective structure in which we are, on the one hand, victimized and, on the other, engaged in a righteous cause rooting out terror, we have to start the story with the experience of violence we suffered.[73]

To begin the narrative elsewhere would open the possibility of an explanation for the attack and undermine the nation's claim to a place within the Cult of True Victimhood.

## Remasculinization

Remasculinizing America by restoring patriarchal power serves as one remedy to the danger posed by at least two feminine archetypes—the victim and the victimizer. During the 2004 presidential campaign, both parties aspired to assume the mantle of masculinity. Republicans peddled the incumbent as the embodiment of strength, virility, and determination. By contrast, they portrayed John Kerry as French-loving, decadent, dithering, and far too cerebral for action. "In a time of fear, the only battle that matters is the broad-stroked cultural cockfight over who's most macho," Frank Rich writes of the "castration warfare" on display at the national conventions. "[W]ith the high stakes of an election at hand, it's not enough to stuff socks in the president's flight suit. Mr. Kerry must be turned into a girl."[74] Meanwhile, Kerry's campaign toiled hard to juxtapose his Vietnam War decorations and tales of heroism with Bush's questionable military record. Democrats vied to convince American voters that their guy was the real man "reporting for duty." Both party conventions celebrated testosterone in a spectacle of muscle.

Worshiping the masculine also featured sentimental praise for men's virtues as well as their buff bodies. Peggy Noonan waxes erotic:

> It is not only that God is back, but that men are back. A certain style of manliness is once again being honored and celebrated in our country since 9/11. . . . I am speaking of masculine men, men who push things and pull things and haul things and build things, men who charge up the stairs in a hundred pounds of gear and tell everyone else where to go to be safe.[75]

The burly men feminist critic Susan Faludi claimed were "stiffed" and dejected by the new global economy, Noonan thinks 9/11 raised to royalty: "I have seen the grunts of New York become kings of the City." How do these allegedly newly empowered grunts rule? With chivalry, swoons Noonan. Rugged and silent, like her beloved Duke, "good men suck it up . . . manliness wins wars . . . but also . . . will bring the return of gentlemanliness."[76] Camille Paglia gushes as well: "I cannot help noticing how robustly, dreamily masculine the faces of firefighters are. They are working-class men, stoical, patriotic. They're not on Prozac or questioning their gender."[77] "After years of male-bashing," Cathy Young chimes in, "it is good to see some appreciation for male heroism and even for the fact that traditional machismo always included not only dominance but protection and rescue."[78] Even the beef and brawn of those who perished on 9/11, such as Todd Beamer on Flight 93 ("The Flight That Fought Back" as the

*Discovery Channel* titled its docudrama), became essential tropes in the official account, as Patricia Leigh Brown notes.[79] The men are strong, fearless, chivalrous, staunchly heterosexual, and above all, they dare not complain.

In this theater of masculine valor, the appearance and sudden disappearance of one female figure merits consideration. The story of the capture and rescue of the nineteen-year-old army supply clerk, Jessica Lynch, received tremendous national attention during the initial stages of the Iraq war. At first, the media simply plastered Jessica's photogenic face onto the pantheon of male warriors, depicting her as a Rambo-like figure "fighting to her death," killing many Iraqis despite being shot and stabbed. Even after modifying the story to accord with actual events—with her M-16 jammed she was unable to fire even before being injured—American television continually replayed the scene of can-do men rescuing the blonde damsel from her captors and their escape in the Black Hawk helicopter.

If not as a hero, Lynch could still serve in the role of demure woman (reports told of how she had won "Miss Congeniality" at a local fair in West Virginia) with an impotent gun. The nation needed some "good news" about the mission in Iraq. In the initial stages, the war relied on "shock and awe" pyrotechnics and other gadgets of military technology. Ever since, it has become a war of attrition, of roadblocks and car bombs. The attempt to glorify Private Lynch highlights what is otherwise deficient in the Iraqi story—evidence of a gallant struggle between good and evil. This war won't be televised, at least not according to the rules that govern Sunday-evening television docudramas.

The release of Lynch's book, *I Am a Solider Too* (on Veterans' Day 2003 no less), clarified little, since in this authorized version Lynch reports to still have no direct recollection of her capture and captivity.[80] But it was only when Lynch refused another tour of duty as the poster girl for the war effort that her erasure from our screens and memory became paramount. Fellow soldiers reportedly sold naked photos of Lynch to *Hustler* magazine publisher Larry Flynt, justifying their action as motivated by the need to expose that "she's not all apple pie."[81] Inevitably, Lynch would be demoted further, from heroic warrior turned precious victim to shameless slut and then the disappeared.

Conversely, the images of Iraqi men terrorized by female soldiers in Abu Ghraib demonstrated, for some, that women have no place in the military. After all, the photos of Private Lyndie England holding a prisoner on a leash did not sit well with the woman-as-victim motif.[82] President of the Center for Military Readiness, Elaine Donnelly, for instance, claims the photographs document the

hatred of men feminism fosters, especially that of "victim feminists" who allege that men oppress all women.[83] "The war between the sexes, provoked by
mutual resentments, has just gone nuclear." Abu Ghraib affords the public a
glimpse at the dystopia feminists aim to bring to our shores. What happened
there also disproves the "the unrealistic theory" that women can perform as
well as men in all military roles. Donnelly additionally discerns in the images of
homosadism enough material for advocating the removal of gays from the military. Accordingly, she advises the Bush administration to enforce the exclusion
of homosexuals from the armed services without the Clinton fudge regarding
asking and telling.[84]

## The Good Victim

President Bush's conception of the post-9/11 geo-moral landscape renders him
a practitioner of anti-victimist victim politics whose main trope is the virtuous
victim. America assumes the positions of both innocent (feminine) victim as
well as its own (masculine) savior. Still, this gendered binary represents only
one modality of the post-9/11 victim discourse. The administration's immer-
sion in anti-victimism is more complex and multifaceted, unfolding in unexpected ways. Even as Washington used the horror of the attack to cast America as a True Victim, it often resorted to another of the anti-victimist models
of venerated victimhood—the victim who rejects victimhood and refuses to be
a victim. True, Bush emphasizes his compassion toward a variety of American
sufferers in moments of political necessity; for instance, the Floridians who endured hurricanes in 2004 and, somewhat belatedly, those left homeless after
Katrina's wrath in 2005. In famous images integrated into the visuals accompanying his 2004 campaign for a second term in office, we see members of a 9/11
victim's family receiving a presidential hug. Bush desires to assure the public
that he can empathize as much as his predecessor Bill Clinton, to show that he
too is capable of feeling others' pain.

Yet Bush's approach to the suffering 9/11 inflicted is a great deal more ambiguous. For a variety of reasons, Bush chose to repackage the post-9/11 wars
in terms of a global pursuit for freedom rather than simply as a response to
(or retribution for) an attack planned and executed by a few individuals. Exi-
gencies of self-defense did not propel America; it was, in fact, responding to a
higher calling. Once again, necessity generated some of the rhetoric and policy.
The war against Iraq was initially peddled as a defensive war to topple a sinister
enemy who possess mighty arms that could devastate the United States. Since

no weapons of mass destruction were located, the war was quickly rescripted as a single instance of a historic struggle against tyranny in which the United States found its groove again by rediscovering its ancient mission, its manifest destiny, as a model to the nations of the world.

Regardless of motives, the White House abandoned explicitly identifying the events of 9/11 as the sole anchor of its moral cause (though, of course, it benefited from voters' misperceptions to the contrary in the 2004 elections).[85] The "war for freedom" has deeper roots in American culture, a long chain of historical myths and icons. It is steeped in a manly heroism that is deeply ambivalent about suffering and sacrifice. Post-9/11 America is juxtaposed not just to a bloodthirsty enemy but also to the liberalism and moral laxity of the Clintons and the "gay" 1990s. In this narrative, the attack represents little more than a turning point in the plot, a moment of reckoning—not a point of origin in need of contemplation and response. Bush's America sees the people who died at the World Trade Center, the Pentagon, and aboard the four planes not as victims but as heroes who—much like the defenders of the Alamo—"died for freedom." It posthumously conscripts or deputizes them to proselytize core American values rather than merely to protect its civilization.

Bush's administration supported efforts to compensate bereaved families generously and, importantly, in record time. (Commentators attribute this more to concern with preserving the airline industry than with the plight of the victims, however.)[86] Otherwise, it rarely granted the victims' families the same public standing that the victims' rights movement bestows upon relatives of victims of crime. The president appears more comfortable in the company of law enforcement officers. In his visits to post-9/11 New York, he met and was continually photographed with the "heroes"—policemen and firemen—not grieving families. When some families began to raise nagging questions about 9/11, the White House labored hard to stifle them. Together with its cadre of dependable pundits, it dismissed the families' call for a comprehensive investigation and was thoroughly unsympathetic to their expressed desire to find release, resolve, or closure in truth-telling rather than in the killing fields of Iraq and Afghanistan.

The devastation inflicted on New York City was also not a source of great concern for Bush and his administration. Shrewdly, the Republican National Committee made Manhattan the site of the party's 2004 convention and gave a stage to Governor Pataki and former Mayor Giuliani, who had the dual assets of being the caretakers of the wounded city and moderate Republicans. At the same time, the president was rather stingy in his gestures toward the city.

The official "biographical" film featured during the convention made Riefen-stahlesque use of the president's strapping body parts while he threw the first pitch at Game Three of the 2001 World Series at Yankee Stadium. But Bush never expressed a sense of affinity that, for instance, Kennedy articulated in Berlin in the early 1960s. Despite a national (and international) outpouring of sympathy toward the city and its loss, Bush never suggested that he too is a New Yorker.

As importantly, the Bush administration remains strangely sluggish in com-memorating fallen soldiers or acknowledging their suffering in other ways. Some of the most poignant moments in Michael Moore's *Fahrenheit 9/11* (2004) were footage of American soldiers being hit by insurgents' bullets or roadside bombs in Iraq. The depiction of the pain inflicted on a family of a fallen soldier was perhaps the most powerful element of the documentary. In our otherwise image-congested culture, injured soldiers and bereaved families have been de-leted somehow. For the longest time, the Bush administration refused to release pictures of coffins of American soldiers or military funerals. Only the specter of a public cry forced the president and the secretary of defense to feign greater empathy toward families of American casualties (including the vacuous gesture of signing by hand the secretary of defense's letters of condolences). Practices of commemoration that have become constitutive of the modern state were left to private initiative. When anchor Ted Koppel decided to read the names and show the photos of all American fatalities in Iraq during a single episode of *Nightline* in April 2003, his gesture was considered overtly political, unpatriotic, and even subversive. The conservative Sinclair Broadcasting Company accordingly pre-empted the live program on its ABC affiliates.

## The Passion of Bush

It was not the case that the events of September 2001 or the war in Iraq were un-documented. However, even as reports and images inundated the public, very little of the wounded and the dead were seen. Perhaps this lacuna is at the root of the immense commercial success of Mel Gibson's *The Passion of the Christ* (2004). Three thousand men and women perished on 9/11 (and many more died during the subsequent wars), but the only body that was not closeted, indeed was offered for public display, was that of Jesus. Detailing the last twelve hours of his life, the *Passion* focuses relentlessly on Christ's traumatized body. Richard Dyer notes in his study of "whiteness" that Christ represents the essence of the white heterosexual male—the paradox of visibility and invisibility—being in the body but not of it.[87] Gibson's Jesus, by contrast, is strongly embodied in a way that is seemingly alien to the Protestant tradition, rendering the enthusiasm with which evangelical America greeted the film ever more puzzling. Christ reminds us of sacrificial suffering, but Gibson's Jesus is unquestionably a man, not a lamb. Journalist Katha Pollitt describes a major scene in the film as a "ten minute homoerotic sadistic extravaganza that no human being could have survived, as if the point was to show how tough Christ was." Another reviewer situates the movie within "the culture of blackshirt and brownshirt pseudomasculinity." [88]

Conceived before 2001, the *Passion* nevertheless became emblematic of the post-9/11 atmosphere as well as of the larger campaign to reconfigure the role of victimization in American public life. Gibson registered on celluloid the perfect model of the Cult of True Victimhood. His victim is subjected to pain that is immediate and visible, verifiable yet immeasurable, and he accepts his torture without reservation or complaint, almost existentially (for the meaning of his sacrifice remained entirely outside the subject matter of the film). As the director, Gibson may also assume the role of anti-victimist victim by claiming, in so many words, that a Jewish conspiracy (and other stock suspects on the political Left) attempts to undermine his art. The *Passion* derives its visual vocabulary from a wide range of sources that came to dominate our cultural conception of tortured bodies, from images of concentration camps to Gibson's own history of filmic violence—especially the brutality and martyrology of the historically fictive *Braveheart* (1995).[89]

Gibson's film seems to correspond particularly well with the vernacular efforts to grapple with the violence of the World Trade Center attack and its victims. Post-9/11 iconography thrived in the memorabilia that vendors sold on the streets of New York and in the new public space of the Internet. Much of this rather sentimental folk art employed national symbols and Christian motifs. Numerous images featured a tearful eagle. Others depicted angels hovering over the inferno of the World Trade Center embracing dying firemen in their wings. Still other illustrations made use of the single remnant of the tall buildings that remained standing for weeks on end, the cluster of mangled steel beams that once supported the building and later towered over the rescue teams, suggesting in their geometrical simplicity the form of the cross. These symbols were blatantly patriotic and partook in the justification of America's belligerence abroad. At the same time, the vernacular crying eagle militated against the official iconography of the aftermath of 9/11 when limited space was granted to any articulation of injury and grief or to open debate over the reasons for and meaning of the attack. Recall that in the maudlin song written and performed by former Attorney General John Ashcroft, "the eagle always soars, like she never soared before."

The image of Jesus appears to sit somewhat uneasily with the more aggressively masculine tropes that flooded the American public sphere after September 11. America's violence abroad not only rejects the Christian imperative to turn the other cheek, it goes far beyond even the cowboy approach of pursuing lowly perpetrators. The United States embraced preemptive strikes as a supra-principle of its foreign policy. Within anti-victim discourse, however, these contrasting models of manhood—the *Terminator*-like preemptor and Christ—cohere, since the first refuses to be a victim, while the latter refuses to be a victimist. Moreover, by finding another anchor for the "war on terror," by dislodging the events of 9/11 as the foundation for U.S. policy, America's mission in Iraq assumes an aura of radical altruism. Our troops are not fighting back retributively; they are "freedom fighters" rescuing tortured men and women from the clutches of a tyrant. As the hunt for Bin Ladin and his Taliban followers receded from the national agenda by 2004, and as Americans prepare to dedicate the World Trade Center site to celebrating "Freedom"—complete with a "Freedom Tower"—the "war on terror" and the "war for freedom" seem to have been America's initiative all along, not a response to a sneak attack.

## Refusing Society

The success of the *Passion* coincided with Bush's repeated invocation of Christ as his mentor or even premiere father figure.[90] Neither formally endorsed by the president nor screened at the White House (at least not as an official event meriting publicity), the timing of the film's release during Bush's reelection campaign still caused many Republicans to welcome it as an antidote to Michael Moore's irreverent anti-Bush *Fahrenheit 911*.[91] Even without formal sanction, the film participated in the making of the Bush phenomenology, in substituting one reality with another and conjuring a bigger messianic or millennial "truth."

Such splitting, doubling, and displacements are symptomatic of antivictimism, as we saw in the previous chapters. These tensions underlined, to give another example, Julius Lester's fantastical self-invention. Lester's racial conversion as well as Bush's conversion to the cause of world freedom are commensurate with a culture that, regardless of political bent, privileges the fluidity of self-making; a culture that engages in endless play with reality, embraces and rejects, commodifies and consumes reality, including the reality of victimiza-

tion. Bush's allegiance to the "vision thing" (which his father mocked) is so entrenched that key aides poke fun at "the reality-based community," comprised
of "those who believe that solutions emerge from . . . judicious study of discernible reality." Obsessed with inconvenient facts and trifling details, plagued
by doubt and an insatiable desire for deliberation, such "realists" seek to sully
Bush's vision. Besides, as one of Bush's aides explained,

> That's not the way the world really works anymore. We're an empire now,
> and when we act, we create our own reality. And while you're studying
> that reality judiciously, as you will—we'll act again, creating new realities,
> which you can study too, and this is how things will sort out. We're histo-
> ry's actors . . . and you, all of you, will be left to just study what we do.[92]

Lester's and Bush's transformations exemplify the potential of anti-
victimism to serve as a vehicle for radical rebirth, predicated upon the death
and eradication of a prior identity. In the wake of 9/11, Bush promised to remake America. Carefully avoiding articulating precisely what ills America or
specifying the abyss from which it needs to climb, he still repeatedly invokes
the grammar of redemption and rejuvenation. (It remains unclear whether the
president thinks our country needs regeneration or just a simple affirmation.)
Journalist Bob Woodward reports that Bush claimed to have discerned "an opportunity" in the horror of 9/11. According to Karl Rove, "Bush's first 8 months
had been middling . . . [9/11 was a] second chance to define himself, an acciden-
tal shot at rebirth . . . [that could] revive Bush's presidency."[93] The opportunity
9/11 afforded Bush to lead the nation reiterates his own experience of conversion, when he reportedly overcame a life of heavy drinking and aimlessness to
become a highly driven, self-possessed individual. After 9/11, Bush's personal
and political merged. To whom was Bush referring when he declared "adversity
introduced us to ourselves"?[94]

The president expresses himself in a redemptive language that both ab-
stracts and anthropomorphizes the nation. What worked for Bush the man
will work for Bush's America. Just as individual character and dogged resolve
determined his fate, so too will it shape that of the country. "This country will
define our times, not be defined by them," Bush instructs us.[95] This sentiment
partakes of the logic of "American exceptionalism" and the notion that unlike
the rest of the world the United States resides beyond history. Whereas Charles
Krauthammer posited that 9/11 ended America's "holiday from history," Bush
determinedly labors to extend the vacation. Similarly, Lynne Cheney encour-

ages educators to teach American schoolchildren her favorite adage by Thomas Paine: "We have in our power to begin the world over again."[96] The conception of individual will that anti-victimism nurtures goes far beyond bootstraps ideology to embrace a fantasy of self-making that exists outside time. Recall that "leaping out of history" was also a central theme in Lester's story of self-invention. As makers of history, we need never be victims, since each of us can choose otherwise, if only we have the right character.

The space between individual self-making and national regeneration is one of the conceptual wrinkles that demands frantic reworking and bridging, especially in a time of national emergency. Thus, Bush incessantly recombines different elements of anti-victimism and the Cult of True Victimhood it spawned. This is typical of the manner in which anti-victimism unfolded in American public life over the course of the last two decades, but Bush's anti-victim pastiche seems remarkably inventive. Even as he propagates fear among the citizenry, Bush promises that the millennial struggle for freedom will be free of sacrifice. While government officials occasionally remind us that the country is at war, they also emphasize that Americans' only civic duty is to consume. The business of warfare was "out-sourced" to an elite group of professional soldiers equipped with cutting-edge technology (or literally out-sourced to civilian companies—as in the case of bodyguard services in Iraq). On the home front Americans should continue to indulge in their rightful prosperity. In fact, perhaps there is not much to worry about since America took the war to the enemy.[97] Bush does not call even for modest financial sacrifice. There is no need to suspend tax cuts to pay for the debts the war continues to accrue. In this way, Bush's America displays the dangers of what Lauren Berlant stresses in her analysis of the rise of "infantile citizenship"—the privatization of the public by which consumerism serves as an alternative to political participation.[98]

The White House conjures a nation devoid of a sense of community, strong social fabric, or collective obligations. This fundamental feature further ties Bush's presidency to 1990s anti-victimism that emerged as the antidote to the "nanny state" and multiculturalism. The president's domestic policies—notably the program to privatize Social Security—are commensurate with his vision of freedom for the world. To put it differently, the "war on terror" partakes in the anti-victimist campaign to individuate American society. It dresses in battle fatigues ideas that sprang from the marketplace.

Even when Bush appeals to the public as a public, he focuses almost exclusively on individual actions in the private sphere. He rarely calls upon the public to "debate policy, volunteer for the armed services, or contribute to bond drives," as rhetoric scholar John Murphy observes in his analysis of Bush's major policy speeches during the year that followed 9/11.[99] The president relates to Americans as coreligionists: good Christians, believers in the free market, or worshipers of American "freedom." The only social camaraderie permitted is akin to charity work and, in the tradition of "compassionate conservatism," is left to individual initiative or civil associations rather than to the state. There are no official policies in this regard. It took Hurricane Katrina in August 2005 to lay bare the pernicious effects of ignoring society and neglecting, under the marquee of "homeland security," to sustain a government infrastructure to assist victims during a devastating crisis. Bush's team may prefer to deal with millennial truth and ideational suffering rather than empirical truth and victimization, but when in the fall of 2005 poor people stood on the rooftops of hurricane-ravaged New Orleans pleading for help, social reality and victimhood could no longer be easily ignored.

# Epilogue

ANTI-VICTIMISM CONGEALED in the early 1990s when politicians and pundits instigated an alarmist campaign, verging on a moral panic, alerting Americans that their society was dangerously deluged by victim claims. As we have seen, tensions and conflicts over victims and victimhood cross the boundaries of political camps and ideologies. The Right upholds both fervent animosity toward victims and the Cult of True Victimhood. The Left also embraces seemingly contradictory and yet mutually constitutive positions. Even when they champion the cause of the most vulnerable, progressives harbor their own version of anti-victimism—associating victimhood with weakness, fatalism, dependency, and passivity. We explored this dynamic in detail within feminism. Feminists' deliberations over how to theorize women's oppression—how women might be both victims of invidious forces beyond their control and sufficiently empowered to become their own liberators—generated a seemingly endless cycle of debates in which each effort to construct some victim-free account of women's condition ultimately met criticism for being too victim-oriented.

In its conservative rendition, anti-victimism castigates victims for shamelessly using their disadvantage, misfortune, or personal failures to plunder the public coffers or to impose rigid codes of behavior, decorum, and even cultural forms on others through means such as hate speech codes, affirmative action, and radically revised university curricula. Such policies and laws allegedly constrict American freedoms and present a punishing burden on national resources. In this way, victimism injures, indeed victimizes, American society.

"Victim" still designates individuals and groups who have been subjected to harm, such as victims of violent crimes or of natural disasters, but anti-victimism affixes new pejorative connotations to the term. This derisive application now taints all forms of victimization that do not adhere to the austere rules of True Victimhood. Seeking recognition of one's victimization is deemed indicative of a deficient character. Victimhood came to represent an all-consuming identity (a stain), not a verifiable claim. This is arguably the most insidious consequence of the anti-victimists' assault.

The dynamics of victimhood-as-identity resonate with Michel Foucault's analysis of the late-nineteenth-century transformation of certain sexual activities into a pathology, which was assigned a label, "homosexuality," and a set of remedial practices deployed by therapeutic professionals and regulated by the state. The medico-juridical discourse of sex among men gave rise to a new comprehensive identity as well as to particularly intrusive forms of discipline.[1] Anti-victimism, in a similar manner, shifts attention from the harm done to victims, to the victim herself, her mental state and character, and calls for her rehabilitation. The medicalization of the victim began in the post–Second World War period, especially with the emergence of the field of victimology, which focused its professional gaze on victims of a wide range of crimes, from rape to genocide. Even after victimology was challenged in the 1970s, a therapeutic logic continued to dominate approaches toward the victimized. Chronicling the history of "blaming the victim" demonstrated this trend. Therapeutic ideas underscored personal responsibility at the expense of collective accountability.

Therapeutics informed the 1990s conception of the victimist as well. Paradoxically, however, the drive against victimism (as well as the assault on the welfare state) seeks to undermine the same post-Enlightenment scientific discourses that Foucault critiqued: the modern social sciences, social welfare, psychology, and other forms of expertise that allegedly were conducive to victimism by being immensely tolerant of transgressive behavior and by shifting attention from the immorality of individuals to structural inequality. Anti-victimism straddles the gap between therapy and antitherapy. Its proponents deploy therapeutic ideas while ostensibly rejecting the therapeutic ethos. Anti-victimists argue that victims are psychologically invested in their suffering, irrevocably attached to their status as victims. For example, in his contribution to the Democratic Leadership Council's journal "Beyond Victimization" issue, Jonathan Rauch warns that "oppression politics" can be dangerously addictive. "What you win through oppression politics you naturally hope to keep; but to keep the winnings of victimhood, you must play the victim. You must prove at every turn that you are less than a full citizen and haven't yet arrived."[2]

Rauch's warning is analogous to the argument that the welfare recipient's dependence on state support diminishes him as a citizen. This deficiency signifies a slippery slope that eventually leads recipients to engage in additional immoral acts such as illegitimacy and even criminality. They abdicate their standing in society and reciprocate society's generosity with deviant behavior. Welfare dependents are not just bogus victims, and a burden on society, but blameworthy because they succumb to, or indulge in, their own weaknesses and desires. Their need for public assistance in the first place signals a character flaw that must be corrected. As George Lakoff reasons, the importance of the "moral strength metaphor" within conservative thought and language renders the welfare state "evil" because it works against self-discipline and self-reliance.[3] "In conservative, strict father morality evil is a palpable thing in the world. To stand up to evil you have to be morally strong. If you're weak, you let evil triumph, so that weakness is a form of evil itself, as is promoting weakness."[4]

Anti-victimists emphasize free will and individual character. Victimhood, if not victimization itself, they insist, is a matter of choice, which is deeply moral. If one is inflicted with a "victim mentality," he can (and should) decide to overcome it, to rid himself of it. Julius Lester's conversion vividly exemplified this view by promoting the idea that Jewishness, blackness, and victimhood are all voluntary affiliations, decisions individuals make, unmake, and remake. While Lester conceives of his conversion as an existential quest, other formulations employ the marketplace (often implicitly) as the template for the process of identity selection.

Anti-victimism also frequently appears as a form of popular sermonizing. For instance, televangelist Joel Osteen, who ministers the largest congregation in the country, preaches in his best-selling book *The Best Life Now* (2004) the message that God too wants us to decide to be "victors not victims."

> [Let] go of the past. . . . It's just an attitude we've got to get up and make a decision every single day. . . . [W]hat so many people today do, they focus on what they don't have instead of what they do have. They focus on what's wrong instead of what's right. And I believe all of us, if we want to, can be happy right where we are. . . . [T]his is where God has me and I'm going to make the most of it.[5]

The eleventh commandment—"Don't be a victim"—thus serves two purposes. It encourages individuals to assert themselves in the marketplace by embracing bootstraps ideology; and conversely, as in Osteen's homily, it instructs them to accept their misfortune as divinely determined should they fail. Regardless of particular emphases, prescriptions to conquer victimhood occlude matters of injustice.

Anti-victimists introduce different recuperative strategies that are decidedly disciplinary and yet fundamentally removed from the nuanced knowledge and skills of the therapeutic expert. They ultimately rely on ethical or pastoral rather than psychological expertise. These methods amount to one or another admixture of crude deterrence, moralism, and the gospel of personal self-making. Anti-victimism itself encapsulates a cure for the social disease it aims to expose, for anti-victimism is not merely an instrument of analysis. It also unleashes rhetorical devices that dislodge victims from their victimhood through the power of humiliation and ridicule. Making a victim claim has become unacceptable or even antisocial behavior. (Babies do cry, but "crybabies" are an embarrassment to themselves and a burden on society.) The shaming of victims has been so successful that even those who seek public acknowledgment of their injury shun the designation. Anti-victimism is consequently more preventative than reformative. Dispensing with the intricacies of addressing root causes, anti-victimists labor instead to convince individuals to cease and desist. As anti-victimism extended after 9/11, the possibility of reforming or rehabilitating victims was rendered all but impossible. The victimists who perpetrate terror are evil Others who deserve nothing less than moral outrage and punishment. President Bush's response to 9/11 makes evident that anti-victimism structures and sustains victim discourse in contemporary American politics within and beyond conflicts over social inequality.

## What Is to Be Undone?

Beyond the affinity of the moral imagination of Left and Right, and the symmetry in the way that victim discourse subsumes the difference between claimers and blamers, anti-victimism emerged in the early 1990s primarily to undermine identity politics, multiculturalism, and the welfare state. All three have been deemed harbingers of victim politics. More recently, anti-victimism contributed to waging war, by disseminating a counterepistemology and counterethics of suffering. The Cult of True Victimhood in particular is a decidedly antiprogressive tool that works to curb and regulate claims of injury and injustice that do not comport with rigid models of victimhood. The Cult amounts to an individuating apparatus (or technology) inimical to collectives—whether racial, ethnic, social, gender, sexual, or economic—and hostile to claims grounded in historical consciousness and historical analysis. Even when the Cult claims to speak for a potential group—unborn children, victims of crime—it rejects the notion of social groups constituted by difference, culture, and historical experience. The legislation aimed at equipping these individuals (and fetuses) with new rights serves to empower them only as individuals, not as a class.

There is one important caveat to this rule, for beyond their loyalty to marketplace individualism conservatives wish to safeguard the nuclear heteronormative family. The Right's selective and ferocious defense of this social unit brings the contemporary Cult of True Victimhood closer to its nineteenth-century precursor, the cult of true womanhood, which, according to historian Barbara Welter (who coined the phrase), rested on four principles—piety, domesticity, purity, and submissiveness.[6] Only victims who restore patriarchal power and enhance the retributive state readily receive recognition as true victims. Most conservatives, therefore, embraced the Violence Against Women Act (which many feminists also supported) since in their conception it expands upon victims' rights legislation. From this vantage point, the unborn victims protection clause is not incoherent, as critics claim; it is simply a natural extension of the law. That the VAWA could be amended in this way reveals how focusing on the isolated, innocent individual victim outside the contexts of inequality that facilitate systematic victimization allows for conservative appropriations of seemingly progressive agendas. We observed similar attempts to graft progressive rhetoric onto a conservative agenda in the Bush administration's response to 9/11.

In addition to critical analysis, then, what might be the proper response to the anti-victimist attack and the pernicious effects of the Cult of True Victimhood? Given the ways that both Left and Right have distorted our understanding of victimhood, is there still a place for the concept of the victim in contemporary struggles against injustice? There is no substantial political literature to guide us in this regard. Over the last fifteen years, there has been a great outpouring of theoretical work on related topics such as oppression, genocide, trauma, loss, melancholy, and mourning, but only a few studies use "victim" as a category of analysis. Two scholars who have explored the dynamics of victim claiming are Judith Shklar and Martha Minow.

Shklar's *The Faces of Injustice* (1990) argues for the political value of "victim" as a concept to designate harm, making the case that theorizing injustice through victimization forces us to challenge the fixity of the boundary between misfortune and injustice. Social responses to the suffering of others rest on this division—the former category refers to suffering that we resign ourselves to, and the latter, that which we might labor to change. Distinguishing between the unfortunate and the unjust is politically necessary, she maintains, but the process of classification relies upon intricate political negotiations. Shklar reminds us that we often neglect cases of injustice that do not neatly conform to established legal and ethical rules.

> [N]one of the usual models of justice offer an adequate account of injustice because they cling to the groundless belief that we can know and draw a stable and rigid distinction between the unjust and the unfortunate. Moreover, this belief inclines us to ignore . . . the full, complex, and enduring character of injustice as a social phenomenon.[7]

Focusing on victimization, she suggests, might enable us to address an expansive range of harms not ordinarily considered within the same analytic framework, from victims of accidents and natural disasters to victims of crimes, victims of discrimination, or even victims of extreme bad luck in the marketplace. Not all instances of injury can or should be similarly ameliorated. However, Shklar cautions against presuming that such differences can be neatly calibrated and predetermined. What may appear to be little more than an unfortunate turn of events to most might be deemed a transparent instance of injustice to those who endured injury. Since the division between injustice and misfortune is contingent and open to challenge, it is important to probe beyond the causes of harm. In doing so, we must take into account the sufferer's point of view, what she calls "the victim's perspective." Shklar seems to envision an exchange that brings together the "irreducibly subjective" victim's perception of injustice and society's own equally subjective investment in relegating injustices to misfortunes.[8]

One way to characterize her proposal, therefore, is that in contrast to campaigns to silence or curb victim talk, Shklar suggests that we need more victim talk (or at least to encourage victims to talk as victims). Her theorization of politically actionable suffering, however, is very preliminary. Where, for instance, did she hope these discussions might take place, how would such encounters navigate the traps of mutual accusations, and to what extent should political decisions incorporate victims' perspectives? Most importantly, Shklar does not consider the extent to which anti-victimism shapes the victim's subjectivity and thereby impedes, if not precludes, the sort of intersubjective dialogue she envisaged.

Minow's work, "Surviving Victim Talk" (1993), wrestles primarily with the complications of adjudicating competing claims of injury. In contrast to

Shklar, Minow worries that victim claims overwhelm the public with excessive petitions, making it very difficult for institutions to arbitrate grievances and differentiate among those that deserve attention and those that do not. Victim language generates only two absolute positions, she argues, victims and victimizers. Since there is nothing beyond this binary, political exchanges degenerate into cycles of figurative shouting matches, with little possibility of resolution. For every claim of victimization two equally troubling counterclaims are possible—a denial ("No, you're not!") or a trump ("No, I'm the real victim here!"). Minow's analysis may provide another explanation for why those who ostensibly oppose victim politics are propelled in effect to adopt it and assume the mantle of victimhood themselves. In a world divided between victims and victimizers, perhaps some seek victim status simply to avoid being viewed as victimizers.

Minow sees great possibility for circumventing the reductive nature of victim talk in the way that tort law allows for a continuum of responsibility. That the injured party (whose legal standing is as a "plaintiff," not a "victim") may have precipitated her own pain and suffering does not undermine her ability to ask for redress, since the modern doctrine of contributory negligence permits degrees in the allocation of compensation.[9] Minow's worthy attempt to introduce nuance to unbending binary oppositions discounts, however, the political context of the contemporary victim debates and the anti-victimist contribution to attaching victimhood to absolute notions of innocence. Her analysis relies on the presumption that these dichotomies are intrinsic to the victim concept. Furthermore, the early 1990s preoccupation with the supposed glut of victim claims seems, in retrospect, overdrawn to say the least.

Minow has since turned her attention to truth and reconciliation commissions as a model for addressing victimization. Such international and national bodies have proliferated in recent years to grapple with atrocities and human rights violations without generating new conflicts in countries such as South Africa, Rwanda, and the former Yugoslavia. Of course, the rise of these forums is as much a product of the inability of conventional courts to handle the sheer range and number of violations as the potential problems in litigating victim claims. Promoting the idea that truth telling itself is a form of justice, many scholars highlight additional benefits for victims, perpetrators, and society. Truth telling, proponents maintain, sublimates vengeance and in doing so, allows for the possibility of forgiveness without forgetting. Testifying before and, as importantly, being heard by such commissions "potentially holds independent value for the individual victims and for the nation," explains Minow. "The process of engaging official listeners in hearing from victims, and broadcasting that process before a listening public, accomplishes some important healing for individuals and for societies." [10]

These forums may be useful to emerging democracies, but their applicability to contemporary American politics is highly questionable. Truth and reconciliation commissions ostensibly depoliticize suffering. There is no need to debate or deliberate collectively, for there will be no compensation or redistribution. The point is to bear witness, to give testimony, to assemble a factual record as well as the therapeutics of the process, the benefits of "healing."

## "We Must Complain"

Most attempts to theorize victimization so far have been rather disappointing—trapped in a liberal calculus of petitions and resources, in the procedures of legalistic discourse, in a therapeutics that reduces grievance to grief, or seeking to eliminate victimhood from politics altogether. [11] It remains unclear how a radical political theory that deploys victimization as its organizing principle might work. How, for example, might "victim" perform differently than other concepts used to designate inequality, such as "discrimination," "exploitation," "racism," "sexism," or "homophobia"? At a minimum, before exploring the potential a grammar of victimization might have for emancipatory politics and social policy, victimhood must first be unshackled from the anti-victimist manacle.

At the same time, a simple point needs reiteration: acknowledging victimization has been and can be the stepping-stone toward emancipation rather than a corridor to despair, fatalism, enduring powerlessness, and eternal dependence. For instance, when in the early 1960s Malcolm X declared that whites victimized blacks, he did not betray weakness or dependency. Rather he made a militant statement for direct political action through conventional means such as voting, a fact strikingly evident to his contemporaries.

> No, I'm not an American. I'm one of the 22 million black people who are the victims of Americanism. . . . I'm speaking as a victim of this American system. And I see America through the eyes of the victim. I don't see any American dream; I see an American nightmare. These 22 million victims are waking up. Their eyes are coming open. They're beginning to see what they used to only look at. They're becoming politically mature. [12]

Perhaps, then, the problem lies not in the absence of a better understanding of victimhood or our need for more sophisticated and precise mechanisms to allocate blame, innocence, punishments, rewards, and protections. Both the enterprises of crafting a theory of victimhood, or seeking to banish victimhood from politics, ignore the actual contexts in which claims of victimization emerge as well as the circumstances under which, over the last decade or so, victims have been demonized. The "trouble with victims" today does not target a Platonic universal victim but contests progressive politics, multiculturalism, major aspects of the Great Society, and the welfare state.

In facing the anti-victimist challenge, therefore, we should neither celebrate victimhood, nor jettison it altogether. Quite the opposite, we must insist on its demystification, its usability, and its propriety in designating social injustice, especially that to which groups, classes, and communities are subjected.[13] It is not that the concept of the victim has an inherent value that is absent in other terms of injustice. In dispensing with "victim," however, we succumb to an ongoing campaign to purge our language, our consciousness, and our public sphere of words and concepts (such as "feminist" or "liberal") that acquired the taint of illegitimacy simply based on their association with progressive politics. In forfeiting our vocabulary, we risk losing our ability to talk about structural inequality, systematic domination, and collective life. We thus diminish our capacity to speak truth to power and to ourselves, and to effectively politicize injustice. W. E. B. DuBois perhaps put it best:

> What must we do? We must complain. Yes, plain, blunt complaint, ceaseless agitation, unfailing exposure of dishonesty and wrong—this is the ancient, unerring way to liberty, and we must follow it. I know the ears of the American people have become very sensitive to . . . complaint of late and profess to dislike whining. Let that worry none. No nation on earth ever complained and whined so much as this nation has, and we propose to follow the example.[14]

Notes

# Notes

## Chapter 1

1. Charles Sykes, *A Nation of Victims: The Decay of the American Character* (New York: St. Martin's Press, 1992).

2. John Taylor, "Don't Blame Me! The New Culture of Victimization," *New York Magazine*, June 3, 1991, 28.

3. Larry Elder, "Attack of the Victicrat," *FrontPage Magazine*, September 4, 1999, www.frontpagemagazine.com.

4. Katherine Finkelstein, "Year After Brick Attack, Refusing to 'Tiptoe Around Life,'" *New York Times*, December 24, 2000.

5. Trisha Meili, *I Am the Central Park Jogger: A Story of Hope and Possibility* (New York: Scribner's, 2003).

6. Marcia Chambers, "Sua Sponte: Victims of Their Own Success," *National Law Journal*, November 22, 1993, 15–16; Wendy Kaminer, *It's All the Rage: Crime and Culture* (Reading, MA: Addison-Wesley, 1995); Sharon Lamb, *The Trouble with Blame: Victims, Perpetrators, and Responsibility* (Cambridge, MA: Harvard University Press, 1996).

7. David Clarke quoted in Heather MacDonald, "Heralds of a Brighter Black Future," *City Journal* 15 (Spring 2005), 27.

8. George W. Bush, "President Discusses War on Terror at National Endowment for Democracy" (speech, Ronald Reagan Building and International Trade Center, Washington, DC, October 6, 2005).

9. Errol Smith, "It's the Values, Stupid," *New Democrat*, November 1993, 12.

10. Michael Rogin, *Ronald Reagan, the Movie: And Other Episodes of Political Demonology* (Berkeley: University of California Press, 1988), 284.

11. Barbara Welter coined the phrase "the cult of true womanhood." Welter, "The Cult of True Womanhood, 1820–1860," in *Dimity Convictions: The American Woman in the Nineteenth Century* (Athens: Ohio University Press, 1976), 21–41.

12. James Bayley, "The Concept of Victimhood," in *To Be a Victim: Encounters with Crime and Injustice*, ed. Diane Sank and David Caplan (New York: Plenum, 1991), 53, 61.

13. Fredrich Nietzsche, *Ecce Homo*, trans. Walter Kaufmann (New York: Vintage, 1969), II-10, 258.

14. Shelby Steele, *The Content of Our Character: A New Vision of Race in America* (New York: St. Martin's Press, 1990).

15. Wendy Brown, *States of Injury: Power and Freedom in Late Modernity* (Princeton, NJ: Princeton University Press, 1995), 21. For an earlier analysis of the hazards of relying on law and courts for addressing social injustice, see Kristin Bumiller, *The Civil Rights Society: The Social Construction of Victims* (Baltimore: Johns Hopkins University Press, 1992).

16. Louis Althusser, "Ideology and Ideological State Apparatuses (Notes Towards an Investigation)," in *Lenin and Philosophy and Other Essays* (London: New Left Books, 1971/1977). Note parallels to Judith Butler's views of subjection (*The Psychic Life of Power: Theories in Subjection* [Stanford: Stanford University Press, 1997]).

17. Judith Shklar, *Ordinary Vices* (New York: Belknap Press, 1984), 17; see also Shklar, *The Faces of Injustice* (New Haven, CT: Yale University Press, 1990).

18. Susan Bickford, "Anti-Anti-Identity Politics: Feminism, Democracy, and the Complexities of Citizenship," *Hypatia* 12 (Fall 1997), 127.

19. Karl Marx, "German Ideology," in *The Marx-Engels Reader*, ed. Robert Tucker (New York: Norton, 1845/1978), 160.

20. Carol Hanisch, "Personal Politics," in *Radical Feminism: A Documentary Reader*, ed. Barbara Crow (New York: New York University Press, 1970/2000), 113.

21. Compare, for example, Stanley Elkins, *Slavery: A Problem in American Institutional and Intellectual Life* (Chicago: University of Chicago Press, 1959) and Lawrence Levine, *Black Culture and Black Consciousness: Afro-American Folk Thought from Slavery to Freedom* (New York: Oxford University Press, 1977).

22. Compare, for example, Kate Millet, *Sexual Politics* (New York: Doubleday, 1970) and Carol Smith-Rosenberg, *Disorderly Conduct: Visions of Gender in Victorian America* (New York: Knopf, 1985).

23. Linda Gordon, "What's New in Women's History," in *Feminist Studies/Critical Studies*, ed. Teresa de Lauretis (Bloomington: Indiana University Press, 1986), 20–30.

24. Robert Elias, *The Politics of Victimization* (New York: Oxford University Press, 1986); Lynne Henderson, "The Wrongs of Victims' Rights," *Stanford Law Review* 37 (April 1985), 937–1021.

25. It is worth noting that "reverse discrimination" is an American coinage. The *Oxford English Dictionary*, for instance, includes "positive discrimination" but has no entry under "reverse discrimination." Reverse discrimination encapsulates the idea of victimists as victimizers.

26. Gertrude Himmelfarb, *The De-moralization of Society: From Victorian Virtues to Modern Values* (New York: Knopf, 1995).

27. David Harvey, *The Condition of Postmodernity: An Inquiry into the Origins of Cultural Change* (New York: Blackwell, 1989).

28. A religious rhetorical form, often referred to as a "political sermon," the jeremiad conceives of its audience as a chosen people who have transgressed from the covenant that graced them. It, therefore, simultaneously identifies sinners and calls for national redemption. Sacvan Bercovitch explains that jeremiads rely upon ideals of "cultural revitalization" and "the terms of the American myth" (*The American Jeremiad* [Madison: University of Wisconsin Press, 1978], 179). Most important for our purposes, morality and immorality, transgression and redemption, are conceived as matters of individual actions and will. The problem rests with discrete individuals, not the system. In fact, adhering more strictly to the system's fundamental values will lead to redemption. Cf., also, Perry Miller, *The New England Mind: From Colony to Province* (Cambridge, MA: Harvard University Press, 1953); John Murphy, " 'A Time of Shame and Sorrow': Robert F. Kennedy and the American Jeremiad," *Quarterly Journal of Speech* 76 (1990), 401–14.

29. Thomas Laqueur, "Bodies, Details, and the Humanitarian Narrative," in *The New Cultural History: Essays*, ed. Lynn Hunt (Berkeley: University of California Press, 1989).

30. Oz Frankel, *States of Inquiry: Social Investigations and Print Culture in Nineteenth Century Britain and the United States* (Baltimore: Johns Hopkins University Press, 2006).

31. Patricia Nelson Limerick, *The Legacy of Conquest: The Unbroken Past of the American West* (New York: Norton, 1987), 47.

32. Tony Horowitz, *Confederates in the Attic: Dispatches from the Unfinished Civil War* (New York: Vintage, 1998).

33. Gaines Foster, *Ghosts of the Confederacy: Defeat, the Lost Cause, and the Emergence of the New South, 1865 to 1913* (New York: Oxford University Press, 1987); David Blight, *Race and Reunion: The Civil War in American Memory* (Cambridge, MA: Harvard University Press, 2002).

34. Randy Roberts and James Olson, *A Line in the Sand: The Alamo in Blood and Memory* (New York: Free Press, 2001).

35. Eyal Naveh, *Crown of Thorns: Political Martyrdom in America from Abraham Lincoln to Martin Luther King, Jr.* (New York: New York University Press, 1990). See also Michael Rogin, "The King's Two Bodies: Lincoln, Wilson, Nixon, and Presidential Sacrifice," in *Ronald Reagan, the Movie*, 81–114.

36. Bernard Bailyn, *The Ideological Origins of the American Revolution* (Cambridge, MA: Harvard University Press, 1967). Historian Edmund Morgan demonstrated how

the American conception of freedom rested upon the institution of slavery, and thus, eighteenth-century Virginia could be both the largest slaveholding colony and the birthplace of the American Revolution (*American Slavery/American Freedom* [New York: Norton, 1975]).

37. David Roediger, *The Wages of Whiteness: Race and the Making of the American Working Class* (London: Verso, 1991).

38. The Assistant Attorney General also invoked King's legacy as he defined his plans to address lingering civil rights disparities but warned against what he called "victim politics" (Assistant Attorney General Ralph Boyd Jr., "Remarks" [speech, University of Missouri, St. Louis, MO, January 20, 2003]).

39. Peter Novick, *The Holocaust in American Life* (New York: Houghton Mifflin, 1999).

40. For instance, see Primo Levi, *The Drowned and the Saved* (New York: Vintage, 1988); Lawrence Langer, *Holocaust Testimonies: The Ruins of Memory* (New Haven, CT: Yale University Press, 1991).

41. Slavoj Žižek, *Welcome to the Desert of the Real! Five Essays on September 11 and Related Days* (London: Verso, 2002).

42. Jacqueline Scherer, "An Overview of Victimology," in *Victimization of the Weak: Contemporary Social Reactions*, ed. Jacqueline Scherer and Gary Shephard (Springfield, IL: Charles C Thomas, 1982), 14.

43. William Ryan, *Blaming the Victim*, 2nd ed. (New York: Vintage, 1976).

44. Raymond Williams, *Keywords: A Vocabulary of Culture and Society* (New York: Oxford University Press, 1983/1976), 22.

45. Ibid., 16.

## Chapter 2

1. Jules Feiffer, "This World," *San Francisco Chronicle-Examiner*, July 11, 1993.

2. Roger Connors quoted in John Taylor, "Don't Blame Me! The New Culture of Victimization," *New York Magazine*, June 3, 1991, 26–34.

3. Peter Hamill, "A Confederacy of Complainers," *Esquire*, July 1991, 26–30. Another essay featured Powell as a "success victim." John Taylor writes, "Blacks—like Colin Powell—who do integrate are sometimes accused of betraying their race by shedding their status as victims" (Taylor, "Don't Blame Me!" 34). Rejecting racial "victocrat dogma" recently found new proponents; see Heather MacDonald, "Heralds of a Brighter Black Future," *City Journal* 15 (Spring 2005), 24–35.

4. In addition to works cited elsewhere in this chapter, cf. Bette Harrison, "Playing the Blame Game," *Cosmopolitan*, November 1988, 232–35; Fredrick Lynch, *Invisible Victims: White Males and the Crisis of Affirmative Action* (New York: Praeger, 1991); Jesse Birnbaum, "Crybabies: Eternal Victims," *Time*, August 12, 1991; Jacob Weisberg, "The Accuser: Kimberly Bergalis, AIDS Martyr," *New Republic*, October 21, 1991,

12–15; David Reiff, "Victim's All? Recovery, Co-Dependency, and the Art of Blaming Somebody Else," *Harper's*, October 1991; Amy Saltzman and Ted Gest, "Your New Civil Rights," *U.S. News & World Report*, November 18, 1991; Thomas Hazlett, "Nobody Here But Us Victims," *Reason*, January 1992; Gretchen Morgenson, "A Whiner's Bible," *Forbes*, March 16, 1992; John Leo, "A 'Victim' Census for Our Times," *U.S. News & World Report*, November 23, 1992; William Farrell, *The Myth of Male Power* (New York: Simon & Schuster, 1993); Ruben Navarrette, "New Victims?" *Change*, March 1993, 8–12; Ruth Shalit, "Romper Room," *New Republic*, March 29, 1993, 13–16; David Gates, "White Male Paranoia," *Newsweek*, March 29, 1993, 48–53; Ellis Cose, "To the Victors, Few Spoils," *Newsweek*, March 29, 1993, 54; Benjamin Wittes and Janet Wittes, "Group Therapy," *New Republic*, April 5, 1993, 15–16; Joel Brinkley, "Lobbying Rule of 1990's: Show the Most Vulnerable," *New York Times*, June 16, 1993; Lino Graglia, "Beyond Racism: Affirmative Discrimination," *National Review*, July 5, 1993, 26–31; Heather MacDonald, "The Diversity Industry," *New Republic*, July 5, 1993, 22–26; Richard Bernstein, "A Publisher of Conservative Books Complains," *New York Times*, July 19, 1993; Bunny Hoest and John Reiner, "Laugh Parade" (cartoon), *San Francisco Examiner*, July 25, 1993; Jon Berry, "Culture of Complaint," *Brandweek*, July 29, 1993, 32–43; Camille Paglia, "A Case for the Reform of Feminism," *San Francisco Examiner*, August 1, 1993; Anna Quindlen, "Tied to the Tracks," *New York Times*, November 14, 1993; Edmund White, "The Politics of Identity," *New York Times*, December 21, 1993; George Fletcher, "Convicting the Victim," *New York Times*, February 7, 1994; Brent Staples, "The Rhetoric of Victimhood," *New York Times*, February 13, 1994; Raspberry, "Problems, Inc.," *Family Circle*, February 22, 1994, 162; Editorial, "Sufferers All," *Economist*, February 26, 1994, 15; Albert Shanker, "Victim History" (advertisement), *New York Times*, April 10, 1994; Cathy Young, "Man Troubles," *Reason*, July 1994, 18–25; Colman McCarthy, "The Harm of Taking Cover in Racial Rift," *Washington Post*, September 13, 1994; William Raspberry, "The Need for Enemies," *Washington Post*, September 18, 1994; Jim Cullen, "Angry White Men and the Polls," *Texas Observer*, October 28, 1994; Berkeley Breathed, "Outland" (cartoon), *Washington Post*, November 12, 1994; Editorial, "White Guys," *Washington Post*, November 22, 1994; Phil McCombs, "The White Guys' Lament," *Washington Post*, December 3, 1994; Ellen Goodman, "White Men Look Back—in Anxiety," *Boston Globe*, December 3, 1994; Richard Goldstein, "Save the Males: The Making of the Butch Backlash," *Village Voice*, March 7, 1995; Clyde Haberman, "Victims Victorious: Angry White Men," *Village Voice*, March 7, 1995; John Leo, "Hey, We're All Victims Here," *U.S. News & World Report*, December 8, 2003, 80.

5. Observing this trend Kurtz suggests that the strategy succeeds because the public "tends to believe [these] victims, not the politician." Howard Kurtz, "Ads Use Crimes' Pain for Candidates' Gain," *Washington Post*, November 2, 1994. See also E. J. Dionne, "Phony Populism," *Washington Post*, November 1, 1994, where he sug-

gests that a primary tactic employed by the Republicans was to cast the entire society as a victim of government; and Richard Lacayo, "Lock 'Em Up!" *Time*, February 7, 1994, 50–53.

6. Shelby Steele, *The Content of Our Character: A New Vision of Race in America* (New York: St. Martin's Press, 1990), 33.

7. For more on the trope of the welfare queen in American politics, see Ange-Marie Hancock, *The Politics of Disgust: The Public Identity of the Welfare Queen* (New York: New York University Press, 2004).

8. Charles Sykes, *A Nation of Victims: The Decay of the American Character* (New York: St. Martin's Press, 1992), 134. See also Trevor Armbrister, "A Good Law Gone Bad," *Reader's Digest*, May 1998; Walter Olson, "Disabling America," *National Review*, May 5, 1997. For a scholarly analysis of ADA, see Thomas Burke, "On the Rights Track: The Americans with Disabilities Act," in *Comparative Disadvantages? Social Regulations and the Global Economy*, ed. Pietro Nivola (Washington, DC: Brookings Institute, 1997), 247–72.

9. John Stossel, *Give Me a Break: How I Exposed Hucksters, Cheats, and Scam Artists and Became the Scourge of the Liberal Media* (New York: HarperCollins, 2004), 203.

10. Dinesh D'Souza, *Illiberal Education: The Politics of Race and Sex on Campus* (New York: Free Press, 1991), 14. The university is a common site of victimism identified in the literature (Sykes, *Nation of Victims*, xiii; Alan Dershowitz, *The Abuse Excuse: And Other Cop-Outs, Sob Stories, and Evasions of Responsibility* [Boston: Little, Brown, 1994], 287–90; Robert Hughes, *Culture of Complaint: The Fraying of America* [New York: Oxford University Press, 1993], 81–152; Steele, *Content of Our Character*, 111–49; Stephen Carter, *Reflections of an Affirmative Action Baby* [New York: Basic Books, 1991], 11–28, 47–98). The connection between multiculturalism, political correctness, Afro-centrism, and other efforts undertaken by universities to support segments of the student population has generated numerous books. Among them, *The Disuniting of America: Reflections on a Multicultural Society* (New York: Norton, 1991) by Arthur Schlesinger Jr. holds a prominent place in this literature, especially his discussion of the victimist uses of history as well as his fear that the university is a bellwether of things to come.

11. Dershowitz, *Abuse Excuse*, 45, 8–11.

12. Wiley, "Non Sequitur," *The Washington Post*, December 11, 1994.

13. Sykes, *Nation of Victims*, xiii, 22, 3–10, 95, 17.

14. Ibid., 11.

15. Ibid., 15.

16. Hughes, *Culture of Complaint*, 162.

17. Since the publication of Hughes's book there have been at least two prominent debates over "victim art." Choreographer Bill T. Jones's use of dancers with AIDS and other terminal illnesses in "Still/Here" was the source of one controversy, cf. Arlene Croce, "Discussing the Undiscussible," *New Yorker*, December 24, 1995, 54–60; "Who's

the Victim? Dissenting Voices Answer Arlene Croce's Critique of Victim Art," *New Yorker*, January 30, 1995, 10–13; Joyce Carol Oates, "Confronting Head On the Face of the Afflicted," *New York Times*, February 18, 1995. For a thoughtful analysis of Croce's reaction, cf. Elizabeth Spelman, *Fruits of Sorrow: Framing Our Attention to Suffering* (Boston: Beacon, 1997), 133–56. A second debate emerged in 1996 after the release of the film *Shine*, which depicted the story of pianist David Helfgott. The fictional account in the film received praise, while the subsequent concert tour by Helfgott sparked dispute. For more on victim art, see M. Christakos, "Dispositions: Undressing Victim Art," *MIX*, Fall 1995; M. Berger, *The Crisis of Criticism* (New York: New Press, 1998).

18. Sykes, *Nation of Victims*, 3, 7, 4–5.

19. Dershowitz, *Abuse Excuse*, 273; D'Souza, *Illiberal Education*, 195, 214, 216, 246–48; see also Carter, *Affirmative Action Baby*, 103, 170; Schlesinger, *Disuniting of America*, 94, 99, 116.

20. D'Souza, *Illiberal Education*, 243.

21. Ibid., 239; see also 6, 49–51, 127, 197, 209.

22. Dershowitz, *Abuse Excuse*, 113, 279–81, 311–13; see also Sykes, *Nation of Victims*, 185.

23. Dershowitz, *Abuse Excuse*, 271.

24. Gates, "White Male Paranoia," 48–53; Cose, "To Victors, Few Spoils," 54; Young, "Man Troubles," 18–25; Cullen, "Angry White Men and the Polls"; Goodman, "White Men Look Back"; Goldstein, "Save the Males," 25–27; Haberman, "Victims Victorious," 31–33.

25. D'Souza, *Illiberal Education*, 203–4; Sykes, *Nation of Victims*, 167; Steele, *Content of Our Character*, 73–74; Carter, *Affirmative Action Baby*, 101–2, 126, 170.

26. Dershowitz, *Abuse Excuse*, 28. Stephen Carter likewise divulges his fear and continuing battles as a "black dissenter" in his meditation on victimhood, *Affirmative Action Baby*, 115, 253.

27. Sykes, *Nation of Victims*, 212–13; Steele, *Content of Our Character*, 157; Hughes, *Culture of Complaint*, 19; Carter, *Affirmative Action Baby*, 187, 215, 220–22; Wendy Kaminer, *I'm Dysfunctional, You're Dysfunctional: The Recovery Movement and Other Self-Help Fashions* (Reading, MA: Addison-Wesley, 1992), 153, 172–74.

28. Steele, *Content of Our Character*, 29, 61.

29. Ibid., 67.

30. Ibid., 23–24, 26.

31. Ibid., 69.

32. Ibid., 10.

33. Dinesh D'Souza, *The End of Racism: Principles for a Multiracial Society* (New York: Free Press, 1995), 528.

34. Steele, *Content of Our Character*, 78–79, 88–91; Shelby Steele, "The Age of White Guilt and the Disappearance of the Black Individual," *Harper's*, November 2002, 33–43.

188 Notes to Chapter 2

35. Sykes, *Nation of Victims*, 50, 60.

36. D'Souza, *Illiberal Education*, 122.

37. Sykes, *Nation of Victims*, 61, 95–96, 212–13. Camille Paglia also describes contemporary (victim) feminism as being stuck in an "adolescent whining mode," an "endless prolongation of childhood . . . coddling and pampering of people who are in fact adults" (*Sex, Art, and American Culture: Essays* [New York: Vintage, 1992], 4, 67, 113. Cf. Chapter 3). Even Martha Minow's careful explication of the paradoxes sustained by victim claims relies upon contrasting "victim-talk" from "grown-up talk" ("Surviving Victim Talk," *UCLA Law Review* 40, 1432).

38. Hughes, *Culture of Complaint*, 8–11, 48, 50–55. See also, Peter Carlson, "Self-Help: America's One True Faith," *Washington Post*, February 12, 1995.

39. Kaminer, *I'm Dysfunctional*, 40.

40. Ibid., 18, 24, 40, 94, 149, 30, xii.

41. Cf., for example, Wendy Kaminer, *It's All the Rage: Crime and Culture* (Reading, MA: Addison-Wesley, 1995); Wendy Kaminer, "Can Someone Be a Victim and Still Be Guilty?" *San Francisco Examiner*, December 23, 1994. Kaminer also appeared on ABC's *Nightline*, along with Dershowitz, arguing this very point. "Is Abuse an Excuse?" *Nightline*, ABC, February 4, 1994.

42. Dershowitz, *Abuse Excuse*, 138. At the end of his book, Dershowitz includes a twenty-page glossary of these syndromes, including the "black rage defense," "nicotine withdrawal syndrome," and the "Twinkie defense," among others (*Abuse Excuse*, 323, 89–92, 331, 339). See also Sykes, *Nation of Victims*, 147–49. For a less polemical consideration of the rise in syndrome defenses, see Donald Downs, *More Than Victims: Battered Women, the Syndrome Society, and the Law* (Chicago: University of Chicago Press, 1996).

43. Dershowitz, *Abuse Excuse*, 42.

44. Some regard anti-victimist texts as part of the self-esteem genre, even those that do not offer specific therapeutic prescriptions or formulas. This is the perspective from which Adolph Reed Jr. reviews *The Content of Our Character*, arguing that "Steele gives racial self-help rhetoric a comforting, all-American frame—inequality as a form of codependency. His analysis is tailor-made for Oprah, Sally Jessy and Phil" ("Steele Trap," *Nation*, March 4, 1991, 279). For a similar critique of Steele's approach, see Yoong Lee, "A Bleak Portrait of Black America," *Indianapolis (IN) Recorder*, September 5, 1992.

45. Kaminer, *I'm Dysfunctional*, 81, xvii–xx.

46. Sykes, *Nation of Victims*, 18–20.

47. *City of Richmond v. J. A. Croson Co.*, S.Ct. 706, 730 (1989).

48. D'Souza, *Illiberal Education*, 33–35.

49. Kaminer, *I'm Dysfunctional*, 82.

50. D'Souza, *Illiberal Education*, 243.

51. Sykes's discussion relies on an essay by political scientist James Q. Wilson. In his 1985 article, "The Rediscovery of Character: Private Virtue and Public Policy," Wilson argued that the most pressing social problems, welfare and crime in particular, could be understood and resolved only through recognizing large-scale "defects in our character formation" (Sykes, *Nation of Victims*, 242–43). Steele does not credit anyone, but I suspect that his work was influenced by Glenn Loury, especially "The Moral Quandary of the Black Community," *Public Interest* 79 (1985). Note also similarities with Orlando Patterson's earlier essay "The Moral Crisis of the Black American," *Public Interest* 32 (1973), where he explains, "There can be no moral equality where there is a dependency relationship among men; there will always be a dependency relationship where the victim strives for equality by vainly seeking the assistance of his victimizer. No oppressor can ever respect such a victim, whatever he may do for him. . . ." (68).

52. Consider how the "Post Traumatic Slave Syndrome" playwright describes her project: "I did not want this to become a blaming session or a 'Woe is me piece.' I was always clear that this was about individual responsibility and looking in the mirror at oneself. I wanted people to recognize their individual illness within this epidemic" (Kamal Sinclair Steele, "NYTheatre Voices," www.nytheatre.com/nytheatre/v_steele .htm [May 28, 2002]).

53. While self-help groups might not conform to conventional conceptions of identity politics, Kaminer echoes many of the complaints regarding the groups' suppression of individuality (Kaminer, *I'm Dysfunctional*, 6). She reports that members are encouraged to see themselves through a lens of the abuse they suffered, as passive recipients, not active agents of change (Ibid., 13; see also 21–22, 28, 164).

54. Steele, *Content of Our Character*, 96.

55. Ibid., 71, 100, 107.

56. Ibid., x, xi.

57. Ibid., 160.

58. Sykes, *Nation of Victims*, 213–15, 219; Hughes, *Culture of Complaint*, 4; Steele, *Content of Our Character*, 71; Carter, *Affirmative Action Baby*, 215.

59. Sykes, *Nation of Victims*, 224.

60. Carter, *Affirmative Action Baby*, 206.

61. D'Souza, *Illiberal Education*, 51.

62. Sykes, *Nation of Victims*, 18–20.

63. Ibid., 71–72.

64. Ibid., 77. Camille Paglia also frequently characterizes victimism (in the women's movement) as Rousseauist to the point that "Rousseauist" functions as an expletive in her text. Cf. Paglia, *Sex, Art*, 66, 103; see also 34, 50, 105–6, 175, 208, 216, 230, 242.

65. Jean-Jacques Rousseau, *On the Social Contract*, ed. Rogers Masters, trans., Judith Masters (New York: St. Martin's Press, 1762/1978).

66. D'Souza, *America*, 154.

67. Sykes, *Nation of Victims*, 75–77. Sykes's analysis of the intellectual origins of victimism draws extensively from Joseph Amato's *Victims and Values: A History and Theory of Suffering* (New York: Greenwood, 1990).

68. Shelby Steele, "Culture Wars: Selma to San Francisco?" *Wall Street Journal*, March 20, 2004.

69. Edward Linenthal, *Preserving Memory: The Struggle to Create America's Holocaust Museum* (New York: Viking, 1995).

70. Sara Bershtal and Allen Graubard, *Saving Remnants: Feeling Jewish in America* (New York: Free Press, 1992).

71. Peter Novick, *The Holocaust in American Life* (New York: Houghton Mifflin, 1999); Alvin Rosenfeld, "The Americanization of the Holocaust," *Commentary*, June 1995, 35–40. Indeed, a lively debate reemerged in the late 1990s about Jews—both American and Israeli—exploiting the memory of the Holocaust; see Zygmunt Bauman, "The Holocaust's Life as a Ghost," *Tikkun* (July/August 1998), 33–39; Leon Wieseltier, "Shrunken," *New Republic*, November 9, 1998, 50. See also the controversy over the field of Holocaust Studies, which some critics refer to as "victim studies." (Cf. Ruth Wisse and Steven Katz, "A Debate about Teaching the Holocaust," *New York Times*, August 8, 1998.) But see Lucy Dawidowicz, "How They Teach the Holocaust," *Commentary*, December 1990, 25–33, who claims that Holocaust studies have been a victim of "oppression studies."

72. Sykes, *Nation of Victims*, 17.

73. The anti-victimist backlash has been remarkably successful in shaming victims. In addition to the other examples mentioned in the chapter, consider the following disavowals of victimhood: Lally Weymouth, "J.C. Watts: No Excuses," *Washington Post*, February 15, 1995; Francis Davis, "One Scats, the Other Doesn't," *New York Times Book Review*, September 25, 1994; and E. R. Shipp, "O.J. and the Black Media," *Columbia Journalism Review* 33 (November/December 1994), 39–41. Also note the renewed interest in shaming as punishment, cf. Pam Belluck, "Forget Prisons: Americans Cry Out for the Pillory," *New York Times*, October 4, 1998, 5.

74. D'Souza, *Illiberal Education*, 18–19, 67, 81; Steele, *Content of Our Character*, 127–48; Sykes, *Nation of Victims*, 73; Dershowitz, *Abuse Excuse*, 45–46, 138; Carter, *Affirmative Action Baby*, 7, 199; Kaminer, *I'm Dysfunctional*, 17, 45–46, 59, 73.

75. Sykes, *Nation of Victims*, 254. Steele, *Content of Our Character*, 23, 54, 61, 99, 100, 108, 112, 122–23, 142, 169. Patricia Williams describes Carter's *Reflections* in similar terms. She detects in his texts symptoms of "intellectual bulimia," finding his fear of criticism unwarranted, indeed "paranoid" ("Nothing but the Best," *Nation*, November 18, 1991, 632–38).

## Chapter 3

1. Katie Roiphe, *The Morning After: Sex, Fear, and Feminism on Campus* (Boston: Little, Brown, 1993), 12.

2. For other examples of the genre, see Elizabeth Fox-Genovese, *"Feminism Is Not the Story of My Life": How Today's Feminist Elite Has Lost Touch with the Real Concerns of Women* (New York: Doubleday, 1996); Ellen R. Klein, *Feminism under Fire* (New York: Prometheus, 1996); Karen Lehrman, *The Lipstick Proviso: Women, Sex, and Power in the Real World* (New York: Anchor, 1997); Daphne Patai and Noretta Koertge, *Professing Feminism: Cautionary Tales from the Strange World of Women's Studies* (New York: Basic Books, 1994).

3. Victim feminists' reign on campuses is the focus of Roiphe's book, but these other writers also identify universities as a central site of victim feminist training, what Hoff Sommers refers to as feminists' "colonization of the liberal academy." Cf. Naomi Wolf, *Fire with Fire: The New Female Power and How It Will Change the 21st Century* (New York: Random House, 1993), 123–26; Camille Paglia, *Sex, Art, and American Culture: Essays* (New York: Vintage, 1992), 170–248; Rene Denfeld, *The New Victorians: A Young Woman's Challenge to the Old Feminist Order* (New York: Warner Books, 1995), 7, 9–10, 210–11, 261, 278–79; Christina Hoff Sommers, *Who Stole Feminism? How Women Have Betrayed Women* (New York: Simon & Schuster, 1994), 50–73, 87–117. See also Christina Hoff Sommers, "Sister Soldiers," *New Republic*, October 5, 1992, 29–33; Patai and Koertge, *Professing Feminism*.

4. Christina Hoff Sommers, "Has Feminism Gone Too Far?" *Think Tank with Ben Wattenberg*, National Public Radio, November 4, 1994. On feminists as a gloomy bunch, cf. Paglia, *Sex, Art*, 33, 37, 61–62, 67, 116, 250, 263; Wolf, *Fire with Fire*, 152–55, 196, 229, 236, 242. For an interpretation of Wolf as telling feminists to "cheer up," see Laura Shapiro, "She Enjoys Being a Girl," *Newsweek*, November 15, 1993, 82; Karen Lehrman, "Women's Hour," *New Republic*, March 14, 1994, 40–45; Michiko Kakutani, "Suggestions for an Era of Practical Feminism," *New York Times*, December 3, 1993.

5. On cosmetics and other adornments for "fashionable feminists," Wolf, *Fire with Fire*, 186–90; Naomi Wolf, "Radical Heterosexuality," *Ms.* (July/August 1992), 28–31; on bridal wear, Naomi Wolf, "Brideland," in *To Be Real: Telling the Truth and Changing the Face of Feminism*, ed. Rebecca Walker (New York: Anchor, 1995), 35–40; on interior decoration, Wolf, *Fire with Fire*, 152–53; on Rhett Butler fantasies, Hoff Sommers, *Who Stole?*, 261–70; see also Roiphe, "The Independent Woman (and Other Lies)," *Esquire*, February 1997, 84–86, but see Roiphe, *Morning After*, 120–30.

6. Wolf, *Fire with Fire*, xvi–xix, 142.

7. Paglia, *Sex, Art*, vii, 5, 11, 26, 30–31, 63, 213.

8. Wolf, *Fire with Fire*, 136.

9. Ibid., 136–37.

10. Ibid., 94. Comparing victim feminism's "protectionist" efforts on behalf of women to Victorian notions of femininity is a common theme of the genre. This analogy constitutes Denfeld's principal thesis.

11. Paglia, *Sex, Art*, 53.

12. Roiphe, *Morning After*, 35.

13. Hoff Sommers, "Has Feminism Gone Too Far?"; see also Hoff Sommers, "A Bureaucracy of One's Own," *Who Stole?*, 118–36, 272–75.

14. Wolf, *Fire with Fire*, 259–60.

15. Ibid., 178.

16. Ibid., 245–46.

17. Denfeld, *New Victorians*, 15.

18. See, for instance, Hoff Sommers, *Who Stole?*, 74–86, 152–56; Denfeld, *New Victorians*, 169–214; Wolf, *Fire with Fire*, 175–77, 274–75; Roiphe, *Morning After*, 5–7, 158, 171.

19. For example, Carol Gilligan, *In a Different Voice: Psychological Theory and Women's Development* (Cambridge, MA: Harvard University Press, 1982); Sara Ruddick, *Maternal Thinking: Toward a Politics of Peace* (Boston: Beacon, 1989); Joan Tronto, *Moral Boundaries: A Political Argument for an Ethic of Care* (New York: Routledge, 1993).

20. Consider Denfeld who, in her criticism of difference feminism, drifts from Carol Gilligan to Mary Daly within a matter of sentences (*New Victorians*, 15–17).

21. Roiphe, *Morning After*, 102. For other examples of AVFers' vision of women as "sexual explorers and renegades," see Wolf, *Fire with Fire*, 185–96; Denfeld, *New Victorians*, 73, 83–89, 118–23, 258–62. Cf. also Hoff Sommers, *Who Stole?*, 209–26; Sarah Crichton, "Sexual Correctness: Has It Gone Too Far?" *Newsweek*, October 25, 1993, 52.

22. In a 1998 Supreme Court case about same-sex harassment, the Court held that Title VII's prohibition against discrimination "because of . . . sex" protects men as well as women, cf. 96–568: *Oncale v. Sundowner Offshore Services Inc.* 66 USLW 4127 (US March 4, 1998). It is also worth noting that male plaintiffs have won more sex discrimination cases before the Supreme Court than women (David Cole, "Strategies of Difference: Litigating for Women's Rights in a Man's World," *Law & Inequality: A Journal of Theory and Practice* 2, 34 [1984], 33–96).

23. Paglia, *Sex, Art*, 51.

24. Rophie, *Morning After*, 68.

25. Catharine MacKinnon, *Feminism Unmodified: Discourses on Life and Law* (Cambridge, MA: Harvard University Press, 1987). On MacKinnon as the archetype victim feminist: Roiphe, *Morning After*, 138–60; Wolf, *Fire with Fire*, 96, 122, 131, 143, 180; Patai and Koertge, *Professing Feminism*, 127–30, 208; Denfeld, *New Victorians*, 8, 12, 27, 55, 78, 93–98, 100–101, 112–15, 238–44; Hoff Sommers, *Who Stole?*, 231ff.

26. Paglia, *Sex, Art*, 31.

27. Wolf, *Fire with Fire*, 68.

28. Paglia, *Sex, Art*, 278, 29, 32.

29. Time/CNN pollsters found that 94 percent of American women support equal pay for equal work, and 74 percent believe that women have benefited from the accomplishments of the women's movement; but only 37 percent of women considered themselves feminists, and among college-age women, the percentage was a meager 16 percent. Tad Friend, "The Rise of 'Do Me' Feminism," *Esquire*, February 1994, 52; A CBS News poll affirmed this datum a year later. See also Denfeld, *New Victorians*, 2–6; Hoff Sommers, *Who Stole?*, 18; Kaminer, "Feminism's Identity Crisis," *Atlantic Monthly*, October 1993, 51–68; Fox-Genovese, *Feminism Is Not the Story*.

30. Wolf, *Fire with Fire*, 61, 68–72, 126–32. Wolf distinguishes between "gutter homophobia" and heterosexual women's "legitimate worries . . . when feminism and lesbianism are synonyms" in public discourse (*Fire with Fire*, 71–72). I find this a highly problematic distinction.

31. Wolf, *Fire with Fire*, 139.

32. Ibid., 53.

33. Ibid., 304–305.

34. Ibid., 298–99.

35. Denfeld, *New Victorians*, 262–65.

36. Paglia, *Sex, Art*, 3–14.

37. Ibid., 48.

38. Wolf, *Fire with Fire*, 304–305, 152–53, 186–89. Several other AVFers seem to share this perspective. For example, see Hoff Sommers, *Who Stole?*, 261–70, and even Roiphe, *Morning After*, 120–30.

39. It is striking that both Wolf and Paglia fashioned pivotal heroes out of the confrontation between Thomas and Hill. Others viewed these hearings as representing competing victim claims. See Toni Morrison, *Racing Justice, Engendering Power: Essays on Anita Hill, Clarence Thomas, and the Construction of Social Reality* (New York: Pantheon, 1992), esp. vii–xxx, 402–40; Nancy Fraser, "Sex, Lies, and the Public Sphere: Some Reflection on the Confirmation of Clarence Thomas," *Critical Inquiry* 18 (Spring 1992), 595–612; Nell Painter, "Who Was Lynched?" *The Nation*, November 11, 1991, 577–600.

40. Reactions among feminists to specific AVFers' arguments vary in their tone of disapproval, but most commentators position AVF within the tradition of antifeminism. Cf. Moira Ferguson, Ketu Katrak, and Valerie Miner, "Feminism and Anti-Feminism: From Civil Rights to Cultural Wars," in *Anti-Feminism in the Academy*, ed. VèVè Clark et al. (New York: Routledge, 1996), 35–66; Nan Maglin Bauer and Donna Perry, *"Bad Girls"/"Good Girls": Woman, Sex, and Power in the Nineties* (New Brunswick, NJ: Rutgers University Press, 1996); Diane Bell and Renate Klein, ed., *Radically*

*Speaking: Feminism Reclaimed* (Melbourne: Spinifex Press, 1996); Susan Faludi, "I'm Not a Feminist But I Play One on TV," *Ms.* 5 (March/April 1995), 30–40.

41. Anne Snitow, "Gender Diaries," in *Powers of Desire*, ed. Anne Snitow, Christine Stansell, and Sharon Thompson (New York: Monthly Review, 1983), 14.

42. Denfeld, *New Victorians*, 267. See also Hoff Sommers, *Who Stole?*, 22–35, 74–86. Such ideas are not confined to this group of writers; see, for example, Karen Lehrman, "Backlash Backfire," *New Democrat*, November 1993, 17.

43. Germaine Greer, *The Female Eunuch* (New York: McGraw-Hill, 1973); Betty Friedan, *The Feminine Mystique* (New York: Norton, 1963).

44. For an analysis of the genre of postmortems on feminism, see Mary Hawkesworth, "The Semiotics of Premature Burial: Feminism in a Postfeminist Age," *Signs* 29 (Summer 2004), 961–86. According to Rosenfelt and Stacey, the first use of the term "post-feminist" was 1982 (Deborah Rosenfelt and Judith Stacey, "Second Thoughts on the Second Wave," *Feminist Studies* 13 [Summer 1987], 341–61; Susan Bolotin, "Voices from a Post-Feminist Generation," *New York Times Magazine* [October 17, 1982], 28–31, 103ff.). See also, Judith Stacey, "The New Conservative Feminism," *Feminist Studies* 9 [Autumn 1983], 559–83; Arlie Hochschild, "Is the Left Sick of Feminism?" *Mother Jones*, August 1983; Wini Breines, Margaret Cerullo, and Judith Stacey, "Social Biology, Family Studies, and Antifeminist Backlash," *Feminist Studies* 4 (February 1978), 43–67.

45. Like 1990s AVF, 1980s neo-feminism also received a mixed reception among feminists, as can be seen in the confusion over how to designate this rupture with the second wave. Cf. Stacey, "New Conservative Feminism"; Hochschild, "Sick of Feminism"; Rosenfelt Stacey, "Second Thoughts"; Susan Faludi, *Backlash: The Undeclared War Against Women* (New York: Crown, 1991), esp. 282–324; Wendy Kaminer, *A Fearful Freedom: Women's Flight from Equality* (Reading, MA: Addison-Wesley, 1990), esp. 1–10, 87–89.

46. Rosenfelt and Stacey, "Second Thoughts," 41; Tania Modleski, *Feminism Without Women: Culture and Criticism in a "Postfeminist" Age* (Boston: Beacon, 1991), 3. Hochschild observes: "The new anti-feminists are not just nostalgic for old-fashioned women. They actively dislike modern women. If women win equality at work, they warn, look at what happens to them. They lose their knack for 'maternal thinking', says Elshtain. They sadly miss their 'potential contribution to homemaking,' says Illich. Paradoxically, each seems to confine women to the home *not because women are frail clinging vines, but because they are mean, tough mamas*" (emphasis added, "Sick of Feminism," 57).

47. Betty Friedan, *The Second Stage* (New York: Summit, 1981), 282.

48. Ibid., 68, 257.

49. I am not suggesting that victim compounds had never been used before to derogate. As I show, Charlotte Bunch first employed the designation "professional vic-

tims" in the early 1970s. Elshtain also presented her criticisms of the antipornography and antirape campaigns in 1982 under the title "The Victim Syndrome" ("The Victim Syndrome: Troubling Turn in Feminism," *The Progressive* [June 1982], 42–47). My point is simply that we see an important shift and tremendous growth in this pejorative use in the early 1990s, such that "victim" becomes a term of derision requiring no modification such as "professional" or "syndrome."

50. Betty Friedan, *"It Changed My Life": Writings on the Women's Movement* (Cambridge, MA: Harvard University Press, 1998), xii. Of course, just as with the AVFers, her repudiation of others' victimism does not prevent her from elevating her personal experiences of mistreatment into a public struggle, as in her later campaign against age discrimination in *The Fountain of Age* (New York: Simon & Schuster, 1993).

51. On the level of style, it is hard to ignore the rhetorical flourishes so typical of early feminist tracts, including Friedan's. However, what the AVFers consider victimism would within Mary Hawkesworth's theorization be classified as "the rhetoric of oppression." Hawkesworth forcefully argues against conflating style and content: the "rhetoric of oppression" is a strategic choice aimed at "creat[ing] radical consciousness without the personal encounter of violence" (*Beyond Oppression: Feminist Theory and Political Strategy* [New York: Continuum, 1990], 113). For more on the political importance of anger, see Audre Lorde, *Sister Outsider* (Freedom, CA: Crossing Press, 1984), 114–23; Marilyn Frye, "A Note on Anger," *The Politics of Reality: Essays in Feminist Theory* (Freedom, CA: The Crossing Press, 1983), 84–94.

52. Friedan, *Feminine Mystique*, 26. In *The Second Stage*, Friedan suggests that it was precisely when feminists' focus shifted away from white middle-class women that they adopted a divisive sexual politics platform (*Second Stage*, 47, cf. also 48–50, 338).

53. Friedan, *Feminine Mystique*, 31. In *The Feminine Mystique*, as well as in interviews in later years, Friedan presents herself as part of the cohort of those plagued by the mystique. However, her biographer, Daniel Horowitz, offers evidence that this self-presentation is quite different from Friedan's actual biography, and that her move toward psychological analyses was in part a rejection of her past involvement in radical politics (Daniel Horowitz, "Rethinking Betty Friedan and the 'Feminine Mystique': Labor-Union Radicalism in Cold War America," *American Quarterly* 48 [March 1996], 1–42).

54. Friedan, *Feminine Mystique*, 185, 356, 384–85; but see 346–47.

55. Ibid., 386.

56. Ibid., 17, 305.

57. Ibid., 71, 73, 75, 181, 52–53, 154, 166, cf. also 127, 128, 135.

58. Ibid., 180, 382, 101, 96–97.

59. Ibid., 37.

60. Ibid., 305–306.

61. Ibid., 364.

62. For examples of Holocaust metaphors, specifically women as Jews, in other feminists' writings, see Mary Daly, *Gyn/Ecology: The Metaethics of Radical Feminism* (Boston: Beacon, 1978); Andrea Dworkin, *Woman Hating* (New York: E. P. Dutton, 1972); MacKinnon, *Feminism Unmodified*; Susan Brownmiller, *Against Our Will* (New York: Simon & Schuster, 1975). Also note that in her first book Wolf deployed similar comparisons to the Holocaust to emphasize the severity and prevalence of eating disorders among women (Naomi Wolf, *The Beauty Myth* [London: Chatto & Windus, 1990], 159–61, 171–72).

63. Friedan, *Feminine Mystique*, 255, 306. This aspect of my reading of Friedan's analysis was certainly influenced by Hanna Pitkin's interpretation of Arendt's conception of the "social." Cf. Hanna Fenichel Pitkin, *The Attack of the Blob: Hannah Arendt's Concept of the Social* (Chicago: University of Chicago Press, 1998).

64. Friedan, *Feminine Mystique*, 17, 305, 314, 207, 204.

65. Friedan is particularly bothered by male homosexuality and uses it as an indicator of social decay throughout her career: in the 1950s she interprets it as a product of frustrated housewives castrating their sons; whereas in the 1980s she claims the visibility and proliferation of homosexuality demonstrates that men too are victims, as much in need of liberation as women (Friedan, *Second Stage*, 276, 271, 273, 275, 280–81).

66. Friedan, *Feminine Mystique*, 307–8. In *The Second Stage*, she also acknowledges that this was a "rather extreme metaphor" but doesn't retract or alter it (46–47).

67. Friedan, *Feminine Mystique*, 309.

68. Stanley Elkins, *Slavery: A Problem in American Institutional and Intellectual Life* (Chicago: University of Chicago Press, 1959).

69. Friedan, *Feminine Mystique*, 277–83, 308.

70. Ibid., 26, 23, 42, 64, 69, 312.

71. Ibid., 61, 77, 79.

72. Ibid., 231.

73. Ibid., 208, 313–14.

74. Ibid., 307, cf. also 317.

75. Ibid., 101, 317, 336.

76. Ibid., 204.

77. Ibid., 181.

78. This tension in Friedan's theory, between accepting a liberal commitment to individual liberty while simultaneously upholding a conception of women as a group, is the crux of what Zillah Eisenstein sees as the "radical potential" of liberal feminism. However, Eisenstein also notes that Friedan's work does not actualize this potential (*The Radical Future of Liberal Feminism* [Boston: Northeastern University Press, 1981], 183, 179). Friedan never conceded this contradiction, embraced the radical perspective, or repudiated liberalism. Indeed, the thesis of her last book, *Beyond Gender*, was that all forms of class politics must be abandoned.

79. Friedan, *Feminine Mystique*, 384.

80. Friedan, *Second Stage*, 50; *Feminine Mystique*, 390.

81. Members of Redstockings, for example, held that what Friedan claimed was a problem with no name had already been named six years earlier, in *The Second Sex*. Unlike Simone de Beauvoir, however, Friedan "left men out of [her] analysis, [she] somehow blamed the psyches and intelligence of women themselves" (Katie Sarachild, "The Power of History," in *Feminist Revolution*, ed. Katie Sarachild [New York: Random House, 1975], 29).

82. Friedan, *Feminine Mystique*, 304, 310.

83. Ibid., 238.

84. Ibid., 122, 125, 186.

85. Despite her reproach of those who subscribe to Freudian theories for "blaming" women, Friedan's argument winds its way back to precisely the same source: both Freudians and Friedan ultimately blame mothers. For an analysis of the perceived threat of Momism during the cold war, see Michael Rogin, "Kiss Me Deadly: Communism, Motherhood, and Cold War Movies," *Ronald Reagan, the Movie: And Other Episodes in Political Demonology* (Berkeley: University of California Press, 1987), 236–71.

86. Friedan, *Feminine Mystique*, 271, cf. also 189, 190–93, 197.

87. Ibid., 386. In *The Feminine Mystique* she suggested that men are victimized not only by the feminine mystique but also by something she called "the masculine mystique." By the time she writes *Beyond Gender*, which received a dust jacket endorsement from Katie Roiphe, Friedan explains that it is men's suffering—that women have done better, while men have done worse—that convinced her that the time had come to transcend gender politics altogether.

88. Friedan, *Feminine Mystique*, 203.

89. Ibid., 282, 271, 273, 275, 302.

90. Ibid., 364.

91. Ibid., 285–86.

92. Ibid., 334, 284.

93. Kate Millet, *Sexual Politics* (New York: Doubleday, 1970). Patriarchy is a concept with different meanings to those who employ it. Compare, for example, Veronica Beechy, "On Patriarchy," *Feminist Review* 3 (1979), 66–82 and Joseph Interrante and Carol Lasser, "Victims of the Very Songs They Sing: A Critique of Recent Work on Patriarchal Culture and the Construction of Gender," *Radical History Review* 20 (1978), 25–41. My point here is to illustrate some of the initial rumblings about an expansionist, ahistorical view of women's oppression.

94. Cf. Zillah Eisenstein, ed., *Capitalist Patriarchy and the Case for Socialist Feminism* (New York: Monthly Review, 1979).

95. Gayle Rubin, "The Traffic in Women: Notes on the 'Political Economy' of Sex," in *Towards an Anthropology of Women*, ed. Rayne Reiter (New York: Monthly Review, 1975).

96. Sheila Rowbotham, "The Trouble with Patriarchy," in *People's History and Social Theory*, ed. Raphael Samuel (London: Routledge & Kegan Paul, 1981), 364–69.

97. Frigga Haug, *Beyond Female Masochism: Memory-work and Politics* (London: Verso, 1992), 8.

98. Linda Gordon, "What's New in Women's History," in *Feminist Studies/Critical Studies*, ed. Teresa de Lauretis (Bloomington: Indiana University Press, 1986), 20–30.

99. Cf. Alice Echols, *Daring to Be Bad: Radical Feminism in America, 1967–1975* (Minneapolis: University of Minnesota Press, 1989). The politicos were committed to dismantling the sex-class system by obliterating gender differences, whereas the cultural feminists aimed at reversing the cultural devaluation of things marked as "female." For a discussion of a similar schism among first wave feminists, see Cott, *Grounding of Modern Feminism*.

100. See, for example, Jean Baker Miller, *Towards a New Psychology of Women* (Boston: Beacon, 1976).

101. Hester Eisenstein, *Contemporary Feminist Thought* (London: Unwin, 1984), 131.

102. Echols, *Daring to Be Bad*, 287.

103. Gordon, "What's New in Women's History," 25.

104. Lynne Segal, *Is the Future Female? Troubled Thoughts on Contemporary Feminism* (London: Virago, 1987), 4. Cf. also Joan Scott, "Deconstructing Equality-versus-Difference: Or, the Uses of PostFeminism," *Feminist Studies* 14 (Spring 1988), 33–48; and Alcoff, "Cultural Feminism," 303–4.

105. Catharine MacKinnon et al., "Feminist Discourse, Moral Values, and Law—A Conversation," *Buffalo Law Review* 34 (1985), 11, 74–75.

106. MacKinnon, *Feminism Unmodified*, 39.

107. Ibid., 8.

108. Drucilla Cornell, *Beyond Accommodation: Ethical Feminism, Deconstruction, and the Law* (New York: Routledge, 1991), 119–64; Wendy Brown, *States of Injury: Power and Freedom in Late Modernity* (Princeton, NJ: Princeton University Press, 1995), 77–95, 128–34.

109. On the limits and transformation of personal politics, see Elizabeth Fox-Genovese, "The Personal Is Not Political Enough," *Marxist Perspectives* 8 (Winter 1979/80), 94–113; Judith Grant, "I Feel Therefore I Am: A Critique of Female Experience as the Basis for Feminist Epistemology," *Women & Politics* 7 (Fall 1987), 29–46; Nancy Adamson, Linda Briskin, and Margaret McPhail, *Feminists Organizing for Change: The Contemporary Women's Movement* (Toronto: Oxford University Press, 1988), esp. 198–298; Teresa de Lauretis, "Feminist Studies/Critical Studies: Issues, Terms, Contexts," *Feminist Studies/Critical Studies*, 1–19.

110. Sarachild, "The Power of History"; Barbara Leon, "Consequences of the Conditioning Line," *Feminist Revolution*. Redstockings' "pro-woman" was in part a rejection of Friedan's claim that women's oppression was a product of their condition-

ing or psychology. They argued that concluding that women need (what Wolf today calls) a "new power psychology" is nothing more than old biological theories about women dressed in new psychological jargon. In both cases women are blamed for their victimization.

111. Echols, *Daring to Be Bad*, 157.

112. Charlotte Bunch, "Self-Definition and Political Survival," *Passionate Politics: Feminist Theory in Action 1968–1986* (New York: St. Martin's Press, 1987), 87–88.

113. Beverly Fisher-Manick, "Race and Class: Beyond Personal Politics," *Building Feminist Theory: Essays from "Quest"* (New York: Longman, 1981), 158; Karen Kollias, "Class Realities: Create a New Power Base," *Essays from "Quest,"* 126.

114. bell hooks, *Feminist Theory: From Margin to Center* (Boston: South End Press, 1984), 43–47. Of course, Audre Lorde had already voiced these concerns in her response to Mary Daly's universalistic portrayal of women's oppression in *Gyn/Ecology* (Lorde, *Sister Outsider*, 70).

115. hooks, *Feminist Theory*, 46; bell hooks, *Ain't I a Woman? Black Women and Feminism* (Boston: South End Press, 1981). In her later work hooks reiterates her reproach of white feminists but offers a more sympathetic reading of African American men's engagement in "victim politics." In addition, she now argues that moving beyond victimization means acknowledging the oppressed's "complicity" (bell hooks, *Killing Rage: Ending Racism* [New York: Henry Holt, 1995], 53, 58–59). At the same time, she criticized Wolf, Roiphe, and Paglia for misappropriating her argument (bell hooks, *Outlaw Culture: Resisting Representations* [New York: Routledge, 1994], 83–108).

116. hooks, *Outlaw Culture*, 14–15.

117. Lorde, *Sister Outsider*, 123, 132; Cherríe Moraga, "La Guerra," in *This Bridge Called My Back: Writings by Radical Women of Color*, ed. Cherríe Moraga and Gloria Anzaldúa (New York: Kitchen Table, 1981), 29.

118. Shane Phelan, *Identity Politics: Lesbian Feminism and the Limits of Community* (Philadelphia: Temple University Press, 1989), 157–58.

119. Angela Weir and Elizabeth Wilson ("The British Women's Movement," *New Left Review* 148 [November/December 1984], 74–104) see this manifested in British feminists' renaming the movement. Replacing "women's liberation movement" with "feminism," they argue, indicates a move away from a commitment to sexual liberation, and perhaps more significantly, from other national liberation movements. Cf. also Nancy Hartsock, "Political Change: Two Perspectives on Power," *Essays from "Quest,"* 3–19.

120. Elly Bulkin, Minnie Bruce Pratt, and Barbara Smith, *Yours in Struggle: Three Feminist Perspectives on Anti-Semitism and Racism* (New York: Long Haul Press, 1984), 99–100.

121. Barbara Smith, ed., *Home Girls: A Black Feminist Anthology* (New York: Kitchen Table, 1983).

122. Moraga and Anzaldúa, eds., *This Bridge Called My Back*, 23.

123. Elizabeth Spelman, *Inessential Women: Problems of Exclusion in Feminist Thought* (Boston: Beacon, 1988), 13, 15; Kimberle Crenshaw, "Mapping the Margins: Intersectionality, Identity Politics, and Violence Against Women of Color," in *After Identity: A Reader in Law and Culture*, ed. Dan Danielsen and Karen Engle (New York: Routledge, 1995), 332–54.

124. Deborah King, "Multiple Jeopardy, Multiple Consciousness: The Context of a Black, Feminist Ideology," *Signs* 14 (Autumn 1988), 58. A substantial literature on the problem of how "identity" was conceptualized and deployed within feminism emerged during this period. Constructs such as "hybridity," "sister outsider," "the new mestiza," and "world traveling" attempted to embrace the malleable, partial, and contradictory nature of identities as liberatory. See Trinh Minh-ha, *Framer Framed* (New York: Routledge, 1992); Lorde, *Sister Outsider*; Gloria Anzaldúa, *Borderlands/La Frontera: The New Mestiza* (San Francisco: Aunt Lute Books, 1987); Maria Lugones, "Playfulness, World Traveling, and Loving Perception," in *Women, Knowledge, and Reality*, ed. Ann Gar and Marilyn Pearsall (Boston: Unwin, 1989). Others sought to revise essentialist notions of identities; see, for example, Naomi Schor and Elizabeth Weed, *The Essential Difference* (Bloomington: Indiana University Press, 1994). Still others theorized feminist collectivity without group identity. See Donna Haraway, "A Manifesto for Cyborgs: Science, Technology, and Socialist Feminism in the 1980s," in *Coming to Terms: Feminism, Theory, Politics*, ed. Elizabeth Weed (New York: Routledge, 1989); Judith Butler, *Gender Trouble: Feminism and the Subversion of Identity* (New York: Routledge, 1990); Iris Young, *Justice and Politics*, chapter 8; and Jodi Dean, *Solidarity of Strangers: Feminism after Identity Politics* (Berkeley: University of California Press, 1996).

125. Barbara Smith, "Between a Rock and a Hard Place: Relationships Between Black and Jewish Women," *Yours in Struggle*, 65–88.

126. Letty Cottin Pogrebin, "Anti-Semitism in the Women's Movement," *Ms.* (June 1982), 45–75.

127. Minnie Bruce Pratt, "Identity: Skin Blood Heart," *Yours in Struggle*, 9–64.

128. Lorde, *Sister Outsider*, 115.

129. Melanie Kaye/Kantrowitz and Irena Klepfisz, *The Tribe of Dina* (New York: Sinister Wisdom, 1986), 274.

130. Paglia, *Sex, Art*, 252; Wolf, *Fire with Fire*, 62.

131. Roiphe quoted in Susan Faludi, "I'm Not a Feminist," 36; Christina Hoff Sommers, "Ms. Information," *Wall Street Journal*, March 25, 2003; Hoff Sommers, *Who Stole?*, 119–36, 244–46, 263.

132. Christina Hoff Sommers, *The War Against Boys: How Misguided Feminism Is Harming Our Young Men* (New York: Simon & Schuster, 2001); Laura Bush "Putting Boys in the Spotlight," *All Things Considered*, National Public Radio, February 9, 2005.

133. Wolf, *Fire with Fire*, 236–43.

134. Ibid., 28–31, 42–44.

135. Ibid., 186.

136. Paglia, *Sex, Art*, xii.

137. Shelby Steele, *The Content of Our Character: A New Vision of Race in America* (New York: St. Martin's Press, 1990), 23–24, 26, 29, 61.

138. Judith Butler, *The Psychic Life of Power: Theories in Subjection* (Stanford: Stanford University Press, 1997).

## Chapter 4

1. National Desk, "Massachusetts U. Raises Censorship Cry," *New York Times*, May 29, 1988, 22. See also "Ambush at Amherst," *New Republic*, June 27, 1988, 10.

2. Julius Lester, "Academic Freedom and the Black Intellectual," *The Black Scholar* (November/December 1988), 20–22. See Julius Lester, *Lovesong: On Becoming a Jew* (New York: Holt, 1988), 134, 137, 140, 208–9, 211.

3. This comment by one of Lester's colleagues was quoted in Philip Lentz, "Ex-Militant Is on Strange Battlefield," *Chicago Tribune*, June 19, 1988.

4. In addition to the reports already cited, cf. Deborah Blum, "Black Professor Accuses His Colleagues of Censorship and Anti-Semitism," *Chronicle of Higher Education*, June 8, 1988; Editorial, "Department Head Rejects UMass Probe," *Boston Globe*, June 16, 1988; Anonymous, "Black Massachusetts University Professor Stirs Censorship Issue," *Jet*, June 1988; W. J. Weatherby, "A Storm in a Teacup at the University of Massachusetts," *Guardian* (UK), July 4, 1988; Elizabeth Mehren, "The Baldwin Blow Up: A Prominent Professor's Criticism of an Icon of Black Literature Sets Off a Major Debate Over Academic Freedom," *Los Angeles Times*, July 10, 1988; Jonathan Kaufman, "At UMass, Comrades Have Become Combatants," *Boston Globe*, July 25, 1988; David Lehman, "A Conversation," *Partisan Review* (Spring 1990), 321–52.

5. Mehren, "Baldwin Blow Up"; see also "Massachusetts U. Raises Censorship."

6. For example, Lester, *Lovesong*; Lester, "Academic Freedom"; Julius Lester, "Man in the Mirror: The Apotheosis of Jesse Jackson," *New Republic*, May 27, 1988, 20–22; Julius Lester, "The Responsibility of the Black Intellectual," *Falling Pieces from a Broken Sky* (New York: Little, Brown, 1990), 180–227.

7. Dinesh D'Souza, *Illiberal Education: The Politics of Race and Sex on Campus* (New York: Free Press, 1991), 194–204.

8. Shelby Steele, *The Content of Our Character: A New Vision of Race in America* (New York: St. Martin's Press, 1990), 73–74; Stephen Carter, *Reflections of an Affirmative Action Baby* (New York: Basic Books, 1991), 109, 133, 195, 209.

9. Charles Sykes, *A Nation of Victims: The Decay of the American Character* (New York: St. Martin's Press, 1992), 167.

10. Angela Dillard coined the term "multicultural conservative." Angela Dillard, *Guess Who's Coming to Dinner Now? Multicultural Conservatism in America* (New York: New York University Press, 2001).

11. For more about black Jews generally, see Katya Gibel Azoulay's *Black, Jewish, and Interracial: It's Not the Color of Your Skin, but the Race of your Kin and Other Myths of Identity* (Durham, NC: Duke University Press, 1997); www.blackandjewish.com.

12. Lester, *Lovesong*, 126.

13. Lester characterizes his memoir as simply "relating my spiritual odyssey to Judaism" ("Academic Freedom," 17); see also *Lovesong*, 1, 26–27, 72, 74–86, 207, 244.

14. Frantz Fanon, *Black Skins, White Masks*, trans. Charles Lam Markmann (New York: Grove, 1952/1967), 111.

15. Since racial masquerade typically conjures images of whites in blackface, Susan Gubar's term, "racechanging," seems most appropriate here. Racechanging refers to "the traversing of race boundaries, racial imitation or impersonation, cross-racial mimicry or mutability, white posing as black or black passing as white, pan racial mutuality" (Susan Gubar, *Racechanges: White Skin, Black Face in American Culture* [New York: Oxford University Press, 1997], 5).

16. Michael Rogin, *Blackface, White Noise: Jewish Immigrants in the Hollywood Melting Pot* (Berkeley: University of California Press, 1996), 147, 73–112. See also, Michael Rogin, "Making America Home: Racial Masquerade and Ethnic Assimilation in the Transition to Talking Pictures," *Journal of American History* (December 1992), 1050–77; Michael Rogin, "The Jewish Jazz Singer," *Critical Inquiry* (Spring 1992), 417–53; Alexander Saxton, "Blackface Minstrelsy," *The Rise and Fall of the White Republic: Class Politics and Mass Culture in Nineteenth-Century America* (London: Verso, 1990); Eric Lott, *Love and Theft: Blackface Minstrelsy and the American Working Class* (New York: Oxford University Press, 1993).

17. "Ethnic transvestism" is Werner Sollors's term to refer to faux Jewish novelists (Werner Sollors, *Beyond Ethnicity: Consent and Descent in American Culture* [New York: Oxford University Press, 1986], 252).

18. Roger Wilkins, "Turning Points: The Spiritual Odyssey of Julius Lester," *Washington Post*, February 14, 1988, X1.

19. Wendy Kaminer, *I'm Dysfunctional, You're Dysfunctional: The Recovery Movement and Other Self-Help Fashions* (New York: Vintage, 1993), 2. Lester's memoir may additionally be considered part of a genre of narratives by displaced leftists, most typically white men, who seek a place for themselves as part of a reconfigured new radical politics, whether Left or Right. A common feature of these works is the centrality of the authors' discovery that they too are victims. Tom Hayden's book, *Irish on the Inside: In Search of Irish America* (New York: Verso, 2001), where he attempts to de-whiten Irishness in an effort to reclaim a place for himself on the post–New Left Left, offers one example. But David Horowitz's anti-victimist writings, where

demonstrating how minorities victimize the white majority serves to justify abandoning progressive politics and embracing neo-conservativism, are the far more common storyline (e.g., David Horowitz, *Radical Son: A Generational Odyssey* [New York:
Simon & Schuster, 1998]). At the same time, blending a "declaration of selfhood" with
political critique may also be regarded as part of African American literary tradition.
As Henry Louis Gates Jr. contends: "'I write myself, therefore I am' could very well be
taken as the motto of 'the race' in this country" ("Introduction: On Bearing Witness,"
*Bearing Witness: Selections from African American Autobiography in the Twentieth Cen-
tury* [New York: Pantheon, 1991], 7). And, as Angela Dillard demonstrates in her study
of multicultural conservativism, the genre prevails regardless of the authors' political
affiliations (*Multicultural Conservatism*).

20. Lester, "Academic Freedom," 233; Lester, *Falling Pieces*, 139.

21. Lester, *Lovesong*, 39.

22. "Massachusetts U. Raises Censorship Cry." For Lester's reaction to reviews
of *Look Out, Whitey!*, see Julius Lester, *All Is Well* (New York: William Morrow, 1974),
148–50.

23. Prior to more recent events, such as the Crown Heights affair, this was considered the "most racially polarizing event in the city's history" (Maurice Berube and
Marilyn Gittell, *Confrontation at Ocean Hill–Brownsville* [New York: Praeger, 1969],
164). For additional examples of the anti-Semitism aroused by the conflict, see Ibid.,
163–214; Philip Green and Stanford Levinson, eds., *Power and Community: Dissenting
Essays in Political Science* (New York: Pantheon, 1970), 247–75.

24. Lester, *Lovesong*, 51.

25. See Jon Kalish, "Julius Lester: The 'Anti-Semite' Who Became a Jew," *Newsday*,
March 10, 1988, 4. The story of what Lester had done not only aroused the interest of the
national press (becoming front-page news) but also reportedly provoked several Jewish organizations, in particular the Jewish Defense League (JDL), to threaten Lester's
life (*Lovesong*, 55, 65). For Jewish militants' perspective on the Ocean Hill–Brownsville
confrontation, as well as their mimicry of Black Panthers, see Janet Dolgin, *Jewish
Identity and the JDL* (Princeton, NJ: Princeton University Press, 1977), 28–30; Berube
and Gittell, *Confrontation at Ocean Hill*.

26. Julius Lester, "A Response," in *Black Anti-Semitism and Jewish Racism*, ed. Nat
Hentoff (New York: Schocken, 1969), 231–32

27. Lester, *Lovesong*, 57.

28. Ibid., 61; Lester, "A Response," 235.

29. Lester, *Lovesong*, 120, 119.

30. Ibid., 123.

31. Ibid., 120.

32. Ibid.

33. Ibid., 126.

34. Lester, *Falling Pieces*, 256.

35. Lester, *Lovesong*, 128.

36. Ibid., 130; Lester, *Falling Pieces*, 143–45, 165.

37. Lester, *Lovesong*, 127.

38. For instance, Lester, *All Is Well*, 127.

39. Lester, *Lovesong*, 132.

40. Ibid., 61, 130.

41. Ibid., 112.

42. Ibid., 39; Lester, *All Is Well*, 124.

43. Lester, *Falling Pieces*, 98, 60–61; Lester, *All Is Well*, 124.

44. Lester, *Lovesong*, 25.

45. Ibid., 43.

46. Ibid., 44.

47. Ibid., 74.

48. Ibid., 7, 8, 133, 178–79, 222.

49. Julius Lester, *Look Out Whitey! Black Power's Gon' Get Your Mama* (New York: Dial Press, 1968), 4, 41, 105–6; Julius Lester, *Revolutionary Notes* (New York: Grove, 1969), 19, 115. Equating nonviolence with playing the victim owes much, I believe, to *The Wretched of the Earth*, especially Sartre's preface (Frantz Fanon, *The Wretched of the Earth*, preface, Jean-Paul Sartre, trans. Constance Farrington [New York: Grove, 1992], 25).

50. Lester, *Look Out Whitey!*, 57, 140, 26, 37, 74, 113; Lester, *Revolutionary Notes*, 41–43.

51. Lester, *Look Out Whitey!*, 107, 30.

52. Ibid., 137.

53. Lester, *Revolutionary Notes*, 70–71, 97; Lester, *All Is Well*, 128–29.

54. Julius Lester, *Search for a New Land: History as Subjective Experience* (New York: Dial Press, 1969), 133.

55. Lester, *Lovesong*, 43.

56. Ibid., 42.

57. Ibid., 58.

58. Observe also how Lester assumes a female voice at his most furious: "We've had our love affair with white America and our virginity is gone. We're tired of whoring so you can wash your guilt in our blood. We're tired of being raped by racism and hatred" (*Look Out Whitey!*, 106).

59. Paul Berman, "The Other and the Same," in *Blacks and Jews: Alliances and Arguments*, ed. Paul Berman (New York: Delacorte, 1994), 5.

60. Lester, *Lovesong*, 61, 63; Lester, *Revolutionary Notes*, 235. See also where Lester reduces the history of black-Jewish relations to one of mutual projections: "The story of blacks and Jews in America is a story of projections. At one time, the projections

were almost all positive; now they are almost all negative. What remains constant is the fact of misperception, for by their very nature projections are not concerned with muddy reality and its murky truths. *Projections use another in an attempt to make one-self whole*" (emphasis added, Lester, "The Outsiders: Blacks and Jews and the Soul of America," *Transitions* 68 [1995], 68).

61. Lester, *Lovesong*, 131.

62. Lester, *All Is Well*, 46.

63. Ibid., 50.

64. Ibid., 312.

65. Lester, *Falling Pieces*, 53.

66. Lester, *All Is Well*, 243–44.

67. Lester, *Lovesong*, 1.

68. W. E. B. DuBois, *The Souls of Black Folks*, ed. David Blight and Robert Gooding-Williams (Boston: Bedford/St. Martin's Press, 1903/1997), 38.

69. Fanon, *Black Skin*, 109–16.

70. Lester, *All Is Well*, 84.

71. Lester, *Lovesong*, 66.

72. Ibid., 67, 72.

73. Ibid., 69.

74. Friedrich Nietzsche, *Gay Science: With a Prelude in Rhymes and an Appendix of Songs*, trans. Walter Kaufman (New York: Vintage, 1887/1974), 270.

75. One way for Lester to justify such violence against himself may actually come from his interpretation of Fanon's ideas (*Falling Pieces*, 135). In *Revolutionary Notes*, Lester, paraphrasing Fanon, wrote, "A man who sees himself only as a reflection in the eyeballs of another is not a man. The colonized must kill themselves and awaken unborn within, before they can address themselves directly to the colonizer" (*Revolutionary Notes*, 153). Whatever ambiguity there was in Fanon's imperative, Lester seems to take it literally. Self-negation is the prescription Lester offers for all blacks, even though he positions himself in stark opposition to the black political movement laboring to bring blacks onto the stage of history. He regards himself as fulfilling the mission of his race by jumping into the "void" of (an imagined) ahistorical time where race does not matter. Jumping away from history would ultimately be achieved for him by converting to Judaism.

76. Lester, *Lovesong*, 1.

77. Rogin, *Jewish Jazz Singer*, 447.

78. On the inadequacy of "ethnos," "race," and "religion" for classifying American Jews, cf. Aron Horowitz, *Striking Roots: Reflections on Five Decades of Jewish Life* (Oakville, ON: Mosaic Press, 1979). On Jews' racial status from the nineteenth century to the post–civil rights era, see Mary Waters, *Ethnic Options: Choosing Ethnic Identity in America* (Berkeley: University of California Press, 1990); Richard Alba, *Ethnic*

*Identity: The Transformation of White America* (New Haven, CT: Yale University Press, 1990); Sander Gilman, *The Jew's Body* (New York: Routledge, 1991), 168–93; Michael Lerner, "Jews Are Not White," *Village Voice*, May 18, 1993; Melanie Kaye/Kantrowitz, "Jews in the US: The Rising Cost of Whiteness," in *Names We Call Home: Autobiography on Racial Identity*, ed. B. Thompson and S. Tyagi (New York: Routledge, 1996); Azoulay, *Black, Jewish*; Daniel Boyarin, *Unheroic Conduct: The Rise of Heterosexuality and the Invention of the Jewish Male* (Berkeley: University of California Press, 1997); Karen Brodkin, *How Jews Became White Folks and What That Says about Race in America* (New Brunswick, NJ: Rutgers University Press, 1998); David Biale, Michael Galchinsky, and Susannah Herschel, *Insider/Outsider: American Jews and Multiculturalism* (Berkeley: University of California Press, 1998). See also Gish Jen, *Mona in the Promised Land* (New York: Vintage, 1996), for an engaging novel about a daughter of Chinese immigrants who converts to Judaism in order to more fully assimilate as American.

79. There is a rich literature on the relationship, past and present, between African Americans and American Jews. For a sampling of writings not mentioned elsewhere in this chapter, see Claybourne Carson Jr., "Blacks and Jews in the Civil Rights Movement," in *Jews in Black Perspectives: A Dialogue*, ed. Joseph Washington (Rutherford, NJ: Fairleigh Dickinson University Press, 1984), 113–31; H. Daughtry, *No Monopoly on Suffering: Blacks and Jews in Crown Heights (and Elsewhere)* (Trenton, NJ: Africa World Press, 1997); Max Geltman, *The Confrontation: Black Power, Anti-Semitism, and the Myth of Integration* (Englewood Cliffs, NJ: Prentice-Hall, 1970); Ben Halpern, *Jews and Blacks: The Classic American Minorities* (New York: Herder & Herder, 1971); Nat Hentoff, *Black Anti-Semitism and Jewish Racism* (New York: Schocken, 1969); Jonathan Kaufman, *Broken Alliances: The Turbulent Times Between Blacks and Jews in America* (New York: Scribner, 1988); Michael Lerner and Cornel West, *Jews and Blacks: Let the Healing Begin* (New York: Putnam, 1995); Michael Lerner and Cornel West, *Jews and Blacks: A Dialogue on Race, Religion, and Culture in America* (New York: Plume, 1996); Jack Salzman, *Bridges and Boundaries: African Americans and American Jews* (New York: George Braziller, 1999). Jeffrey Melnick provides an insightful overview of this literature, comparing the two waves of interest (from the mid-1960s to mid-1970s, and then reemerging in the 1990s) demonstrating how both waves focus on political alliance and disillusion, eliding economic and cultural tensions between African Americans and American Jews. Melnick also points out that the idealized vision of alliance (shared oppression and political alliance) and subsequent disappointment presently "is organized and mobilized to serve a neo-conservative agenda" ("Black & Jew Blues," *Transitions* 62 [1993], 114).

80. Lester, *Lovesong*, 131, 142, 144, 145, 239.

81. Lester has written numerous award-winning books for children. Some are compilations of slaves' stories culled from Northern abolitionist groups before the

Civil War and those gathered by the Federal Writers' Project in the 1930s (e.g., *To Be a Slave* [New York: Scholastic, 1968], *Long Journey Home: Stories from Black History* [New York: Puffin, 1972]); others are fictional narratives about black tricksters—from his controversial reissuing of four books of Uncle Remus's Tales, and his *Sam and The Tiger* (New York: Dial Books for Young Readers, 1996) (a retelling of the infamous *Little Black Sambo*), to the more revered *Black Folktales* (New York: Grove, 1991). Children's literature is the one genre in which Lester claims he writes "as a black for blacks." He explains that he hopes to teach black children the lessons he learned from Amos 'n' Andy (who were "not stereotypes, but models of survival") (*All Is Well*, 14).

82. Lester, *Lovesong*, 174.

83. Ibid., 173.

84. Ibid., 6.

85. Ibid., 167, 193, 199, 211.

86. Ibid., 160.

87. Ibid., 143, 167, 20, 37, 117, 192, 203.

88. On the "jungle," see Andrew Ross, *No Respect: Intellectuals and Popular Culture* (New York: Routledge, 1989), especially chapter 3: "Hip and the Long Front of Color."

89. Lester, *Lovesong*, 206.

90. Ibid., 215.

91. Ibid., 37. For an interesting fictional account of a women's decision to tattoo numbers on her arm in order to participate in the venerated victimhood of concentration camp survivors, see Emily Prager, *Eve's Tattoo* (New York: Random House, 1991).

92. Lester, *Lovesong*, 32–33.

93. For Lester on Baldwin, see "James Baldwin (1924–1987)," *Falling Pieces*, 94–122. Lester admires Baldwin but criticizes him for having suffered "a failure of moral nerve" in the 1960s, for taking refuge in his victim status and allowing himself to become "a prisoner of race." Anti-Semitism was part of this imprisonment (Ibid., 97). Note, however, the similarities between Baldwin's and Lester's understandings of roots of black anti-Semitism. The reason blacks are anti-Semitic, or at least espouse anti-Semitism, according to Lester, is because Jews are the only ones who will listen (Lester, "The Lives People Live," *Blacks and Jews: Alliances and Arguments*, 171). Cf. James Baldwin, "Negroes Are Anti-Semitic Because They're Anti-White," *Black Anti-Semitism and Jewish Racism*.

94. Lester, *Lovesong*, 9, 23, 7.

95. Ibid., 6.

96. Ibid., 14.

97. Ibid., 103.

98. Ibid., 120.

99. Lester, *All Is Well*, 17.

100. Lester, *Lovesong*, 8.

101. Ibid., 11, 218.

102. Ibid., 217, 220.

103. Ibid., 7.

104. Lester, *All Is Well*, 12–13.

105. Lester, *Lovesong*, 37, 113, 138, 143, 114; Lester, *Search for a New Land*, 185, 189, 191.

106. Lester, *All Is Well*, 19, 207.

107. Ibid., 164.

108. Lester, *Lovesong*, 233, 144; Lester, *Falling to Pieces*, 137–39.

109. Lester, *Lovesong*, 25.

110. Ibid., 90-91.

111. Ibid., 91.

112. Ibid., 97, 116.

113. Lester, *Revolutionary Notes*, 132–35, 140–43, 188.

114. Lester, *Lovesong*, 159.

115. Ibid., 152, 155, 183–84.

116. Ibid., 95.

117. Ibid., 161.

118. Ibid., 179; Lester, *All Is Well*, 13–14.

119. Lester, *Lovesong*, 215, cf. also 163, 168, 170, 183, 202.

120. Jewish identity is conventionally divided between Jews by descent and Jews by assent. Although the convert to Judaism is a Jew by assent, that is, belief, in Jewish law, *Halakhah*, being Jewish is determined by maternal descent. For a discussion of this distinction, see Michael Krausz, "On Being Jewish," in *Jewish Identity*, ed. David Theo Goldberg and Michael Krausz (Philadelphia: Temple University Press, 1993), 264–78. See also Biale, *Insider/Outsider*, who argues that in a post-ethnic era, all Jews are Jews by choice. Of course, it is not uncommon for converts or those who return to religion to characterize their transformations in terms of rebirth, but in Lester's description his journey into Judaism often sounds like a womb, a prenatal state (cf., for example, *Lovesong*, 165, 175). At times, Lester appears to want to convince the reader (and probably himself) that his Jewishness was a matter of predestination determined by forces greater than himself (Ibid., 22, 27, 29–31, 159).

121. Lester, *Lovesong*, 160.

122. Ibid., 1, 172.

123. Ibid., 217.

124. Lester, *All Is Well*, 9.

125. Ibid., 10.

126. Ibid., 35. This sort of explicit violence against women is usually absent in Lester's other writing. He typically situates sexual matter in traditionally "romantic"

settings. See, for instance, *Two Love Stories* (New York: Dial Press, 1972). Still, it makes one wonder about his more recent children's book, *When Dad Killed Mom* (San Diego, CA: Harcourt, 2001).

127. Lester, *All Is Well*, 34.

128. Ibid., 169.

129. Ibid., 35, cf. also 83.

130. Ibid., 24, 28.

131. Lester, *Lovesong*, 21–2.

132. Ibid., 54.

133. James Baldwin, "Fifth Ave Uptown," *The Price of the Ticket* (New York: St. Martin's Press, 1985).

134. Leslie Fiedler, *Fiddler on the Roof: Essays on Literature and Jewish Identity* (Boston: David R. Godine, 1994), 18–21.

135. Ibid., xvii–xviii.

136. Lester, *Lovesong*, 189.

137. On circumcision as an archive, see Jacques Derrida, *Circumfession*, trans. Geoffrey Bennington (Chicago: University of Chicago Press, 1993); Jacques Derrida, *Archive Fever: A Freudian Impression*, trans. Eric Prenowitz (Chicago: University of Chicago Press, 1996); as an embodied sign, see Daniel Boyarin and Jonathan Boyarin, "Self-Exposure as Theory: The Double Mark of the Male Jew," in *Rhetorics of Self-Making*, ed. Deborah Battaglia (Berkeley: University of California Press, 1995); as a practice that destabilizes masculinity, cf. Boyarin, *Unheroic Conduct*; Daniel Boyarin, "'This We Know to Be Carnal Israel': Circumcision and the Erotic Life of God and Israel," *Critical Inquiry* (Spring 1997).

138. Fanon, *Black Skins*, 170.

139. Cf., for example, Michele Wallace, *Black Macho and the Myth of the Super-woman* (New York: Dial Press, 1979); Eldridge Cleaver, *Soul on Ice* (New York: Dell, 1968). Cleaver, for instance, describes rape as "an insurrectionary act." Cf. also Fanon's discussion of the benefits of interracial sex for black men in *Black Skin*, chapter 3. For more on the complicated relationship among skin color, genitals, and the phallus, cf. Diana Fuss, *Essentially Speaking: Feminism, Nature, and Difference* (New York: Routledge, 1989), chapters 1 and 4; Boyarin, *Unheroic Conduct*.

140. Lester, *All Is Well*, 135.

141. Ibid., 168, 210, 261.

142. Sigmund Freud, "Analysis of a Problem in a Five Year Old Boy," *The Standard Edition of the Complete Works of Sigmund Freud*, Volume 10, ed. and trans. James Strachey and Anna Freud (London: Hogarth, 1955), 198.

143. Boyarin, *Unheroic Conduct*, 84–85. Boyarin finds feminist potential in Jewish men's status as a "third sex," since the cross-gender identification he envisions involves neither female impersonation nor appropriation, but rather a destabilizing of masculinity and femininity. Lester, by contrast, finds antifeminism. Perhaps, then, Lester's

transformation may be better understood through Derrida's reading of circumcision. Whereas the primal father is central to Freud's conception of circumcision as a symbolic substitute for castration, Derrida turns the mother from an object of desire to one of betrayal by emphasizing the role of Moses's wife Zipporah (Derrida, *Circumfession*). For more on racializing sex and sexualizing race, cf. Ann Pellegrini, "Whiteface Performance: 'Race,' Gender, and Jewish Bodies," in *Jews and Other Differences: The New Jewish Cultural Studies*, ed. Jonathan Boyarin and Daniel Boyarin (Minneapolis: University of Minnesota Press, 1997). Also note Patraka's provocative reading of the Washington, DC, Holocaust museum's portrayal of Jews and Jewish history as the feminized victim allowing the United States to assume the role of the masculinized liberator (Vivian Patraka, "Situating History and Difference: The Performance of the Term *Holocaust* in Public Discourse," *Jews and Other Differences*, 54–78).

144. Julius Lester, *All Our Wounds Forgiven* (San Diego: Harcourt Brace, 1994), 118–19.

145. Lester, *Lovesong*, 17; 148–49.

146. Ibid., 19.

147. Ibid., 20.

148. Ibid., 6.

149. Lester, *All Is Well*, 312.

150. Lester, *Lovesong*, 172, 170–71, 174–75, 165–66, 243.

151. Ibid., 172, 17; Lester, *Falling Pieces*, 244–50.

152. Lester, *Lovesong*, 22, 27, 29–31, 159.

153. Ibid., 41; Lester, *All Is Well*, 293–95.

154. Eric Erikson, *Young Man Luther: A Study in Psychoanalysis and History* (New York: Norton, 1962), 204–6.

155. Lester, *Look Out Whitey!*, xi; Lester, *All Is Well*, 293; Lester, *Falling Pieces*, 138. The outhouse may also signify the closet. For more on the relationship between Jewishness and homosexuality as closeted identities, see Daniel Itzkovitz, "Secret Temples," *Jews and Other Differences*, 176–202.

156. For examples of race-bending, cross-dressing, and border-crossing as politically subversive, see Gloria Anzaldúa, *Borderlands/La Frontera: The New Mestiza* (San Francisco: Aunt Lute Books, 1987); Judith Butler, *Bodies That Matter: On the Discursive Limits of "Sex"* (New York: Routledge, 1993); Judith Butler, *Gender Trouble: Feminism and the Subversion of Identity* (New York: Routledge, 1990); Marjory Garber, *Vested Interests: Cross-Dressing and Cultural Anxiety* (New York: Routledge, 1992); Gubar, *Racechanges*.

157. Lester, *All Is Well*, 181, 275.

158. Ibid., 181–221.

159. Stuart Hall, "What Is This 'Black' in Black Popular Culture?" in *Black Popular Culture*, ed. Gina Dent and Michelle Wallace (Seattle: Bay Press, 1992), 29.

160. Sara Bershtal and Allen Graubard, *Saving Remnants: Feeling Jewish in America* (New York: Free Press, 1992); Jim Young, *The Texture of Memory: Holocaust Memorials and Meaning* (New Haven, CT: Yale University Press, 1993). See also Alan Dershowitz, *Chutzpah* (New York: Simon & Schuster, 1991), 130–81; Letty Pogrebin, *Deborah, Golda, and Me: Being Female and Jewish in America* (New York: Anchor, 1991), 94, 117, 139, 160, 195, 210, 216, 252, 303–4, 331.

161. Patraka, "Situating History."

162. Stephen Steinberg, "The Politics of Memory," *Turning Back: The Retreat from Racial Justice in American Thought and Policy* (Boston: Beacon, 1995), 156–63.

163. Novick, *Holocaust in America*, 192.

164. Consider, for instance, Patricia Williams's description of a dream she had in which she inserted her great-great-grandmother (a slave) into the bare patch of canvas left in a painting by an Auschwitz survivor (Patricia Williams, *The Rooster's Egg: On the Persistence of Prejudice* [Cambridge, MA: Harvard University Press, 1995], 209). Beyond the symbolic power of "the Jews" after the Holocaust, African Americans have long identified with the suffering of Jews in the Old Testament, some even claim to be the "true Jews" (James Baldwin, "Harlem Ghetto," *The Price of the Ticket*; Lester, "The Lives People Live," 169; Lester, *Falling Pieces*, 160–62; Henry Louis Gates, "The Uses of Anti-Semitism, with the Memoirs of an Anti-Anti-Semite," *Blacks and Jews*, 227). Khalid Abdul Muhammad, the national assistant of Minister Louis Farrakhan and the Nation of Islam, for instance, asserts that blacks "are the true Jew. [Blacks] are the true Hebrew. [Blacks] are the ones who are in line with the Bible prophecy and scripture" (Berman, "The Other and the Same," 2, 22–23). In even more abridged terms the Jew boy poet reiterates this sentiment: "Jew boy you took my religion and adopted it for you. But you know that black people were the original Hebrews" (*Lovesong*, 51).

165. Simone de Beauvoir, *The Second Sex*, trans. H. M. Parshley (New York: Vintage, 1952/1974); Betty Friedan, *The Feminine Mystique* (New York: Simon & Schuster, 1963/1983); Naomi Wolf, *The Beauty Myth* (London: Chatto & Windus, 1990).

166. Hannah Arendt, *The Jew as Pariah: Jewish Identity and Politics in the Modern Age*, ed. Ron H. Friedman (New York: Grove, 1978); Isaac Deutscher, *The Non-Jewish Jew and Other Essays*, ed. Tamara Deutscher (New York: Oxford University Press, 1968); J.-P. Sartre, *Anti-Semite and Jew* (New York: Schocken, 1948/1976); J.-F. Lyotard, *Heidegger and "the jews,"* trans. Andreas Michel and Mark S. Roberts (Minneapolis: University of Minnesota Press, 1990).

167. For additional examples of Holocaust metaphors in the works of feminists, specifically women as "Jews," cf. Andrea Dworkin, *Women Hating* (New York: Dutton, 1972); Susan Brownmiller, *Against Our Will* (New York: Simon & Schuster, 1975); Mary Daly, *Gyn/Ecology: The Metaethics of Radical Feminism* (New Haven, CT: Yale University Press, 1978); Catharine MacKinnon, *Feminism Unmodified: Discourse on*

*Life and Law* (Cambridge, MA: Harvard University Press, 1987). For a critique of ways in which even progressive constructions of "the jew" occlude "spiritual" Jews, see Daniel Boyarin and Jonathan Boyarin, "Diaspora: Generation and Ground of Jewish Identity," *Critical Inquiry* (Summer 1993); Itzkovitz, "Secret Temples." On the problems with analogical thinking, see Elizabeth Spelman, *Inessential Women: Problems of Exclusion in Feminist Thought* (Boston: Beacon, 1988); Elizabeth Spelman, *Fruits of Sorrow: Framing Our Attention to Suffering* (Boston: Beacon, 1997).

168. Lester differs slightly from the other anti-victimists who retell his story (e.g., Steele, D'Souza, Carter, Sykes), for he does not promote the entrepreneurial, self-made, liberal individual as the antidote to the oppressive collectivism of victim politics, preferring instead Zarathustrian individualism. Otherwise, Lester fully participates in the recent demonization of victims.

169. Lester, *Look Out Whitey!*, 139, 142; Lester, *Revolutionary Notes*, 44–47.

170. Lester, *Search for a New Land*, 194.

171. Jean-Paul Sartre, *Being and Nothingness* (New York: Washington Square Press, 1943/1992), 68, 707–709.

172. Lester, *All Is Well*, 260.

173. Lester, *Falling Pieces*, 103. Lester explores the theme of forgiving victimizers through a fictional account of the life of Martin Luther King Jr. In *All Our Wounds Forgiven*, Lester alters King's real biography by fusing it with his own. Specifically, "John Calvin Marshall," while married to a black woman, found real love and comfort in the body of a white woman. "She and Cal were joined by pain" (Ibid., 68). Where the young Lester criticized King for asking blacks to emulate Christ when they could not, claiming that adhering to King's philosophy of nonviolence required denying black men's manhood, the older Lester now embraces King's legacy by reducing his vision of racial integration and equality to sexual intercourse (Lester, *Revolutionary Notes*, 153; Lester, *All Is Well*, 234–35). As the ghost of Lester's King asks in the novel: wasn't the "real work of the Civil Rights Movement . . . interracial sex?" (Lester, *All Our Wounds Forgiven*, 71). In the novel Lester not only promotes liquidating race and racism through miscegenation, as Norman Podhoretz famously proposed, but also counsels that victims must heal themselves (Norman Podhoretz, "My Negro Problem—and Ours," *Blacks and Jews*, 1964/1994, 91; Lester, *All Our Wounds Forgiven*, 56, 125, 178, 198, 224, 212–13).

174. Sartre, *Being and Nothingness*, 585.

175. Sartre, *Anti-Semite and Jew*, 78–79.

## Chapter 5

1. Bette Harrison, "Playing the Blame Game," *Cosmopolitan*, November 1988, 232–35. For a more recent example of this ever-popular genre, see the best seller, *The 8th Habit: From Effectiveness to Greatness* by Stephen Covey (New York: Free Press, 2004),

where he explains that "the power to choose is your greatest gift. This power and free-dom stand in stark contrast to the mind-set of victimism and the culture of blame so prevalent in society today" (41).

2. On the relationship between blame and punishment, see Cheshire Calhoun, "Responsibility and Reproach," *Ethics* 99 (January 1989), 389–406; John Plamenatz, "Responsibility, Blame, and Punishment," in *Philosophy, Politics, and Society*, ed. Peter Laslett and W. G. Runcman (New York: Blackwell, 1976), 173–93. On the question of when we blame, see Richard Brandt, "Blameworthiness and Obligation," in *Essays in Moral Philosophy*, ed. A. I. Melden (Seattle: University of Washington Press, 1958); Thomas Nagel, *The View from Nowhere* (New York: Oxford University Press, 1986); Kelly Shaver, *The Attribution of Blame: Causality, Responsibility, and Blameworthiness* (New York: Springer-Verlag, 1985); Melvin Lerner, *The Belief in a Just World: A Fundamental Delusion* (New York: Plenum, 1980). On the relationship between blame and moral luck, see Claudia Card, *The Unnatural Lottery: Character and Moral Luck* (Philadelphia: Temple University Press, 1996), 21–48. On the relationship among blame, causality, and responsibility, see Jonathan Glover, *Responsibility* (London: Routledge & Kegan Paul, 1970); R. Sorabji, *Necessity, Cause, and Blame: Perspectives on Aristotle's Theory* (Ithaca, NY: Cornell University Press, 1980); Marion Smiley, *Moral Responsibility and the Boundaries of Community: Power and Accountability from a Pragmatic Point of View* (Chicago: University of Chicago Press, 1992); Martha Minow, "Surviving Victim Talk," *UCLA Law Review* 40 (August 1993), 1411–45; Donald Alexander Downs, *More Than Victims: Battered Women, the Syndrome Society, and the Law* (Chicago: University of Chicago Press, 1996); Sharon Lamb, *The Trouble with Blame: Victims, Perpetrators, and Responsibility* (Cambridge, MA: Harvard University Press, 1996).

3. I use this distinction only to clarify what these writers mean when they employ the term "blaming." Otherwise, I agree with Marion Smiley's argument that the line between causality and responsibility is malleable and reflects particular political interests (*Moral Responsibility*).

4. Marc Gallanter found no use of the phrase "blaming the victim" in newspapers, journals, or magazines before 1970. By 1985, however, use had "mushroomed" (Gallanter referenced in Downs, *More Than Victims*, 24–25). My own LexisNexis search suggests that in the 1990s, use of "blaming the victim" waned. As of September 12, 2001, however, the phrase came back into use to reproach critics of the Bush administration's post-9/11 policies (cf. Chapter 6).

5. The range of reports and programs Ryan includes in his analysis is extensive, from the Kerner and McCone reports on the Watts riots to Hollingshead and Redlich's study of the relationship between social class and mental health and the FBI's crime report.

6. See, for example, William Ryan, *Blaming the Victim* (New York: Vintage, 1976), 36, 44, 63–88, 97–107, 140.

7. Ibid., 11; Karl Mannheim, *Ideology and Utopia* (New York: Harcourt, Brace, 1936); C. W. Mills, "The Professional Ideology of Social Pathologists," *American Journal of Sociology* 49 (1943), 165–80.

8. Ryan, *Blaming*, 17, 20, 173–74.

9. Ibid., 25.

10. Ibid., 70.

11. Ibid., 161. See also 6–7, 23, 28, 304–6; William Ryan, *Distress in the City: Essays on the Design and Administration of Urban Mental Health Services* (Cleveland, OH: Case Western Reserve University, 1969), 263.

12. Ryan, *Blaming*, 76–77.

13. I have found one exception. Christopher Hitchens and Edward Said title their analysis of U.S. policies toward Palestinians, *Blaming the Victims: Spurious Scholarship and the Palestinian Question* (New York: Verso, 1988).

14. Cf. note #2.

15. To emphasize his contempt, Ryan italicizes the word "culture" throughout much of his text. He maintains that the variance victim blamers observe are "adaptive" or "ideological" not cultural (Ryan, *Blaming*, 124–25, 321). Despite changed views among progressives regarding the importance of distinctive cultures, Ryan remains steadfastly opposed to cultural difference theories (M. Brinton Lykes, *Myths about the Powerless: Contesting Social Inequalities* [Philadelphia: Temple University Press, 1996], 356–57).

16. Ryan, *Blaming*, 7–8.

17. Ibid., 32–33, 44–54.

18. Christopher Holliday argues that Ryan mistakes causal attributions for instances of moral condemnation ("The Elusive Victim: Conceptual Orientations," in *Victimization of the Weak: Contemporary Social Reactions*, ed. Jacqueline Scherer and Gary Shephard [Springfield, IL: Charles C Thomas, 1982], 213–31). On the differences among causality, responsibility, and blame, cf. note #1.

19. William Ryan, "Many Cooks, Brave Men, Apples, and Oranges: How People Think about Equality," *American Journal of Community Psychology* 22 (1994), 25.

20. See, for instance, Joe Klein, who claims that the charge "blaming the victim" has become an epithet ("The True Disadvantage," *New Republic*, October 28, 1996, 32–36).

21. Beyond the peculiarities of contemporary political debates, blaming is conceptually tied to our notion of victims and victimhood. Indeed, according to the *Oxford English Dictionary*, the first recorded use of "victim" denoted a scapegoat, "the living creature killed or sacrificed as an offering to a deity." Thus, the "victim" may be regarded as a receptacle of collective blame, and blaming the victim may be not so much an offense as a tautology. (Cf. Chapter 1.)

22. Ryan, *Blaming*, 27.

23. Ryan, "Many Cooks," 35.

24. Ryan, *Blaming*, 71.

25. This point was overlooked in the clamor over the prospect of an official apology. Most opponents argued that apologizing for slavery would be a flaccid gesture benefiting only the apologizers. Interestingly, however, supporters, such as the bill's author, Tony Hall, justified the apology in therapeutic terms. Cf. John Leo, "So Who's Sorry Now?" *U.S. News & World Report*, June 30, 1997; Deborah Sontag, "Too Busy Apologizing to Be Sorry," *New York Times*, June 29, 1997; Russell Baker, "Sorry about That," *New York Times*, July 1, 1997; Patricia Williams, "Apologia Qua Amnesia," *Nation*, July 14, 1997; Tony Hall, "An Apology Long Overdue," *Christian Science Monitor*, July 9, 1997. See also how critics of President Clinton's Initiative on Race likewise criticize it for turning therapeutic, Steven Holmes, "The Fire Wasn't This Time: Two Race Reports," *New York Times*, October 4, 1998; "Feeling Findings," *New Republic*, October 25, 1998, 8. For reactions to the Senate's 2005 apology to the victims of lynching, see Sheryl Stolberg, "The Senate Apologies, Mostly," *New York Times*, June 19, 2005; Rob Christensen, "Racial Wrongs Retracted," *News & Observer*, June 19, 2005; William Rasberry, "Lynching Apology a Good Start," *Times (NY) Union*, June 20, 2005; James Cobb, "Sins of the Past Still Haunt," *Newsday*, June 26, 2005; Bob Herbert, "An Empty Apology," *New York Times*, July 18, 2005.

26. Melvin Lerner, *The Belief in a Just World*, 106–111. See also Melvin Lerner, "The Justice Motive in Social Behavior: Some Hypotheses as to Its Origins and Forms," *Journal of Personality* 45 (1977), 1–52. Note that Lerner's experimental findings, made available before the publication of his book, have been supported by the work of other social psychologists. See, for example, E. Walster, "The Assignment of Responsibility for an Accident," *Journal of Personality and Social Psychology* 3 (1966), 73–79; Kelly Shaver, "Defensive Attribution: Effects of Severity and Relevance on the Responsibility Assigned to Accidents," *Journal of Personality and Social Psychology* 14 (1970), 101–13; Ronnie Janoff-Bulman and Irene Hanson Frieze, "A Theoretical Perspective for Understanding Reactions to Victimization," *Journal of Social Issues* 39 (1983), 1–17; Carolyn Hafer, "Why We Reject Innocent Victims," in *The Justice Motive in Everyday Life*, ed. Michael Ross and Dale Miller (Cambridge, UK: Cambridge University Press, 2002), 109–26.

27. Hannah Arendt, *Lectures on Kant's Political Philosophy*, ed. Ronald Beiner (Chicago: University of Chicago Press, 1982); John Rawls, *A Theory of Justice* (Cambridge, MA: Harvard University Press, 1971).

28. Lerner, *Belief in a Just World*, 136.

29. Melvin J. Lerner, "Pursuing the Justice Motive," *The Justice Motive in Everyday Life*, 11–12.

30. Kurt Weis and Sandra Borges, "Victimology and Rape: The Case of the Legitimate Victim," in *Rape Victimology*, ed. LeRoy Schultz (Springfield, IL: Charles C Thomas, 1975), 93.

31. Ibid., 104–8; P. B. Campbell, "Are We Encouraging Rape?" *Crisis Intervention* 6 (1975), 20–27. Of course, men may also be raped; indeed, Dershowitz claims that the prevalence of male rape victims has reached epidemic proportions (cf. Chapter 2). Nevertheless, the reproach of blaming the rape victim has been used by those most concerned with raped females, and therefore my discussion addresses only female victims and male offenders.

32. Susan Brownmiller, *Against Our Will* (New York: Simon & Schuster, 1975), 309.

33. Germaine Greer, *The Female Eunuch* (New York: McGraw-Hill, 1971/1975), 376, 388.

34. Susan Griffin, *Rape: The Power of Consciousness* (San Francisco: Harper & Row, 1979), 6.

35. Andrea Medea and Kathleen Thompson, *Against Rape: A Survival Manual for Women: How to Avoid Entrapment and How to Cope with Rape Physically and Emotionally* (New York: Farrar, Straus & Giroux, 1974).

36. Brownmiller, *Against Our Will*. Also note that Brownmiller employs the term "scapegoat" to describe the treatment of raped women (62–64). Some of the transformations in thinking about victims and blame may be observed in the changes in Brownmiller's work; compare her "Rashomon in Maryland," *Esquire* (1968), 130–32, 145–47, *Against Our Will*, and "Hedda Nusbaum, Hardly a Heroine," *New York Times*, February 2, 1989.

37. Camille LeGrand, "Rape and Rape Laws: Sexism in Society and Law," *California Law Review* 61 (1973), 67–87; Gail Sheehy, "Nice Girls Don't Get into Trouble," *New York Magazine* (February 1971), 26–30; Carol Bohmer and Audrey Blumberg, "Twice Victimized: The Rape Victim and the Court," *Judicature* 58 (1975), 391–99; Susan Estrich, *Real Rape: How the Legal System Victimizes Women Who Say No* (Cambridge, MA: Harvard University Press, 1987); Lee Madigan and Nancy Gamble, *The Second Rape: Society's Continued Betrayal of the Victim* (Lexington, MA: Lexington, 1992).

38. Weis and Borges, "Victimology and Rape," 102. For more on rape shield laws, see Vernon Wiehe and Ann Richards, *Intimate Betrayal: Understanding and Responding to the Trauma of Acquaintance Rape* (Thousand Oaks, CA: Sage, 1995), 94–95, 102–7. Note that rape shield laws do not apply in civil cases.

39. The most recent illustration of the enduring power of blaming the rape victim, despite the introduction of shield laws, is probably how the media covered the woman who charged celebrity basketball player Kobe Bryant with rape. On the limits of rape shield laws in the Bryant case, see Dahlia Lithwick, "The Shield That Failed," *New York Times*, August 8, 2004; Kirk Johnson, "Judge Limiting Sex-Life Shield at Bryant Trial," *New York Times*, July 24, 2004.

40. W. Holloway, "Gender Difference and the Production of Subjectivity," in *Changing the Subject: Psychology, Social Regulations, and Subjectivity*, ed. J. Henriques et al. (London: Methuen, 1984), 26–59; P. Sanday, *Fraternity Gang Rape* (New York: New York University Press, 1990).

41. Michelle Fine et al., "Insisting on Innocence: Accounts of Accountability," in *Myths about the Powerless*, 128–58.

42. Sheehy, "Nice Girls"; Brownmiller, *Against Our Will*, 418–20; LeGrand, "Rape Laws"; Maxine Margolis, "Blaming the Victim: Ideology and Sexual Discrimination in the Contemporary United States," in *Anthropology 91/92*, ed. E. Angeloni (Guilford, CT: Dushkin, 1991).

43. Lynda Lytle Holmstrom and Ann Wobert Burgess, *The Victim of Rape: Institutional Reactions* (New Brunswick, NJ: Transaction, 1984), 217. Blaming the rape victim is especially prevalent among women. Some explain this gender gap by claiming that women blame rape victims to deny their own vulnerability (cf. Jacqueline Scherer, "The Myth of Passion: Redefinition of Rape," *Victimization of the Weak*, 163; B. Thornton, M. Robbins, and J. Johnson, "Social Perception of the Rape Victim's Culpability: The Influence of Respondents' Personal-Environmental Causal Attributions," *Human Relations* 34 [1981], 225–37).

44. Brownmiller, *Against Our Will*, 449–50.

45. Camille LeGrand and Jay Reich, *Forcible Rape: An Analysis of Legal Issues* (Seattle: Battelle Law & Justice Center, 1977), 74.

46. For example, the Colorado state court ruled that referring to Kobe Bryant's accuser as a "victim" would be prejudicial and therefore denied her that legal standing in court. Although lawyers for the defense petitioned to refer to her as the "complaining witness," the judge decided on the designation "the alleged victim." See *People v. Bryant* Case No. 03-CR-204 (Dist. Ct. Eagle County, Colo. 2004); Steve Lispher and Howard Pankratz, "Definition Fuels Dispute," *Denver (CO) Post*, April 27, 2004; Kirk Johnson, "Judge Rules Accuser May Not Be Called 'Victim,'" *New York Times*, June 2, 2004.

47. For studies showing that rape victims typically blame themselves for their victimization, cf., Sandra Sutherland Fox and Donald Scherl, "Crisis Intervention with Victims of Rape," *Rape Victimology*, 232; Ronnie Janoff-Bluman, "Characterological versus Behavioral Self-Blame," *Journal of Personality & Social Psychology* 37 (1979), 1798–1809; Julia Schwendinger and Herman Schwendinger, *Rape and Inequality* (Beverly Hills, CA: Sage, 1983); Robin Warshaw, *I Never Called It Rape: The Ms. Report of Recognizing, Fighting, and Surviving Date and Acquaintance Rape* (New York: Harper & Row, 1988), 56–58.

48. LeGrand, *Forcible Rape*, 71. RTS has been used in some courts as circumstantial evidence that a rape occurred. But other courts have ruled RTS inadmissible. (Cf. Susan Murphy, "Assisting the Jury in Understanding Victimization: Expert Psychol-

ogy Testimony on Battered Woman Syndrome and Rape Trauma Syndrome," *Columbia Journal of Law and Social Problems* 25 [1992], 277.)

49. Weis and Borges, *Victimology and Rape*, 92.

50. Robert Elias, *The Politics of Victimization* (New York: Oxford University Press, 1986), 24.

51. Ibid., 59; Jacqueline Scherer, "An Overview of Victimology," *Victimization of the Weak*, 21. Scholars disagree about precisely who originated victimology and whether studies of the criminal-victim relationship conducted before Mendelsohn coined the word "victimology" also should be credited as foundational work. Cf. Stephen Schafer, *The Victim and His Criminal: A Study in Functional Responsibility* (New York: Random House, 1968), 1–6, 50–51.

52. Ibid., 45.

53. Ibid., 51.

54. Ibid., 40.

55. Marvin Wolfgang, "Suicide by Means of Victim Precipitated Homicide," *Journal of Clinical and Experimental Psychopathology and Quarterly Review of Psychiatry and Neurology* 20 (1959), 265.

56. William Berg and Robert Johnson, "Assessing the Impact of Victimization: Acquisition of the Victim Role Among the Elderly and Female Victims," in *Perspectives on Victimology*, ed. William Parsonage (London: Sage, 1979), 61–62.

57. Schafer, *Victim and His Criminal*, 138, 152–54.

58. Menachem Amir, *Patterns in Forcible Rape* (Chicago: University of Chicago Press, 1971), 258.

59. Menachem Amir, "Forcible Rape," *Rape Victimology*, 43.

60. Ibid., 107.

61. Weis and Borges, *Victimology and Rape*, 112. Emphasizing the victim's role and risk, victimologists employed a variety of terms in addition to "precipitation," including "responsibility," "culpability," "guilt," "facilitation," "provocation," and "blame." See Henri Ellenberg, "Psychological Relationship Between the Criminal and His Victim," *Archives of Criminal Psychodynamics* 2 (1955), 256–90; Walter Reckless, *The Crime Problem* (New York: Appleton, Century, Crofts, 1967), 142; LeRoy Schultz, "The Victim-Offender Relationship," *Crime and Delinquency* 14 (1968), 135; C. Ray Jeffrey, *Crime Prevention Through Environmental Design* (Beverly Hills, CA: Sage, 1971), 208–9.

62. Scherer, *Overview of Victimology*, 160.

63. Ibid., 154.

64. Weis and Borges, *Victimology and Rape*, 230.

65. Andrew Karmen, "The Controversy over Shared Responsibility: Is Victim-Blaming Ever Justified?" in *To Be a Victim: Encounters with Crime and Injustice*, ed. Diane Sank and David Caplan (New York: Plenum, 1991), 395–408; Ezzat Fattah, "Recent Developments in Victimology," *Victimology: An International Journal* 4 (1979),

198–213. For examples of critiques of victim precipitation as victim blaming, see LeGrand, "Rape Laws," 925; Robert Silverman, "Victim Precipitation: An Examination of the Concept," *Victimology: A New Focus* (Lexington, MA: Heath, 1974), 99; Brownmiller, *Against Our Will*, 353; Clyde Franklin and Alice Franklin, "Victimology Revisited," *Criminology* 14 (1976), 134; Margaret Anderson and Christine Renzetti, "Rape Crisis Counseling and the Culture of Individualism," *Contemporary Crisis* 14 (1980), 325; Christopher Birkbeck, "'Victimology Is What Victimologists Do': But What Should They Do?" *Victimology: An International Journal* 8 (1983), 270–75; Martha Burt, "A Conceptual Framework for Victimological Research," *Victimology: An International Journal* 8 (1983), 261–69; Emilio Viano, "Victimology: The Development of a New Perspective," *Victimology: An International Journal* 8 (1983), 17–30.

66. Israel Drapkin and Emilio Viano, *Victimology: A New Focus* (Lexington, MA: Heath, 1973), xv.

67. Ibid., vi.

68. Richard Quinney, "Who Is the Victim?" *Criminology* 10 (1972), 315.

69. Emilio Viano, ed. *The Victimology Handbook* (New York: Garland, 1990), xvii. The variety of papers presented at the Jerusalem conference indicate both of these trends, but the debate over whether the scope of the discipline could encompass victims of persecution and prejudice figured prominently. Cf. Drapkin and Viano, *Victimology*.

70. Anne McLeer, "Saving the Victim: Recuperating the Language of the Victim and Reassessing Global Feminism," *Hypatia* 13 (Winter 1998), 42.

71. Ibid., 51.

72. By employing "social victims" here, I am following radical victimologists' distinction between victims who suffer the consequences of actions prohibited by law and those who, because of their affiliation with particular social groups, suffer the consequences of actions or inactions not considered criminal. For more on social groups as distinguished from other forms of collectives, see Iris Young, *Justice and the Politics of Difference* (Princeton, NJ: Princeton University Press, 1990), 42–48.

73. John Vasconcellos, "Preface," in *The Importance of Self-Esteem*, ed. Andrew Mecca, Neil Smelser, and John Vasconcellos (Berkeley: University of California Press, 1989), xiv.

74. Ibid., xxi.

75. Neil Smelser, "Self-Esteem and Social Problems," *Importance of Self-Esteem*, 6–8.

76. Vasconcellos, *Importance of Self-Esteem*, xi.

77. Andrew Mecca, "Forward," *Importance of Self-Esteem*. For a more recent review of studies indicating a weak causal link between self-esteem and social behavior, see Kirk Johnson, "Self-Image Is Suffering from Lack of Esteem," *New York Times*, May 5, 1998.

78. Molefi Kete Assante, *Afrocentricity* (Buffalo, NY: Amulefi Publishing, 1980); Diane Ravitch, "Cultural Pluralism," in *From Different Shores: Perspectives on Race and Ethnicity*, ed. Ronald Takaki (New York: Oxford University Press, 1991), 288–92; Gerald Early, "Understanding Afrocentrism," *Civilization* (July/August 1995), 31–39.

79. Cited in Mary Lefkowitz, *Not Out of Africa: How Afrocentrism Became an Excuse to Teach Myth as History* (New York: Basic Books, 1997), 125.

80. Ravitch, "Cultural Pluralism," 290.

81. We may observe this shift in the activities of cultural feminists (Alice Echols, *Daring to Be Bad: Radical Feminism in America, 1967–1975* [Minneapolis: University of Minnesota Press, 1989]). For examples of self-esteem politics, cf. Sasha Alyson, *Young, Gay, and Proud* (Boston: South End Press, 1985); Jawanza Kunjufu, *Developing Positive Images and Discipline in Black Children* (Chicago: African American Images, 1984); Linda Sanford and Mary Ellen Donovan, *Women and Self-Esteem: Understanding and Improving the Way We Think and Feel about Ourselves* (New York: Anchor/Doubleday, 1984). For criticism of the depoliticizing nature of self-esteem exercises, cf. Wendy Simonds, *Women and Self-Help Culture: Reading Between the Lines* (New Brunswick, NJ: Rutgers University Press, 1992); Elayne Rapping, *Media-tions: Forays in the Culture and Gender Wars* (Boston: South End Press, 1994); Celia Kitzinger, "Therapy and How It Undermines the Practice of Radical Feminism," in *Radically Speaking: Feminism Reclaimed*, ed. Diane Bell and Renate Klein (Melbourne: Spinifex, 1996).

82. Charles Sykes, *A Nation of Victims: The Decay of the American Character* (New York: St. Martin's Press, 1992), 106.

83. Ryan, *Blaming*, xiii–xiv.

84. Sykes, *Nation of Victims*, 106–13; Downs, *More Than Victims*, 24.

85. Friedrich Nietzsche, *On the Genealogy of Morals*, trans. Walter Kaufmann and R. J. Hollindale (New York: Vintage, 1969), III–15, 126–28.

86. Shelby Steele, *The Content of Our Character: A New Vision of Race in America* (New York: St. Martin's Press, 1990), 23–35.

87. Sykes, *Nation of Victims*, 42–43.

88. Camille Paglia, *Sex, Art, and American Culture: Essays* (New York: Vintage, 1992), 51–56; Richard Cohen, "Shades of Blame," *Washington Post*, March 1, 1992.

89. Locus of control is a personality archetype measured by the individual's tendency to view occurrences in her life as an outcome of her own behavior or individual traits (internal locus of control), or conversely, determined by circumstances beyond her control, such as luck, other individuals, or groups (external locus of control). This is a simplified version of ideas that have been influential in therapy, psychology, pedagogy, and other behavioral studies. (Herbert Lefcourt, *Locus of Control: Current Trends in Theory and Research* [New York: Halsted, 1976].)

90. Joannie Schrof, "No Whining," *U.S. News & World Report*, July 14, 1997.

91. Even the anti-victimists who campaign against the proliferation of victims as blamers express support for increasing the rights of victims of crime. See, for instance,

Naomi Wolf, *Fire with Fire: The New Female Power and How It Will Change the 21st Century* (New York: Random House, 1993), 18, 140, 192.

92. Lynne Henderson, "The Wrongs of Victims' Rights," *Stanford Law Review* 37 (1985), 937–1021; Henderson, "Co-Opting Compassion: The Federal Victims' Rights Amendment," *St. Thomas Law Review* 579 (Spring 1998); Henderson, "Exploiting Trauma: The So-Called Victims' Rights Amendment," *Nevada Lawyer* 18 (April 2001); Elias, *Politics of Victimization*; Viano, *Victimology Handbook*.

93. President Ronald Reagan launched the "decade of crime victims" in 1981. The promotion of victims' rights has received bipartisan support ever since. In 1996, President Clinton proposed a Victims' Rights Constitutional Amendment. In 2001, President George W. Bush reiterated executive support for the measure, but the proposed federal amendment is still pending in Congress. One area of dispute remains the language of the proposal, specifically whether the amendment should be limited to victims of violent crimes. Meanwhile, some thirty-three states have enacted a victims' rights amendment to their state constitutions.

94. Brent Smith, John Sloan, and Richard Ward, "Public Support for the Victims' Rights Movement," *Crime and Dependency* 36 (1990), 488–502; Brent Smith and Ronald C. Huff, "From Victim to Political Activist: An Empirical Examination of a Statewide Victims' Rights Movement," *Journal of Criminal Justice* 20 (1992), 201–5.

95. This resembles what Stephen Carter terms "bilateral individualism"—seeing victimization only as "the result of concrete, individual acts by identifiable transgressors"—in his analysis of the Bernhard Goetz case (Stephen Carter, "When Victims Happen to Be Black," *Yale Law Journal* 97 [1988], 421).

96. Bandes, "Empathy," 395.

97. *Booth*, 482 U.S. at 496, 507; Stevens, *Payne*, 501 U.S. at 858.

98. *Booth*, 482 U.S. at 517.

99. *Payne*, 501 U.S. at 823.

100. *Booth*, 482 U.S. at 506.

101. Abraham Abramovsky, "Victim Impact Statement: Adversely Impacting upon Judicial Fairness," *St. John's Journal of Legal Commentary* 8 (1992), 32. In those cases in which the victim can be portrayed as a model member of the community, critics argue that VIS promote retaliatory retribution in their emotional appeal to the jury (Henderson, "Wrongs of Victims' Rights," 995). Susan Bandes observes that VIS incite not only "sympathy, pity and compassion for the victim . . . [but also] hatred, fear, racial animus, vindictiveness, undifferentiated revenge, and the desire to purge collective anger" (Susan Bandes, "Empathy, Narrative, and Victim Impact Statements," *University of Chicago Law Review* 63 [1996], 405–6).

102. Angela Harris, "The Jurisprudence of Victimhood," *The Supreme Court Review* (1991), 77–102.

103. J. Adler, N. Biddle, and B. Shenitz, "Bloodied but Unbowed," *Newsweek*, April 4, 1995, 54–56; D. Thigpen, "Confronting the Killer," *Time*, April 3, 1995, 50.

104. Henderson, "Wrongs of Victims' Rights," 962. See also Paul Gewirtz, "Victims and Voyeurs at the Criminal Trial," *Northwestern University Law Review* 90 (1996), 882; R. Davis and B. Smith, "Victim Impact Statements and Victim Satisfaction," *Journal of Criminal Justice* 21 (1994), 1–15. For the pro-VIS argument, see Seymour Halleck, "Vengeance and Victimization," *Victimology: An International Journal* 5 (1982), 99–109; M. McLeod, "Victim Noncooperation in the Prosecution of Domestic Assault," *Criminology* 21 (August 1986), 21; Carrie Mulholland, "Sentencing Criminals: The Constitutionality of Victim Impact Statements," *Missouri Law Review* (Summer 1995), 60.

105. Encouraging victims to be blamers also includes victims blaming themselves. Psychologist Sharon Lamb, for instance, maintains that self-blame is an integral step in victims' recovery (*Trouble with Blame*). Blaming oneself in such formulations amounts to an expression of individual agency; that is, the victim is thought to regain a sense empowerment by seeing how she made choices. The question of what cognitive course speeds victims' emotional recovery is perhaps best left to others. Nevertheless, I worry that proscriptions compelling victims to view their suffering as a matter of individual choice obscure addressing the larger structures that facilitate victimization and victim blaming. I, therefore, remain both admiring of and deeply hesitant about the recent projects undertaken by feminist legal scholars to rethink the victimization/agency dichotomy especially as it relates to battered women (e.g., Martha Mahoney, "Victimization or Oppression? Women's Lives, Violence, and Agency," in *The Public Nature of Private Violence: The Discovery of Domestic Abuse*, ed. Martha Fineman and Roxanne Mykitiuk [New York: Routledge, 1994], 59–92; Elizabeth Schneider, "Feminism and the False Dichotomy of Victimization and Agency," 38 *New York Law School Law Review* 387 [1993]; Kathryn Abrams, "Ideology and Women's Choices," 24 *Georgia Law Review* 761 [1990]). More recently, the popular press advanced the notion that repression may be the best route to "recovery": Lauren Slater, "Forget about It: The Virtues of Repression," *New York Times Magazine*, February 23, 2003, 48–53.

106. The University of California Regents' new admission policy offers another example of this change from social groups to individual victims. While ending affirmative action for underrepresented racial groups, the Regents concurrently expanded the scope of "disadvantage" or "dysfunction" that an individual might present for special consideration. (Cf. Michel Feher, "Empowerment Hazards: Affirmative Action, Recovery Psychology, and Identity Politics," in *Race and Representation: Affirmative Action*, ed. Richard Post and Michael Rogin [New York: Zone, 1998], 175–84.)

107. Among the first to challenge therapeutic culture was Christopher Lasch. He derided the new emphasis on psychic well-being over objective achievements and moral considerations, and the consequent relinquishing of authority to experts and institutions that promise to provide gratification (*The Culture of Narcissism: American*

*Life in an Age of Diminishing Expectations* [New York: Norton, 1979], 7). See also Philip Rieff's *The Triumph of the Therapeutic: Uses of Faith after Freud* (New York: Harper & Row, 1966). But note that both Rieff and Lasch attack therapeutic culture from a psychoanalytic point of view.

108. Sigmund Freud, "Mourning and Melancholia" (1917), *The Standard Edition of the Complete Psychological Works of Sigmund Freud*. trans. and ed., James Strachey, Vol. 14 (London: Hogarth, 1957), 237–58.

109. Cf. Marcia Chambers, "Sua Sponte: Victims of Their Own Success," *National Law Journal*, November 22, 1993, 15–16; Wendy Kaminer, *It's All the Rage: Crime and Culture* (Reading, MA: Addison-Wesley, 1995); Lamb, *Trouble with Victims*.

110. For examples of the victim/victor dichotomy, see Mari Frank, *From Victim to Victor: A Step-by-Step Guide for Ending the Nightmare of Identity Theft* (Laguna Niguel, CA: Porpoise Press, 2005); J. A. Williams, *Victim to Victor: A Certain Woman's Journey* (Pittsburg, PA: Dorrance, 2002); Yvonne Martinez, *From Victim to Victor: A Biblical Recipe for Turning Your Hurt into Healing* (Centralia, Washington: RPI, 1993); Shirley Azen, *Moving Tales: My Journey from Victim to Victor* (Philadelphia: Xlibris, 2001); B. Kay Coulter, *Victim/Victor: It's Your Choice* (Longwood, FL: Xulon, 2002); Floyd Barackman, *Victors Not Victims* (Grand Rapids, MI: Kregel, 1993). On the victim/survivor pairing, see Juliann Mitchell and Jill Morse, *From Victim to Survivor: Women Survivors of Female Perpetrators* (Toronto, ON: Taylor & Francis, 1998); Nancy Poling, ed., *Victim to Survivor: Recovering from Clergy Sexual Abuse* (Cleveland, OH: United Church Press, 1999); Cheryl Karp et al., *Treatment Strategies for Abused Adolescents: From Victim to Survivor* (Thousand Oaks, CA: Sage, 1998).

111. Primo Levi, *The Drowned and the Saved* (New York: Vintage, 1988). See also Lawrence Langer, *Holocaust Testimonies: The Ruins of Memory* (New Haven, CT: Yale University Press, 1991).

112. Jennifer Hyland Wang, "'A Struggle of Contending Stories': Race, Gender, and Political Memory in *Forrest Gump*," *Cinema Journal* 39 (Spring 2000), 107.

113. See, for example, Mary Ann Glendon's comparative study of abortion and divorce laws in Western democracies as well as her more theoretical discussion of "rights talk" (Glendon, *Abortion and Divorce in Western Law* [Cambridge, MA: Harvard University Press, 1987]; Glendon, *Rights Talk: The Impoverishment of Political Discourse* [New York: Free Press, 1991]).

114. Herbert Gans, *The War Against the Poor: The Underclass and Antipoverty Policy* (New York: Basic Books, 1995); see also Kofi Buenor Hadjor, *Another America: The Politics of Race and Blame* (Boston: South End Press, 1993), 61–88. On the relationship between blame and women's moral agency, see Barbara Houston, "In Praise of Blame," *Hypatia* 7 (Fall 1992), 128–47.

115. Lykes, *Myths about the Powerless*, 354–55.

116. Ibid., 366.

## Chapter 6

1. Dinesh D'Souza, *What's So Great about America* (Washington, DC: Regnery, 2002), 70.

2. Ibid., 24.

3. In a gesture of political equity, he also criticizes anti-immigrant sentiments on the Right and objects to the Reverend Jerry Falwell's vitriol about New Yorkers' decadence. Nevertheless, D'Souza reserves most of his ire for the Left.

4. D'Souza, *What's So Great*, 28.

5. For other examples of dismissing the reparations movement as "victimist," see Shelby Steele, ". . . Or a Childish Illusion of Justice? Reparations Enshrine Victimhood, Dishonoring Our Ancestors," *Newsweek*, August 27, 2001, 23; John McWhorter, "Against Reparations," *New Republic*, July 23, 2001, 32; Armstrong Williams, "Presumed Victims," in *Should America Pay? Slavery and the Raging Debate on Reparations*, ed. Raymond Winbush (New York: HarperCollins, 2003), 165–71.

6. D'Souza, *What's So Great*, 102.

7. Ibid., 127.

8. Ibid., 192–93.

9. William Bennett, *Why We Fight: Moral Clarity and the War on Terrorism* (Washington, DC: Regnery, 2001/2003), 2.

10. Ibid., 7.

11. Ibid., 105.

12. Ibid., 54.

13. Ibid., 27.

14. Charles Krauthammer, "Holiday from History," *Washington Post*, February 14, 2003, A31.

15. David Frum and Richard Perle, *An End to Evil: How to Win the War on Terror* (New York: Random House, 2003), 9.

16. Jonah Goldberg, "Bring Back the Horror," *National Review Online*, March 20, 2002, www.nationalreview.com/goldberg/goldberg032002.asp. Rather than rage, Richard Cohen understands his own post-9/11–induced emotional vulnerability as comparable to "people who survived the Holocaust and made a life for themselves" (Richard Cohen, "Tears of a Nation," *Washington Post*, September 18, 2001).

17. Elie Wiesel, "Peace Isn't Possible in Evil's Face," *Los Angles Times*, March 11, 2003. Cf. also Gary Scott, "Nobel Peace Prize Winner Supports Bush," *San Gabriel Valley Tribune*, March 4, 2003.

18. George W. Bush, "Address to Joint Session of Congress and the American People," September 20, 2001.

19. On the first President Bush, Michiko Kakutani, "How Books Have Shaped U.S. Policy," *New York Times*, April 5, 2003; On Defense Secretary Donald Rumsfeld, *Fox*

*Special Report with Brit Hume*, transcript #081901cb.254, August 19, 2002; On National Security Advisor Condoleezza Rice, Vincent Morris, "Rice Warns Against a Hitler Mistake," *New York Post*, February 17, 2003; On Undersecretary of State John Bolton, Deborah Orin, "Bush Man: Iraq Must be De-Nazified," *New York Post*, October 16, 2002. Note that Britain Prime Minister Tony Blair as well as Senators Ted Stevens, John Warner, and Joseph Lieberman also made this comparison in their respective defenses of the plan to attack Iraq. On Blair, "Blair Likens Saddam to Hitler," *CNN.com*, March 1, 2003; On Stevens, "Stevens Speaks Out on Iraq," October 7, 2002, *Presidential Campaign Press Materials*; on Lieberman and Warner, Joe Conason, "Red-Hot Rhetoric Getting Dangerous," *New York Observer*, October 14, 2002.

20. George W. Bush, "President Discusses War on Terrorism" (speech, World Congress Center, Atlanta, GA, November 8, 2001). For more on the echoes of Winston Churchill, see D. T. Max, "The Making of the Speech," *New York Times Magazine*, October 7, 2001, 32.

21. Craig Smith, "Liberators and Survivors Recall the Auschwitz That Was," *New York Times*, January 28, 2005.

22. www.whitehouse.gov/news/releases/2005/01/20050126-6.html.

23. www.unitedinmemory.net/healing.html.

24. Marita Sturken, *Tangled Memories: The Vietnam War, the AIDS Epidemic, and the Politics of Remembering* (Berkeley: University of California Press, 1997).

25. Mary Hawkesworth, "Theorizing Globalization in a Time of War," *Studies in Political Economy* 75 (Spring 2005), 132.

26. Terry Gross, *News Special*, National Public Radio, September 11, 2001.

27. As a consequence of conceiving of victimization in this way, the victim can restore or redeem himself only through retaliation, a counteremasculating of the victimizer, as Puar and Rai, among others, propose. Cf. Jasbir Puar and Amit Rai, "Monster, Terrorist, Fag: The War on Terrorism and the Production of Docile Patriots," *Social Text* 72 (Fall 2002), 117–48.

28. www.nytimes.com/2002/05/04/arts/04TANK.html.

29. Jonathan Alter, "Blame America at Your Peril," *Newsweek*, October 15, 2001.

30. Christopher Hitchens, "Blaming Bin Laden First," *The Nation*, October 22, 2001.

31. Noam Chomsky, *9-11* (New York: Seven Stories Press, 2001). For Falwell's comments, see Eric Alterman, "The Uses of Adversity," *Nation*, October 8, 2001, www.thenation.com/doc/20011008/alterman.

32. Neil Lewis, "Ashcroft Defends Anti-Terror Plan," *New York Times*, December 7, 2001. Mayor Rudolph Giuliani had already warned: "There is no moral equivalent to this attack. There is no justification for it . . . to suggest that there is any justification for it only invites this happening in the future" (*Forbes.com*, October 11, 2001).

33. Cf. Nikki Craft, "A Call on Feminists to Protest the War Against Afghanistan," in *After Shock: September 11/Global Feminist Perspectives*, ed. Susan Hawthorne and Bronwyn Winters (Vancouver: Raincoast Books, 2002), 180–85.

34. Laura Bush, "Radio Address" (November 17, 2001).

35. George W. Bush, "President Signs Afghan Women and Children Relief Act" (December 12, 2001).

36. Lewis, "Ashcroft Defends."

37. George W. Bush, "State of the Union Address" (January 29, 2002).

38. Zillah Eisenstein, "Imperial Democracy/Imperial Repression and Polyversal Feminisms" (lecture, Ithaca, NY, 2005), 4. Laura Flanders makes a similar point, though she focuses on the role of the media and therefore uses the term "media decoys" (*The W Effect: Bush's War on Women* [New York: Feminist Press, 2004], xi–xxi). See also Flanders, *Bushwomen: Tales of a Cynical Species* (New York: Verso, 2004). Jennifer Lawless provides empirical evidence that as masculine protectionism dominates politics, women candidates' electoral prospects diminish. Cf. Jennifer Lawless, "Women, War, and Winning Elections: Gender Stereotyping in the Post-September 11th Era," *Political Research Quarterly* 57 (September 2004), 479–90.

39. It is also worth noting that the administration selected the conservative, explicitly anti-victim feminist Independent Women's Forum (IWF)—whose membership includes Christina Hoff Sommers, Lynne Cheney, and Wendy Lee Gramm—as the main organization to promote "women's rights" at home and abroad. Shortly after 9/11, the IWF received ten million dollars to generate initiatives for women in Iraq as well as to lobby against the VAWA, Equal Pay Act, Title IX, and so forth, on the domestic front. The IWF's Web site defines its mission as "combat[ing] the women-as-victims, pro-big government ideology of radical feminism."

40. Cynthia Enloe, *Maneuvers: The International Politics of Militarizing Women's Lives* (Berkeley: University of California Press, 2000).

41. Iris Young, "The Logic of Masculinist Protection: Reflections on the Current Security State," *Signs* 29 (Autumn 2003), 9, 13. Seeing a comparable dynamic that reaches beyond women and children to fetuses, Lauren Berlant theorizes the rise of "infantile citizenship" ("The Theory of Infantile Citizenship," *The Queen of American Goes to Washington; Essays on Sex and Citizenship* [Durham, NC: Duke University Press, 1997], 25–53).

42. Mary Hawkesworth, "Theorizing Globalization," 131.

43. George W. Bush, "President Addresses Nation" (speech, Fort Bragg, NC, June 28, 2005).

44. Bush, September 20, 2001.

45. George W. Bush, "President Discusses War on Terror at National Endowment for Democracy" (speech, Ronald Reagan Building and International Trade Center Washington, DC, October 6, 2005).

46. Stanley Fish, "Condemnations Without Absolutes," *New York Times*, October 15, 2001.

47. Cf. Corey Robins, "Closet-Case Studies," *New York Times Magazine*, December 16, 2001, 23–24.

48. Thomas Friedman, "9/11 Lesson Plan," *New York Times*, September 4, 2002.

49. Jerrold Post, "Notes on a Psychodynamic Theory of Terrorist Behavior," *Terrorism* 7 (1984), 241–56. See also Post, "Terrorist Psycho-Logic: Terrorist Behavior as a Product of Psychological Forces," in *Origins of Terrorism: Psychologies, Ideologies, Theologies, States of Mind*, ed. W. Reich (Cambridge, UK: Cambridge University Press, 1990), 25–40.

50. Puar and Rai, "Monster, Terrorist, Fag," 117. Anne Norton frames the same point somewhat differently by drawing attention to the "redoubled masculinity" of Arab men in the Western imagination. It is "marked out from the norm by an exaggeration of masculine traits: strength, willfulness and domestic power." Writing about the Gulf War and the first President Bush's encounter with Saddam Hussein, Norton observes how "fears of Iraq combined Orientalism with homophobia" ("Gender, Sexuality, and the Iraq of Our Imagination," *Gender and Politics* 173 [November/December 1991], 26–28).

51. R. Danielle Egan, "Cowardice," in *Collateral Language: A User's Guide to America's New War*, ed. John Collins and Ross Glover (New York: New York University Press, 2002), 54.

52. Bill Maher, *Politically Incorrect*, ABC, September 17, 2001, www.abc.go.com/primetime/politicallyincorrect/transcripts/transcripts_20010917.html.

53. Bill Press, "Don't Let the Terrorists Kill Free Speech," *CNN.com*, October 9, 2001, www.cnn.com.

54. Mickey Kaus, "Does Welfare Cause Terrorism?" *Slate*, December 17, 2001, www.slate.msn.com/id/2059799. See also James Taranto, "Opinion Journal," *Wall Street Journal.Com*, March 22, 2002, www.opinionjournal.com.

55. Mark Steyn, "Wake Up Folks—It's War!" *Spectator*, July 30, 2005.

56. Bush, October 6, 2005.

57. Stephen Dinan, "GOP Defends Rove's 9/11 Criticisms of Liberals," *Washington Times*, June 25, 2005.

58. Ibid. While Rove claims the Left dispenses therapy, some charge that it is the Bush administration who seeks a therapeutic salve. Cf. Susan Sontag, "Talk of the Town," *New Yorker*, September 24, 2001; Stanley Fish, "Condemnations"; Paola Bacchetta, Tina Campt, Inderpal Grewal, Caren Kaplan, Minoo Moallem, and Jennifer Terry, "Transnational Feminist Practices Against War," *W Effect*, 263–68.

59. Lynne Cheney, "Teaching Our Children about America" (speech, Dallas Institute of Humanities and Culture, Dallas, TX, October 5, 2001). The dispute proliferates in cyberspace. In 2002, William Bennett launched the Americans for Victory

Over Terrorism Web site (www.avot.org), which tracks dissenting voices as "internal threats."

60. Dinan, "GOP Defends Rove."

61. Michael Rogin, *Ronald Reagan, the Movie: And Other Episodes of Political Demonology* (Berkeley: University of California Press, 1988), 80.

62. George W. Bush, "Remarks at United Nations General Assembly" (September 12, 2002).

63. Bush, September 20, 2001.

64. Bush, November 8, 2001. The vice president reiterated this sentiment three years later: "The President and I understand that America requires an aggressive strategy against these enemies—not merely to prosecute a series of crimes, but to fight and win a global campaign against the terror network. Such an enemy cannot be deterred, cannot be contained, cannot be appeased, or negotiated with, it can only be destroyed." Remarks by the Vice President at a Luncheon for Congressional Candidate Sam Graves, Kansas City, MO (April 23, 2004).

65. Bush, November 8, 2001.

66. Renana Brooks, "A Nation of Victims," *The Nation*, June 30, 2003.

67. George W. Bush, "President Calls for Crime Victims' Rights Amendment" (April 16, 2002).

68. See, for instance, www.klaaskids.org.

69. Ray LaHood, report by Nancy Marshall, *Weekend Edition*, National Public Radio, September 15, 2002.

70. David Corn, "The Blame Game," *Nation*, March 1, 2004.

71. George W. Bush, "My Fellow Americans, Let's Roll" (Address to America Before Representatives of Firemen, Law Enforcement Officers, and Postal Workers, Atlanta, GA, November 8, 2001).

72. Sturken, *Tangled Memories.*

73. Judith Butler, "Explanation and Exoneration, or What We Can Hear," *Grey Room* 07 (Spring 2002), 59.

74. Frank Rich, "How Kerry Became a Girlie-Man," *New York Times*, November 5, 2004. See also Stephen Ducat, *The Wimp Factor: Gender Gaps, Holy War, and the Politics of Anxious Masculinity* (New York: Beacon, 2004), who diagnoses in the Bush administration's domestic and foreign policies evidence of "femiphobic masculinity."

75. Peggy Noonan, "Welcome Back, Duke," *Wall Street Journal*, October 12, 2001.

76. Susan Faludi, *Stiffed: The Betrayal of the American Man* (New York: William Morrow, 1999); Noonan, "Welcome Back."

77. Camille Paglia quoted in Patricia Leigh Brown, "Heavy Lifting Required: The Return of Manly Men," *New York Times*, October 28, 2001.

78. Cathy Young, "Feminism's Slide Since Sept. 11," *Boston Globe*, September 16, 2002.

79. Brown, "Heavy Lifting."

80. Tony Leonard, "Heroine Tells of Ordeal," *Daily Star*, November 11, 2003.

81. David Li, "Fellow GIs Sold Nude Pix to Smear Jessica," *New York Post*, November 12, 2003.

82. Zillah Eisenstein notes how the men at Abu Ghraib were continually referred to as having been humiliated, not tortured or raped, as if the real travesty were about challenging their masculinity rather than about their victimization ("Sexual Humiliation, Gender Confusion, and the Horrors at Abu Ghraib," *ZNet | Gender* [June 22, 2004]; "Imperial Democracy," 3). Exploiting gendered tactics to torment prisoners of war is nothing new, as Tim Kaufmann Osborn shows ("Gender Relations in the Age of Neo-Liberal Empire: Interrogating Gender Equality Models" [paper presented at the Western Political Science Association, Oakland, CA, March 2005]).

83. David Thibault, "Abu Ghraib Abuse Is a Feminist's Dream, Says Military Expert," *CNSNews.com* (May 10, 2004), www.cnsnews.com/.

84. "Questions about Abu Ghraib," *Center for Military Readiness*, May 18, 2004, www.cmrlink.org/culture.asp?DocID=225. Linda Chavez, president of the Center for Equal Opportunity, similarly contends that the abuses at Abu Ghraib vividly reveal how women in uniform generate intense sexual tension that can only find release through the sexual harassment of female soldiers or of POWs (Mary Leonard, "Abuse Raises Gender Issues, Women's Soldiers' Role Is Debated," *Boston Globe*, May 16, 2004). Abu Ghraib becomes for Chavez proof of the disciplinary decay women's participation in this man's war produces.

85. On June 29, 2005, however, Bush returned to 9/11 as the moment when those who "murder in the name of a totalitarian ideology that hates freedom, rejects tolerance, and despises all dissent . . . reached our shores" and therefore the prime rationale for his "global war on terror."

86. Lisa Belkin, "Just Money?" *New York Times Magazine*, December 8, 2002, 94–97, 122, 148–49.

87. Richard Dyer, *White* (New York: Routledge, 1997).

88. Katha Pollitt, "The Protocols of Mel Gibson," *Nation*, March 29, 2004; Christopher Hitchens, "Schlock, Yes; New, No; Fascism, Probably," *Slate*, February 27, 2004.

89. Cf. Frank Rich, "Mel Gibson Forgives Us for His Sins," *New York Times*, March 7, 2004; Elvis Mitchell, "Mel Gibson's Longstanding Movie Martyr Complex," *New York Times*, February 8, 2004.

90. Ron Suskind, "Without a Doubt: Faith, Certainty, and the Presidency of George W. Bush," *New York Times Magazine*, October 17, 2004, 44–51, 64, 102, 106.

91. Reports were strangely vague. Cf., "Bush Wants to See 'The Passion of the Christ,'" *NewsMax*, February 20, 2004, www.newsmax.com/archives/ic/2004/2/20/171201.shtml; Scott McClellan, "Press Briefing," News Release, February 25, 2004, www.whitehouse.gov/news/releases/2004/02/20040225-7.html.

92. Suskind, "Faith, Certainty, and the Presidency"; Cf. also Ken Auletta on the Bush administration's relationship with the press, "Fortress Bush," *New Yorker,* January 19, 2004.

93. Max, "Making of the Speech," 34. Cf. also Bob Woodward, *Bush at War* (New York: Simon & Schuster, 2002), 32.

94. George W. Bush, "Address to Nation" (September 14, 2001).

95. Bush, September 20, 2001.

96. Lynne Cheney, "Teaching for Freedom" (speech, Princeton University, Princeton, NJ, November 29, 2001).

97. Bush, June 29, 2005.

98. Berlant, "Theory of Infantile Citizenship." For more on the theme of patriotic indulgences, cf. Naomi Klein, "Buying a Gladiatorial Myth," and Cynthia Peters, "What Does Feminism Have to Say?" *After Shock,* 244–45, 149–55.

99. John Murphy, "'Our Mission and Our Moment': George W. Bush & September 11th," *Rhetoric & Public Affairs* 6 (Winter 2003), 616.

## Epilogue

1. Michel Foucault, *The History of Sexuality: An Introduction* (New York: Vintage, 1978).

2. Jonathan Rauch, "Act Down," *New Democrat,* November 1993, 15.

3. George Lakoff, "Metaphor, Morality, and Politics, or, Why Conservatives Have Left Liberals in the Dust," *Social Research* 62 (Summer 1995), 177–214.

4. George Lakoff, "Metaphors of Terror," www.press.uchicago.edu/News/911lakoff.html, September 16, 2001, 5.

5. "Interview with Joel Osteen," *CNN Larry King Live,* June 20, 2005, http://transcripts.cnn.com/TRANSCRIPTS/0506/20/lkl.01.html.

6. Barbara Welter, "The Cult of True Womanhood, 1820–1860," in *Dimity Convictions: The American Woman in the Nineteenth Century* (Athens: Ohio University Press, 1976), 21–41.

7. Judith Shklar, *The Faces of Injustice* (New Haven, CT: Yale University Press, 1990), 9.

8. Ibid., 37, 49, 51–54.

9. Martha Minow, "Surviving Victim Talk," *UCLA Law Review* 40 (August 1993), 1411–45.

10. Martha Minow, "The Hope for Healing: What Can Truth Commissions Do?" in *Truth v. Justice: The Morality of Truth Commissions,* ed. Robert Rotberg and Dennis Thompson (Princeton, NJ: Princeton University Press, 2000), 240. Many scholars have been engaged in fruitful work probing the possibilities of acknowledging massive systematic injustice without recourse to either a litigious "factity" or to therapeutics. Minow's earlier works examined this issue in the U.S. and international contexts, re-

spectively (Minow, *Not Only for Myself: Identity, Politics, and the Law* [New York: New Press, 1997]; Minow, *Between Vengeance and Forgiveness: Facing History after Genocide and Mass Violence* [Boston: Beacon, 1998]). See also Judith Butler, *Antigone's Claim: Kinship Between Life and Death* (New York: Columbia University Press, 2000); David Eng and David Kazanjian, *Loss: The Politics of Mourning* (Berkeley: University of California Press, 2003); Anne Anlin Cheng, *The Melancholy of Race: Psychoanalysis, Assimilation, and Hidden Grief* (New York: Oxford University Press, 2001).

11. In fact, such hesitations about politicizing suffering have a long tradition. Hannah Arendt, for example, argued that suffering does not lend itself to the sort of multiple perspectives, active exchange, and reasoned judgment that politics necessitates. She also cautioned that it might be easily appropriated and misused (*On Revolution* [New York: Penguin, 1977/1963], 85–88).

12. Malcolm X, "Ballot or the Bullet" (speech, April 3, 1964).

13. Notwithstanding her views on the role of subjection in subject formation, Judith Butler makes a congruous point about terms such as "queer" and "women" ("Critically Queer," *Bodies That Matter: On the Discursive Limits of Sex* [New York: Routledge, 1993], 229). But see Susan Bickford for a compelling critique of the theory/practice divide underlying "strategic" interventions like Butler's ("Reconfiguring Pluralism: Identity and Institutions in the Inegalitarian Polity," *American Journal of Political Science* 43 [January 1999], 86–108).

14. W. E. B. DuBois, "The Niagara Movement," *Voice of the Negro* 2 (September 1905), 621.

# Index

Page numbers followed by *n* indicate notes.

abortion, 10–11

Abu Ghraib prison, 160–61, 229*n*82–84

"abuse excuse" defenses, 25, 32–33, 42, 131, 188*n*42

*Abuse Excuse, The: And Other Cop-Outs, Sob Stories, and Evasions of Responsibility* (Dershowitz), 21

ADA (Americans with Disabilities Act), 23–24, 186*n*8

affirmative action, 6, 11, 23, 24, 30, 35, 42, 54, 126, 163, 169, 222*n*106

Afghanistan, war in, 150–52

Afghan Women and Children Relief Act (AWCRA), 150, 151

African Americans: and anti-Semitism, 79–80, 83–85, 88, 91–93, 100, 203*n*25 (*see also* Julius Lester); roles as victims and victimizers, 81; and victim blaming, 111–16, 131; and victim identity, 37; as victims, 23, 30; and women's oppression, 71–72. *See also* blacks

*Aids Quilt Project*, 148

Alamo, the, 14, 162

*All Is Well* (Lester), 93, 98, 100

*All Our Wounds Forgiven* (Lester), 101

American Alliance for Rights and Responsibility, 20–21

Americans with Disabilities Act (ADA), 23–24, 186*n*8

Amir, Menachem, 125; *Patterns in Forcible Rape*, 125

"angry white men," 12, 22, 28–29, 185*n*5, 187*n*24

antifeminism, 97, 151, 193*n*40, 194*n*44, 194*n*46, 209*n*141, 209*n*143

antipornography, 25, 28, 53, 195

anti-Semitism: and blacks, 79–80, 83–85, 88, 91–93, 100, 203*n*25; feminists and, 74; Ocean Hill-Brownsville confrontation, 83–84

antisexual harassment, 53, 192*n*22

antiterror campaign. *See* war on terror

anti-victim feminism (AVF), 49–78; assumptions of, 57; beginnings of, 57; and character rebuilding, 55–57; difference feminism, 68–70; difference theories in, 52–54; and patriarchy, 67–68; and personal politics, 70–71; race and, 71–75

anti-victimism: beliefs of, 3–4, 107; characteristics of, 6–8, 19–20, 170; Friedan and, 66; history of, 10–16, 45–46; origins of, 10–16, 169; overview of, 3–8; recuperative strategies of, 171; responses to effects of, 173–76. *See also* anti-victim feminism (AVF)

Anzaldúa, Gloria, 73, 200*n*124, 210*n*156

Arendt, Hannah, 63, 106, 117, 231*n*11, 196*n*63

Ashcroft, John, 165

Assembly Bill 3659, 128

Atta, Muhammad, 154

authenticity, 105, 107
AVF. *See* anti-victim feminism

*Bakke, Regents of the University of California v.*, 11
Baldwin, James, 93, 100, 207*n*93, 211*n*164
Bandes, Susan, 135, 221*n*101
battered women's syndrome, 25, 156, 222*n*105
Bayley, James, 5–6
*Beauty Myth, The* (Wolf), 76
Beauvoir, Simone de, 106, 197*n*81
Bennett, William, 145–46, 227*n*59; *Why We Fight*, 145
Bentham, Jeremy, 11
Berlant, Lauren, 167, 226*n*41
*Best Life Now, The* (Osteen), 170
Bickford, Susan, 8, 231*n*13
"blackface," 90–91
*Blackface, White Noise* (Rogin), 81–82
blacks: Black Power movement, 39, 43, 83, 86–87, 100–101; and Jews, 79–80, 82–85, 88, 91, 105, 204*n*60, 206*n*79; pariah status of, 91–92; and politics, 79, 85, 86–87; redefining of, 90; as victims, 23. *See also* African Americans
black victimism, 43, 45
black women, 71–73
blame: meaning of, 110; self, 122, 217*n*47, 222*n*105; therapeutics of, 109–43; use of term, 113, 213*n*2–3
"Blame America at Your Peril" (Alter), 150
blame game, 109, 141, 154, 157
"blaming the victim," 1, 11, 16–18, 53, 109–43, 170; impact on rape victims, 122–23; Lester and, 96; meaning of expression, 113–16, 214*n*21; used in reference to 9/11, 149–50. *See also* victim blaming
*Blaming the Victim* (Ryan), 111–18, 131, 142
Bloom, Allan, 24
*Booth v. Maryland*, 135–36
Boyarin, Daniel, 101
Brown, Wendy, 7, 182*n*15
Brownmiller, Susan, 63, 118, 120, 216*n*36
Bunch, Charlotte, 71–72, 74, 194*n*49
Burgess, Ann Wobert, 120, 122
Bush, George W., 168; and 2004 presidential campaign, 159; antifeminism of, 151; Bennett on, 146; Christianity of, 165; and "compassionate conservatism," 12; denial of victimization,

146; and innocence of U.S., 156–57; on motives of terrorists, 154; and opportunity of 9/11, 166; portrayal of compassion, 161; portrayal of war, 167; as practitioner of victim politics, 156; promise to remake America, 166; response to 9/11, 161–63; on terrorism, 3, 147, 152; victimist portrayal of U.S., 156
Bush, Laura, 150
Butler, Judith, 77, 158, 182*n*16, 231*n*13

California Task Force to Promote Self-Esteem and Personal and Social Responsibility, 128–29, 133
Carmichael, Stokely, 39, 83
Carter, Jimmy, 85
Carter, Stephen, 37–38, 80, 187*n*26, 221*n*95; *Reflections of an Affirmative Action Baby*, 37
castration complex, 101
Cheney, Dick, 147–48, 228*n*64
Cheney, Lynne, 155, 166
Chomsky, Noam, 149
Christianity, 13, 14–15, 41, 87, 101–103, 163–65
circumcision, 92–93, 100–101, 209*n*143
*City of Richmond v. J.A. Croson Co.*, 34
civil liberties, 10, 28, 156
civil rights movement: African Americans and, 15, 23, 37, 39; feminists and, 68; Lester and, 29, 85, 212*n*173; protections of, 42, 43; and victimist claims, 27; and victims' rights movement, 137
Civil War, 13
classification of anti-victimist critique, 42–44
class issues in feminism, 71
Clausen, Jan, 73
Clinton, Bill, 116, 162, 215*n*25, 221*n*93
Coleman, James, 114, 116; Coleman Report, 114
Combahee River Collective, 73
comparative victimism, 37–39, 72, 74
compassionate conservatism, 12, 168
consciousness-raising, 8, 9, 32, 70–71,
Convention on the Elimination of All Forms of Discrimination against Women (CEDAW), 151
Crenshaw, Kimberle, 73
*Criminal and His Victim, The* (von Hentig), 123

criminality, 3, 127, 220*n*95; and blame, 113; and victim impact statements, 135; and welfare state, 153, 171
criminals: representation of as victims, 25; rights of, 10
Crow, Jim, 15
cult of true womanhood, 151, 173, 181*n*11
cultural difference theories, 112, 113
cultural feminists, 68, 69, 198*n*99
*Culture of Complaint: The Fraying of America* (Hughes), 21, 26
culture of poverty, 111–16, 142
*Curb Your Enthusiasm*, 138–39

David, Larry, 138–39
Democratic Leadership Council, 4
demonology, political, 4–6, 146, 155–56
Denfeld, Rene, 48, 51, 56, 58, 77, 192*n*20; *New Victorians, The*, 48
Dershowitz, Alan, 21, 24–25, 28–29, 32–33, 188*n*42; *Abuse Excuse, The*, 21
Deutscher, Isaac, 106
difference feminism, 52–54, 57, 68–70, 74–75, 77, 192*n*20
discrimination, reverse, 10–11, 42, 182*n*25
Donnelly, Elaine, 160–61
Drapkin, Israel, 126–27
D'Souza, Dinesh, 41, 77; on 9/11, 144; *The End of Racism*, 30; *Illiberal Education*, 21; on Julius Lester, 80; victim comparison, 35; on "victim's revolution," 24; *What's So Great about America*, 144
DuBois, W. E. B., 79, 86, 90, 99, 177
Dworkin, Andrea, 58, 63, 196*n*62, 211*n*167
Dyer, Richard, 163

Echols, Alice, 69
Eisenstein, Zillah, 151, 196*n*78, 229*n*82
Elkins, Stanley, 64; *Slavery*, 64
emancipation of women, 77. *See also* feminism
emotional recovery of victims, 137, 222*n*105
*End of Racism, The* (D'Souza), 30
England, Lyndie, 160–61, 229*n*82, 229*n*84
Enloe, Cynthia, 151

*Faces of Injustice, The* (Shklar), 173
*Fahrenheit 9/11*, 163, 165
Faludi, Susan, 159
Falwell, Jerry, 149

Fanon, Franz, 81, 90, 100, 107, 205*n*75, 209*n*139
Fattah, Ezzat, 126
federal apology for slavery, 116, 215*n*25
Feiffer, Jules, 20
*Feminine Mystique, The* (Friedan), 18, 49, 58–67, 195*n*53, 197*n*87
feminism: academic, 52; class issues in, 71; contemporary, 49–50, 54–55; "equality," 58; Lester and, 96–97; liberal, 58, 69, 196*n*78; market-focused, 56; neo, 59, 194*n*45; second wave, 48, 50, 58–59, 63, 67; third wave, 57–58; victim, 48–78, 161, 188*n*37, 191*n*3
feminists: of color, 73, 200*n*124; cultural, 68, 69, 198*n*99; infighting among, 74–75; liberal, 49, 58, 196; radical, 49, 58, 67–70, 226*n*39; relational, 69; as victimizers, 28; work with rape victims, 117
*Feminist Theory: From Margin to Center* (hooks), 71
Fiedler, Leslie, 100
*Fire with Fire: The New Female Power and How It Will Change the 21st Century* (Wolf), 48, 76, 193*n*30
Fleischer, Ari, 153
*Forrest Gump*, 139–40
Freud, Sigmund, 97, 101, 112, 116, 117, 138
Friedan, Betty, 18, 49, 106, 195*n*50–53, 197*n*87; *Feminine Mystique, The*, 58–67; Holocaust metaphor of women's oppression, 62–63, 64, 81, 106; and homosexuality, 196*n*65; *It Changed My Life*, 59; and liberalism, 196*n*78; and radical politics, 195*n*53; *Second Stage, The*, 59
Friedman, Thomas, 153
Frum, David, 147

Gans, Herbert, 142
*Gathers, South Carolina v.*, 135–36
*Genealogy of Morals* (Nietzsche), 132
Gibson, Mel, 163–65
Gilligan, Carol, 69; *In a Different Voice*, 69
Gingrich, Newt, 12, 140
Giuliani, Rudolph, 162
Gordon, Linda, 69
"Gray Areas Report," 111
Greer, Germaine, 58, 118
Griffin, Susan, 119

ground zero, 19, 147
Gubar, Susan, 81, 202*n*15

Hamill, Peter, 21
Hanisch, Carol, 9
Haug, Frigga, 68
Hawkesworth, Mary, 148, 152, 194*n*44, 195*n*51
Hawk Federation Youth Development and
    Training Program, 129–130
Helms, Jesse, 26
Hentig, Hans von, 123–24
Hill, Anita, 50, 56, 57, 75, 193*n*39
Himmelfarb, Gertrude, 11
Hiroshima, 15, 147
Hitchens, Christopher, 149, 214*n*13
Hoff Sommers, Christina, 48–51, 75, 77,
    191*n*3, 226*n*39; *War against Boys, The*, 75;
    *Who Stole Feminism?*, 48
Holmstrom, Lynda Lytle, 120, 122
Holocaust: and African American/Jewish
    relations, 81, 84–85, 105–106, 211*n*164;
    compared to war on terror, 146–48,
    224*n*16; and concept of survival, 139;
    Friedan's views on, 62–63, 64, 81; and
    Jewish identity, 44, 106, 190*n*71; Lester's
    preoccupation with, 81, 84–85, 89, 93,
    104, 105; metaphors of, 196*n*62, 210*n*143,
    211*n*167; pervasiveness of, 15–16, 190*n*71;
    as standard of true victimization, 16, 81
"Holocaust envy," 106
homeland security, 157, 168
hooks, bell, 71–72, 199*n*115; *Feminist Theory*,
    71
Hughes, Karen, 151
Hughes, Robert, 21, 25–26, 32, 40, 44, 77;
    *Culture of Complaint*, 21, 26
Human Potential Fund, 129
Hurricane Katrina, 168

*I Am a Soldier Too* (Lynch), 160
iconography of September 11, 164
identity, conceptions of, 105
identity politics, 6–10, 23, 38–39, 73, 86, 129,
    172
*Illiberal Education: The Politics of Race and
    Sex on Campus* (D'Souza), 21, 80
*I'm Dysfunctional, You're Dysfunctional: The
    Recovery Movement and Other Self-Help
    Fashions* (Kaminer), 32
*In a Different Voice* (Gilligan), 69
"infantile citizenship," 167

inner child, role in victimism, 31–32
innocence, construction of, 5–6; pursuit of,
    30–31; of United States, 157–58
intersectionality, 73
Iraq war, 160–68
*It Changed My Life* (Friedan), 59

jeremiad, 12, 22, 183*n*28
Jews: and blacks, animosity between, 91;
    in feminists' writings, 106; oppres-
    sion of, 62–63, 64; pariah status of, 91;
    racial classification of, 91; as symbols of
    victimhood, 106; victimization of, 44,
    81. *See also* Holocaust
just-world hypothesis, 116–17

Kaminer, Wendy, 32, 33, 35, 82, 189*n*53; *I'm
    Dysfunctional, You're Dysfunctional*, 32
Karmen, Andrew, 126
Kassebaum, Nancy, 129
Kaus, Mickey, 153–54
Kaye/Kantrowitz, Melanie, 74
Kerry, John, 159
keywords, 16–17
King, Martin Luther, Jr., 14, 29, 39–40, 87,
    158, 212*n*173
King, Rodney, 12
Koppel, Ted, 163
Krauthammer, Charles, 146–47, 166

LaHood, Ray, 157
Lakoff, George, 171
Latin Americans, 4, 15, 40, 73
legitimate victim, 119, 216*n*39. *See also* victim
    blaming
Lerner, Melvin, 109–10, 116–18
Lester, Julius, 18, 79–108; *All Is Well*, 93, 98,
    100; *All Our Wounds Forgiven*, 101; and
    anti-Semitism, 79, 83–85, 88, 91–93, 100,
    203*n*25; attraction to Jewishness, 92–93;
    background, 29, 82–83, 94; and chil-
    dren's literature, 91–92, 206*n*81, 208*n*126;
    and Christ, 101–3; and circumcision,
    92–93, 100–101; conversion to Judaism,
    84–86, 107, 170, 208*n*120; drift from
    black politics, 85; *Falling Pieces*, 212*n*173;
    family ties to Judaism, 94–95; female
    identity of, 98–99, 204*n*58; and James
    Baldwin, 93, 100, 207*n*93; *Look Out,
    Whitey! Black Power's Gon' Get Your
    Mama*, 83, 104; *Lovesong: On Becoming a*

Jew, 79–108; *Michele*, 89; "On the Uses of
Suffering," 88–89; preoccupation with
Holocaust, 84–85; on rage of blacks, 90,
205*n*75; role in black politics, 86–87;
self-invention of, 165; on victimhood,
107; views on women, 94–99, 208*n*126;
"Who I Am," 104
Levi, Primo, 139
liberal feminism, 58, 69, 196*n*78. *See also*
Friedan; Greer
Lincoln, Abraham, 14
locus of control, 134, 220*n*89
*Look Out, Whitey! Black Power's Gon' Get
Your Mama* (Lester), 83, 104
Lorde, Audre, 74, 195*n*51, 199*n*114
*Lovesong: On Becoming a Jew* (Lester),
79–108
Lynch, Jessica, 160; *I am a Soldier Too*, 160
Lyotard, François, 106

MacKinnon, Catharine, 28, 54, 58, 63, 69–70,
192*n*25
Madonna, 56
Maher, Bill, 153
Malcolm X, 43, 87, 176
Mannheim, Karl, 111
Marx, Karl, 8–9, 10, 40, 54
*Maternal Thinking* (Ruddick), 69
McLeer, Anne, 127
Mendelsohn, Benjamin, 123–25, 218*n*51
*Merchant of Venice, The* (Shakespeare), 99
*Michele* (Lester), 89
Millet, Kate, 67, 182*n*22; *Sexual Politics*, 67
Mills, C. W., 63, 111
Minow, Martha, 173–76, 188*n*37, 230*n*10;
"Surviving Victim Talk," 174–76
Moore, Michael, 163, 165
Moraga, Cherríe, 73
*Morning After: Sex, Fear, and Feminism on
Campus, The* (Roiphe), 48
Moussaoui, Zacarias, 153
Moynihan, Daniel Patrick, 11, 111, 116, 131;
Moynihan Report, 130
multiculturalism, 45–46, 167, 177, 186*n*10; in
education, 24; feminists and, 55; and
guilt, 144–45
multicultural conservatives, 80

Nagasaki, 147
National Commission on Human Resource
Development, 129

National Endowment for the Arts, 26
National Organization of Victim Assistance,
126
"Nation of Victims, A" (Brooks), 156–57
*Nation of Victims: The Decay of the American
Character* (Sykes), 21, 186*n*10, 189*n*51,
190*n*67
Native Americans, 13, 15, 20, 145
*Negro Family: The Case for National Action,
The* (Moynihan), 111
neo-feminism, 57–59, 194*n*45, 194*n*46
neo-liberalism, 12, 36, 46
*New Victorians, The: A Young Woman's
Challenge to the Old Feminist Order, The*
(Denfeld), 48
Nietzsche, Friedrich, 7, 41, 90, 132; *Genealogy
of Morals*, 132
*Nightline*, 163
Noonan, Peggy, 159
Novick, Peter, 15, 106
"No Whining" (Schlessinger), 134

Ocean Hill-Brownsville teachers' strike, 83,
100, 203*n*23, 203*n*25
Oedipal triangle, 97–98
"On the Uses of Suffering" (Lester), 88–89
oppression: of blacks, 37, 71–72 (*see also* slavery); vs. discrimination, 72; as identity,
72–75; of Jews, 62–63, 64 (*see also* anti-
Semitism; Holocaust); of poor, 111–16;
rhetoric of, 195*n*51; vocabularies of, 14; of
women, 18, 49–78, 118, 150–52
Osteen, Joel, 170; *Best Life Now, The*, 170

Paglia, Camille, 50, 75–77, 188*n*37, 189*n*64;
on masculinity, 159; on rape, 53; on
re-blaming victims, 132; *Sex, Art, and
American Culture*, 48
*Passion of the Christ*, 14, 163–65
Pataki, George, 162
Patraka, Vivian, 106, 210*n*143
patriarchy, 67–68, 70–71, 118, 159–60, 197*n*93
Patriot Act, 156
*Patterns in Forcible Rape* (Amir), 125
*Payne v. Tennessee*, 136
Pell, Claiborne, 129
Perle, Richard, 147
personal politics, 9, 70–71, 73, 198*n*109
Pogrebin, Letty Cottin, 74
politicos, 68, 198*n*99
Pollitt, Katha, 164

Post, Jerrold, 153
poverty, 111–16, 131, 133, 142. *See also* welfare
    state
Powell, Colin, 21, 184*n*3
power feminism, 50, 55, 56–57
Pratt, Minnie Bruce, 74
presidential campaign: of 2000, 12; of 2004,
    156, 159, 161, 162
pro-life movement, 13, 15, 26, 55
psychoanalysis, 66, 112
psychologization of American society, 31–33
psychotherapy: and consciousness-raising,
    71; criticism of, 31–33; and litigiousness,
    32. *See also* therapeutic culture; thera-
    peutics of blame
Puar, Jasbir, 153, 225*n*27

*Quest*, 71

"racechanging," 81–82, 202*n*15
radical feminists, 49, 58, 67–70, 68
Rai, Amit, 153, 225*n*27
rape: burden of proof in, 141; as catalyst for
    change, 141; emotional recovery from,
    137, 222*n*105; prevention of, women's
    responsibility for, 53, 120; psychological
    impact of, 122; September 11 compared
    to, 148–49; victim blaming in, 118–23
rape shield laws, 119, 216*n*39
rape trauma syndrome (RTS), 122, 217*n*48
rape victims: assistance for emotional
    trauma, 122; behavioral traits of, 122;
    blaming of, 118–23; sexual history of,
    119–21
Rauch, Jonathan, 170–71
Reagan, Ronald, 10–11, 146, 221*n*93
Reconstruction, 13–14
recovery movement, 31–33, 35, 128, 137
Redstockings, 48, 70–71, 197*n*81, 198*n*110
*Reflections of an Affirmative Action Baby*
    (Carter), 37
*Regents of the University of California v.
    Bakke*, 11
remasculinization, of America, 36, 159–61
responsibility: continuum of, 175; evasion of,
    21, 25, 33, 37, 53, 115, 132; personal, 5, 18,
    19, 23, 43, 110, 139, 170; for sexual behav-
    ior, 53–54; for victimization, 66
*ressentiment*, 7, 132
*Ressentiment* (Scheler), 132
reverse discrimination, 10–11, 42, 182*n*25

revolution of 1776, 15
Rice, Condoleezza, 151, 225*n*19
Rich, Frank, 159
*Roe v. Wade*, 10–11
Rogin, Michael, 4–5, 81–82, 91, 155, 197*n*85;
    *Blackface, White Noise*, 81–82
Roiphe, Katie, 48, 51–54, 75, 77, 197*n*87,
    199*n*115; *Morning After*, 48
Rousseau, Jean Jacques, 41, 189*n*64
Rove, Karl, 150, 154–55, 166, 227*n*58
Rowbotham, Sheila, 68
Rubin, Gayle, 67–68
Ruddick, Sara, 69; *Maternal Thinking*, 69
Ryan, William, 16, 109–22, 129–33, 141–43,
    213*n*5, 214*n*15; *Blaming the Victim*, 111–18,
    131, 142

Sartre, Jean Paul, 99, 106, 107, 204*n*49
scarcity theory of political struggle, 74
Schafer, Stephen, 124; *Victim and His Crimi-
    nal, The*, 124
Scheler, Max, 132
Scherer, Jacqueline, 126
Schlessinger, Laura, 134; "No Whining,"
    134
Schumer, Charles, 157
*Second Stage, The* (Friedan), 59, 195*n*52
second victimization, 149–50
second wave feminism, 48, 50, 58, 59, 63, 67
Segal, Lynn, 69
self-esteem: enhancement of, 128–30, 219*n*77;
    *Social Importance of Self-Esteem, The*
    (Smith), 129; women and, 51, 54
separatism, 43
September 11, 144–68; aftermath of, 18, 172,
    173; compared to Holocaust, 147–48;
    compared to rape, 148–49, 225*n*27;
    iconography after, 164; as opportunity
    for Bush, 166, 229*n*85; *Passion of the
    Christ* and, 164; and remasculinization
    of America, 159–61
*Sex, Art, and American Culture* (Paglia), 48
*Sexual Politics* (Millet), 67
Shakespeare, William, 99; *Merchant of
    Venice, The*, 99
shaming of victims, 2, 44–45, 160, 171, 190*n*73
Shelley, Percy Bysshe, 99
Shklar, Judith, 8, 173–75; *Faces of Injustice,
    The*, 173
Sinclair Broadcasting Company, 163
slavery, 9, 14–15, 116, 145, 184*n*36, 215n25

*Slavery: A Problem in American Institutional and Intellectual Life* (Elkins), 64
South, post-Confederate, 13–14
*South Carolina v. Gathers*, 135–36
Spelman, Elizabeth, 73, 187*n*17
Steele, Shelby, 7; on black victimism, 23, 37–39, 43, 45, 77; *Content of our Character, The: A New Vision of Race in America*, 21; on Julius Lester, 80; and therapeutic culture, 30–31, 188*n*44
Steinberg, Stephen, 106
Stossel, John, 24, 46
Stowe, Harriet Beecher, 13
Student Non-Violent Coordinating Committee (SNCC), 83, 87
suffering: archetypes of, 10–11; and Christianity, 14–15; depoliticizing of, 175–76, 231*n*11; hierarchy of, 35; politics of, 12–16; psychological investment in, 7, 170; responsiveness to, 1–2
"Surviving Victim Talk" (Minow), 174–76. *See also* oppression
*Survivor*, 139
survivors: of 9/11, 148; compared to victims, 2–3, 16, 137–40; of Holocaust, 15–16, 81, 211*n*164
Sykes, Charles: on *Blaming the Victim* (Ryan), 131; on Julius Lester, 80; *A Nation of Victims: The Decay of American Character*, 21, 25–27; on pessimism, 45; on rise of victimism, 39–41; on therapeutic culture, 31; on victim claims, 33–34

Take Back the Night, 137
terrorism, 3, 147–48, 153–54. *See also* September 11; war on terror
therapeutic culture, 134–39, 222*n*107. *See also* psychotherapy
therapeutics of blame, 109–43
therapy. *See* psychotherapy
third wave feminism, 47, 57–58
Thomas, Clarence, 50, 56, 57, 75, 193*n*39
True Victimhood: Cult of, 35, 136–37, 141, 151, 158, 164, 167; defined, 5–6; description of, 172–73; historical context, 10–12; responses to effects of, 173–76
truth and reconciliation commissions, 175–76
Turner, Nat, 87

Unborn Victims of Violence Act of 2004, 4
*Uncle Tom's Cabin* (Stowe), 13
United in Memory Quilt Project, 148

Vasconcellos, John, 128
Viano, Emilio, 127
*Victim and His Criminal, The* (Schafer), 124
victim blaming: and African Americans, 111, 116; and delayed gratification, 117; explanations for, 112–18; in litigation of rape cases, 119–22, 216*n*46; and the poor, 111–16; as racism, 112; therapeutic effects of, 115–16
victim claims, 5–6, 133; dynamics of, 173–76; litigation of, 175–76; in rape cases, 141; therapy and, 31, 33–34, 137
victim feminism: arguments against, 48–78; characteristics of, 50, 59; compared to difference feminism, 68; and manipulation, 51–52
victimhood: as identity, 7, 18, 169–70; Jewish, 81, 84, 93; Lester on, 107; psychological incentives of, 30, 42–43; role in women's movement, 70; vilification of, 2
victim identity, 37–38, 189*n*53
victim impact panels, 137
victim impact statement (VIS), 135–37, 221*n*101
victimism: in academia, 24; in art, 26, 186*n*17; of blacks, 43, 45; comparative, 37–39; conceptualization of, 22–46; context of term, 27; in criminal courts, 24; deception vs. delusion, 29; Hamill on, 21; origins of, 39–41; psychology of, 7; and racial politics, 24; sites of, 23–26; Sykes on, 25
victimists: cynical, 29–31, 34; deluded, 29–31, 34; portrayal of, 36; rewards sought by, 42–43
victimization: and 9/11, 146–68; addressing of, 175–76; benefits of acknowledgment, 175–76; culture of, 20–21; by exploitation of generosity, 23; false claims of, 27; by feminists, 28; inversion of, 22; of Jews, 44, 81 (*see also* Holocaust; anti-Semitism); psychological incentives of, 30; social, 127, 128, 141; of women, 49–57, 118–23, 150–52
victimology: history of, 123–27, 170, 218*n*51; Holocaust and, 81; radical, 123–27, 219*n*72

victimology-mongers, 145
victim precipitation, 109, 123–27, 218*n*61
victims: behavior of, 77, 114–15; as blamers, 134–37; boys as, 75; classification
of, 33–36; compared to survivors, 16,
137–40; complicity of, 65; defined, 16;
gendering of, 152; hierarchy of, 136;
legitimate, 119; Middle Eastern women
as, 151–53; needs of, 126; "otherness"
of, 111–12; perspective of, 126, 141, 174;
poor as, 111–16, 142–43; portrayal of, 22;
professional, 71; of rape, 118–23; real vs.
bogus, 29–31, 33–36; recovery of, 140–41;
responsibility of, 131; revictimizing of,
149–50; scapegoating of, 16, 115, 116, 118,
214*n*21; shaming of, 2, 44–45, 171, 190*n*73;
U.S. as virtuous victim, 161–63; as victimizers, 14, 28, 66–67, 80
victims' rights movement (VRM), 4, 134–37,
141, 162, 220*n*91, 221*n*93
victim status: benefits of, 38; disavowment
of, 2–3; exploitation of, 26–27; public
display of, 45; self proclaimed, 21, 71
Victorian moralism, 11
*Village Voice, The*, 88
Violence Against Women Act of 1994
(VAWA), 151, 173, 226*n*39. *See also* Unborn Victims of Violence Act of 2004
von Hentig, Hans: *Criminal and His Victim,
The*, 123

Wade, Roe v., 10–11
*War against Boys: How Misguided Feminism
is Harming Our Young Men, The* (Hoff
Sommers), 75

"war for freedom". *See* Iraq war
war on terror: compared to Holocaust, 147–
48; excuses for, 165, 167; welfare and, 154.
*See also* September 11; Iraq war
weapons of mass destruction (WMD), 147,
158, 162
welfare state, 8, 11, 12, 23–24, 170–72, 189*n*51;
anti-victim feminism and, 54, 77; and
terrorism, 153–54; and therapeutics of
blame, 133, 142;
Welter, Barbara, 173, 181*n*11
*What's So Great about America* (D'Souza),
144
"Who I Am" (Lester), 104
*Who Stole Feminism? How Women Have
Betrayed Women* (Hoff Sommers), 48
*Why We Fight: Moral Clarity and the War on
Terrorism* (Bennett), 145
Wiesel, Elie, 147
Williams, Raymond, 17
Wolf, Naomi, 48, 50–57, 75–77, 106, 196*n*62;
*Beauty Myth, The*, 76; *Fire with Fire*, 48,
76, 193*n*30
women's rights, in Afghanistan, 150–52,
226*n*39
*Women's Ways of Knowing* (Belenky), 69
Woodward, Bob, 166

X, Malcolm, 43, 87, 176

Young, Andrew, 85
Young, Cathy, 159

Žižek, Slavoj, 16